PRAISE FOR HARO[LD]
HELL'S PI[RINCESS]

D0503496

Hell's Princess can take its place among Schechter's other true-crime classics as the definitive rendering of one of the most beguiling and brutal of all female serial killers. His gruesome page-turner about Belle Gunness, grounded in meticulous historic research, confirms his reputation as one of the top true-crime writers of our time."

—Katherine Ramsland, bestselling author of
Confession of a Serial Killer

"Harold Schechter's *Hell's Princess* had me on the edge of my seat to the last page! Like Sir Arthur Conan Doyle's *The Hound of the Baskervilles*, Schechter's hound that is always ready to pounce is Belle Gunness, America's most notorious female serial killer. Schechter's achievement is humanizing this inhuman monster, while making us feel the sexual neediness and loneliness urging Belle's victims to give up everything to get into her bed. How the case ultimately turns out is a seminal event in jurisprudence written by one of America's greatest storytellers and historians."

—Fred Rosen, author of *Murdering the President: Alexander Graham Bell and the Race to Save James Garfield*

"Harold Schechter demonstrates why he is the dark prince master of American true-crime history, in this first definitive account of notorious female serial killer Belle Gunness and her 'human slaughterhouse murder farm.'"

—Peter Vronsky, author of *Serial Killers: The Method and Madness of Monsters*

HELL'S PRINCESS

HELL'S PRINCESS

THE MYSTERY OF BELLE GUNNESS, BUTCHER OF MEN

HAROLD SCHECHTER

Published by Little A, New York
www.apub.com

Amazon, the Amazon logo, and Little A are trademarks of Amazon.com, Inc., or its affiliates.

ISBN-13: 9781477808955 (hardcover)
ISBN-10: 1477808957 (hardcover)
ISBN-13: 9781477808948 (paperback)
ISBN-10: 1477808949 (paperback)

Cover design by Faceout Studio

Printed in the United States of America

First edition

For
CHRISTOPH KELLER

Belle Gunness was a lady fair
In Indiana State.
She weighed about three hundred pounds,
And that is quite some weight.
That she was stronger than a man
Her neighbors all did own;
She butchered hogs right easily,
And did it all alone.
But hogs were just a sideline
She indulged in now and then;
Her favorite occupation
Was a-butchering of men.

—Anonymous, "The Ballad of Belle Gunness"

Prologue

BLUEBEARD'S DOOR

Fairyland, as every child knows, is a terrifying place, populated by all manner of nightmarish beings: the snaggletoothed witch who lusts for the fattened flesh of little children; the bloodthirsty giant ready to roast any trespassing human on a spit; the smooth-talking wolf with a sweet tooth for tasty young girls. Of all the scary stories told about that realm of dark enchantment, however, none more closely resembles a modern-day horror movie than the tale of Bluebeard.

Though scholars have identified variants of this folktale in societies throughout the world, the version best known in our own culture was originally put into writing by French author Charles Perrault in his 1697 classic, *Mother Goose Tales* (*Contes de ma mere l'Oye*). Supposedly modeled on the infamous fifteenth-century sadist Gilles de Rais—Joan of Arc's onetime field marshal, accused of the torture-murder of countless peasant children—Perrault's Bluebeard is a highborn serial wife slayer whose creepy castle contains a locked secret chamber in which he stores the dismembered body parts of his fatally curious brides. To test her obedience, each new wife is left alone with a complete set of keys and a warning not to enter the mysterious room. In every case but one, however, the temptation proves too strong. No sooner has her husband gone than she runs down to the forbidden chamber and, with trembling hand, unlocks the door—*"ouvrit en tremblant la porte,"* as Perrault writes.[1]

Not many years before Perrault set down his harrowing tale of the grisly horrors hidden behind Bluebeard's door, one of his countrymen, the famed explorer Rene-Robert Cavelier de La Salle, undertook an expedition around the Great Lakes. While passing through a stretch of present-day Indiana—then part of the Potawatomi nation—he and his men followed an old Indian trail that cut through a dense hardwood forest before opening onto a rolling tall-grass prairie. To La Salle and the early French fur traders who came after him, this opening became known as "the door"—"la porte," in their language.[2]

For the next century and a half, the area remained devoid of white inhabitants. "In all the West, prolific in beauty, there was not a lovelier region," writes an early historian, "but it was in the sole possession of the red man, who roamed at will over the prairies and encamped in the groves, living on the game and fish which were abundant on the land and in the sparkling lakes."[3]

It wasn't until 1829 that the first white pioneers appeared: a widow named Miriam Benedict, her seven grown children, and a son-in-law, Henly Clyburn. By the beginning of 1832, more than a hundred other families had settled in the territory. In April of that year, the county of La Porte, consisting of 462 square miles, was officially incorporated by an act of the state legislature. After casting his vote, one crusty old lawmaker demanded to know the meaning of the new county's "outlandish name." Informed that it was French for "the door," he indignantly proposed that the "high-flown" foreign word be replaced with something more suitably American. Happily, observes one chronicler, "his advice was not followed; and the county received the beautiful name 'La Porte,' instead of being forever known to the world as Gateville or Doorburg."[4]

Seeking a site to establish a county seat, a few enterprising settlers acquired a particularly choice tract of land, 450 acres in size and adorned with a "chain of small lakes, gem-like in their dazzling beauty."[5] A courthouse and jail were promptly erected and a government land office opened. Within a few years, the new county seat—also named La Porte—had grown from a tiny village of scattered log buildings into a flourishing town with "all the departments of human life which go to make a thriving community": churches and schools, taverns and hotels, merchants and mechanics, doctors and lawyers, as well as two newspapers, one promoting the Whig Party, one the Democratic.[6]

In 1852, the town of La Porte was upgraded to a city. By then its population had grown to roughly five thousand. The following decades witnessed the construction of a waterworks plant, the installation of street lighting, the introduction of a telephone system, and successive waves of other civic improvements. Roads were paved, cement sidewalks laid down, dozens of old wooden buildings demolished and handsome brick ones erected in their places. Besides several large drugstores and dry goods emporiums, La Porte's places of business included twenty-five grocery stores, six flour and feed stores, six furniture dealers, four bakeries, ten butcher shops, four hardware merchants, six boot and shoe firms, twenty-six tobacco shops, four sewing machine dealers, nine milliners and dressmakers, two book and stationery stores, nine boardinghouses, twenty-four saloons, six billiard rooms, six barbers, seven livery stables, two tanneries, and three undertakers.[7] Its residential streets were lined with so many trees that it became known as "the Maple City." Altogether, crowed one lifelong resident, the city of La Porte—"with her magnificent court-house, excellent city hall, and splendid school buildings, her fine streets, her beautiful adjacent lakes, her spacious outlying country, and her excellent railroad facilities"—was "the fit capital of one of the best counties in the state."[8]

It wasn't only the physical attributes of the place that made the county and city of La Porte so exceptional in the eyes of its boosters but the caliber of its residents. La Porteans have always taken pride in the achievements of their most distinguished fellow citizens. Among the notables celebrated in local histories were Jacob J. Mann, manufacturer of a harvesting machine that predated the famous McCormick reaper; Dr. F. T. Wrench, creator of a collapsible "sanitary toothbrush"; Antipas J. Bowell, inventor of a dog-powered butter churn; Dr. S. B. Collins, discoverer of the Collins' Painless Cure for Opium Eaters; and such local literati as Benjamin F. Taylor and Mrs. Clara J. Armstrong, authors, respectively, of the poetry volumes *Old-Time Pictures and Sheaves of Time* and *La Porte in June*.[9] In later decades, La Porte would be the home of other, even more widely known figures, including Zerna Sharp, cocreator of the "Dick and Jane" books that taught reading to generations of American schoolchildren; Frederick C. Mennen, inventor of Jiffy Pop popcorn (as well as a patented instrument for detecting gonorrhea); William Mathias Scholl, our nation's preeminent manufacturer of foot-care products; singer Dorothy Claire, who performed with the Glenn Miller and Tommy Dorsey bands and starred in the 1948 Broadway smash *Finian's Rainbow*; and Brewster Martin Higley, lyricist of the American standard "Home on the Range."[10]

Of course, even its most ardent champions had to concede that, along with these and other luminaries, La Porte had produced its share of criminals. In early 1836, a resident of the county named Pelton was waylaid, murdered, and robbed of "a considerable sum of money" by an acquaintance named Staves, who was promptly apprehended, tried, and sent to the gallows. Two years later, in February 1838, nineteen-year-old Joshua M. Coplin, a native of La Porte Township who had just returned home from Virginia, where he had collected a long-overdue debt, was shot to death and robbed of the money—six hundred dollars in gold and silver coins—by his traveling companion, a young man named David Scott. Tracked down, jailed, and tried in La Porte, Scott was hanged before an approving crowd a few months later.[11]

In December 1841, tavern keeper Charles Egbert, "enraged against" a rival named James Smith who had opened a competing establishment that had "taken all the trade away from Mr. Egbert's place of business," went to Smith's bar-room armed with a newly purchased dirk knife and stabbed the latter to death. Arrested and held on $5,000 bail, Egbert managed to come up with the money, then promptly fled to Texas—still a part of Mexico—where, according to later reports, he underwent a religious conversion and became "a Methodist class leader."[12]

"A most remarkable murder" took place in 1862. Following the discovery of the newly slain corpse of a German émigré named Fred Miller, suspicion fell upon his wife. A group of Miller's male friends, intent on "extorting a confession," strung the woman up by the neck from a tree limb until she gasped out the identity of the ostensible culprit: a man named John Poston, who—so she claimed—had murdered her husband "in her presence and had promised to marry her if she would not denounce him." Though Poston was promptly arrested and brought to trial, his accuser's testimony, having been coerced through torture, was deemed to be invalid, and the presiding magistrate "felt constrained to acquit him."[13]

Three years later, another German farmer, John Lohm, while driving his wagon back home after a day of husking corn, encountered a pair of strangers, James Woods and William Fulton, who—having spent the afternoon in a local saloon—were "in that condition when whisky most inflames the blood and leads its victims to the most desperate ends." Some sort of altercation ensued, instigated by the two intoxicated men. When Lohm attempted to continue on his way, Woods drunkenly "drew a revolver and discharged it . . . inflicting a mortal wound" upon the unarmed farmer. Convicted of second-degree murder, Woods was sentenced to "the term of his natural life" in the state penitentiary, while Fulton, guilty of manslaughter, was given a term of thirteen years.[14]

During the last weeks of 1902, the people of La Porte County were lashed into a fury by a particularly heinous killing that occurred in the town of Westville. The victim was sixteen-year-old Wesley Reynolds, a "trusted clerk" at the Westville State Bank, who doubled as the watchman, "sleeping in the institution at night with three revolvers within reach." At daybreak on the morning of Sunday, November 30, Reynolds was startled awake when a beer keg came crashing through the rear window of the bank building. Leaping to his feet, a pistol in each hand, the young man confronted a pair of heavily armed robbers and opened fire. In the ensuing gun battle, Reynolds was struck three times, one bullet passing through his chin and lodging at the base of his brain, another entering his neck and exiting between his shoulder blades, the third striking him directly in the heart, killing him instantly. Fleeing the bank empty-handed, the two desperadoes—one badly wounded by the "heroic youth" (as he would be hailed in newspapers throughout the country)—stole a horse and surrey from a nearby barn and fled.

Young Reynolds's funeral, held on December 3, was attended by the entire population of Westville, and a fund, overseen by State Senator Charles E. Herrold, was immediately established to erect a monument in his honor. A large reward was also offered for the apprehension of his killers, but—despite the involvement of Pinkerton detectives who were put on their trail—the culprits were never apprehended.[15]

Two weeks after the people of Westville turned out to pay their last respects to the martyred young bank teller, the *Fort Wayne Daily News* ran a story on a sudden epidemic of crime that seemed "to be reigning in La Porte County." Besides the Reynolds murder, there had been the recent armed robbery of two local young men "by negro footpads," an "attempt to administer poison to a La Porte woman by means of arsenic," and the "killing of Albert Bader of La Porte by a train, following his attempt to escape arrest after breaking into" a lakeside boathouse.

The immediate occasion of the news article, however, was the violent death of a local farmer that had occurred the previous day and whose circumstances were so bizarre that the town official called to the scene instantly suspected foul play.[16] In the end, the death was ruled a tragic accident. Another six years would pass before the official's initial impression was confirmed. The supposedly accidental death of the farmer, a Norwegian émigré named Peter Gunness, would be recognized as the sinister handiwork of one of the most monstrous killers in the history of the state, if not of the entire nation. Casting about for comparisons, newspaper articles would invoke not only Charles Perrault's fairy-tale ogre Bluebeard but his ostensible historical prototype, Gilles de Rais.[17] Unlike those earlier figures, however—and adding to the horror of the case—this midwestern serial murderer was a woman. Like Fall River, Massachusetts, and Plainfield, Wisconsin—the homes, respectively, of two of the country's criminal legends, Lizzie Borden and Ed Gein—La Porte, Indiana, would become a macabre tourist destination, forever identified not as the birthplace of such proud native sons as William Mathias Scholl and Brewster Martin Higley but as the site of an unspeakable horror: the ghastly "murder farm" of Belle Sorenson Gunness, the Lady Bluebeard.

PART ONE

BELLA

1.

PAUL'S DAUGHTER

Reduced to charred ruins by the Great Conflagration of 1871, Chicago roared back to life in the following years, a phoenix of limestone, granite, and brick reborn from the ashes. By the early 1880s, a decade after being laid waste by the disaster, it had resurrected itself as the "gem of the prairies," the "most American of America's cities": a vast, teeming "magnet metropolis," drawing hordes of eager young men and women in flight from their stultifying midwestern small towns, villages, and farms.[1]

Along with these "life-hungry" seekers pouring in from the provinces,[2] great tides of immigrants swept into the rebuilt city: Germans and Poles, Scots and Irish, Italians and Jews. By 1890, according to one eminent historian, close to 80 percent of the city's population "was of foreign parentage, drawn from every civilized quarter of the globe."[3]

A significant percentage of these foreign-born newcomers hailed from Norway. Indeed, Norwegians were among the earliest settlers to the area, establishing a colony there when Chicago was nothing but a cluster of crude timber buildings planted on the swampy shores of Lake Michigan—a frontier "mud-hole" where fetid muck oozed up from beneath the wood-planked sidewalks, and the unpaved streets were such quagmires that wagons would sink to their axles and remain stuck for days.[4] In 1850, there were 562 Norwegians living in Chicago, making them the third-largest immigrant group, after the German and Irish. Ten years later, that number had increased threefold. By 1870, Norwegian-born Chicagoans numbered more than eight thousand.[5]

Like their fellow Scandinavian immigrants, the Norwegians of Chicago were widely regarded as a frugal, industrious, and upstanding people, who enhanced the moral character of the metropolis. "We get no better population," one early editorialist declared of them, "and we most cordially welcome them to the land of 'liberty, equality, and fraternity.'"[6] Their native honesty and integrity were epitomized by the inspirational tale of little Knud Iverson, recounted by the turn-of-the-century historian A. T. Andreas. On the sweltering day of Tuesday, August 3, 1856, as Andreas tells it, ten-year-old Knud had gone down to the river to swim, when he encountered a gang of teenaged ruffians who attempted to force him to sneak into the garden of a gentleman named Elston and "steal fruit for the larger boys to eat." When Knud refused to do so "because of the consciousness in his own mind that to steal was wrong," the older boys drowned him in the river. Reported in the national press, the tragedy inspired the inimitable P. T. Barnum to contribute two hundred dollars toward the erection of a monument to "the immortal child": an "enduring memorial" (so the showman proclaimed in his typically bombastic style) that would "be for ages the Mecca to which pilgrims from every quarter of this great continent will gladly flock with their little ones, who may be thus fully impressed with the important and glorious principle so feelingly taught in the cruel death of this infantile martyr, that 'it is better to die than to steal!'"[7]

Norwegians could point with pride to other members of their ethnic community, men of enormous enterprise and ambition who seemed the living validation of the American dream. One of the most prominent was Iver Lawson, who rose from day laborer to millionaire by investing every penny of his hard-won savings into vacant city lots; enjoyed a sterling political career as city council member and state legislator; and—among his other contributions to his countrymen—helped organize the First Norwegian Evangelical Lutheran Church and the Scandinavian Emigrant Aid Society.[8] Another local icon of self-made success was Christian Jevne. Emigrating to the United States as a twenty-five-year-old, the determined young man clerked in a grocery store by day while attending night school to improve his English and study bookkeeping. With two hundred dollars in savings that he painstakingly accumulated, he eventually opened his own business, which he ultimately "built into the largest wholesale and retail grocery concern in Chicago," importing "coffee direct from Sumatra and Arabia; tea from China and Ceylon; wine from Europe; cheese, fish, canned goods, and aquavit from Norway, Sweden, and Denmark."⁹ And then there was John Anderson, who arrived in Chicago at the age of nine and worked his way up from newspaper delivery boy to cofounder (with Iver Lawson) of *Skandinaven*, the most widely read and influential Norwegian-language newspaper in the country: a journal so vital to America's Norwegian population that, for his services as publisher, Anderson would ultimately be knighted by King Oscar II.[10]

Even as they pursued their new lives in America, the members of Chicago's Norwegian community found frequent occasions to honor their ethnic heritage. They celebrated Norway's Independence Day each May 17, threw a massive outdoor party on the millennium of Norway's unification under the Viking king Harald Fairhair, and turned out by the thousands in July 1875 for an open-air gala to commemorate the sailing of the sloop *Restauration*, the so-called Norwegian *Mayflower* that carried the first boatload of immigrants from the coastal town of Stavanger to the United States fifty years earlier. One of the highlights of Chicago's great World Columbian Exposition of 1893 was the arrival of the dragon-prowed longship *Viking*, which—in emulation of Leif Eriksson's epochal voyage—had been sailed across the Atlantic by an intrepid crew under the command of Captain Magnus Andersen: a feat that stirred "elated feelings of pride in the hearts of Norwegians throughout the United States."[11]

By the time of the World's Fair, Chicago's Norwegian population (which would eventually grow to be the "the third-largest . . . in the world, after Oslo and Bergen") numbered slightly over twenty thousand. The wealthiest among them—doctors, lawyers, businessmen, and bankers—had turned the neighborhood of Wicker Park into such a tightly knit ethnic enclave that, among themselves, they referred to it as *Hommansbyen*, after a fashionable residential district of Oslo.[12] Their less affluent countrymen—the merchants, shop owners, skilled laborers, and craftsmen—congregated in the neighborhoods of Humboldt Park and Logan Square.[13] As had been the case since the earliest days of their arrival, serious crime was strikingly rare in their community. Official reports issued by the Chicago Department of Police show that, between 1880 and 1890, Norwegians accounted for a mere 1 percent of arrests in the city, generally for infractions no worse than drunk and disorderly conduct. This "enviable record," as one historian writes, was shining proof of one of the most admirable traits of Chicago's Norwegian population: their "deference to law and order."[14]

Among the more than twenty-five thousand Norwegians who came to these shores in 1881—the start of a great wave of migration from Norway that would not subside until the decade's end—was a twenty-two-year-old woman from Selbu on the country's west coast, not far from the city of Trondheim. Her most famous photograph shows a stout, grim-faced matron fixing the camera with a baleful glare—although to be fair, that picture was taken years later, when she had settled into a hard-bitten middle age. Even in her twenties, however—as an earlier photo attests—she was a notably unlovely young woman, with a large head, small eyes, short nose, and a wide, fat-lipped mouth that, when set in a frown, bore resemblance to a frog's. She was christened Brynhild Paulsdatter—Brynhild daughter-of-Paul—to which was added, in accordance with custom, the name of the farm on which her family lived and worked, making her full Norwegian name Brynhild Paulsdatter Størset.

Unsurprisingly, very little is known about her earliest years. Apart from a few official documents laboriously dug up by later historians—confirmation records, census reports, and the like—reliable facts about her background are virtually nonexistent. Born on November 11, 1859, she grew up in Inngbya, one of several tiny hamlets within the district of Selbu. Her sharecropper father, Paul Pedersen Størset, a native of the area and one of its poorer members, leased an acre or so of the Størset farm, where he raised a few cows, sheep, and goats and grew just enough crops—barley, oats, and potatoes—to keep his wife, Berit, and their seven children from starving.[15] During the winter months, he supplemented his meager income by working as a stonemason. Even so, his situation was sometimes so dire that, on at least one occasion, he was compelled to apply for public welfare, receiving ten kroners of poor relief from town coffers.[16]

Like other peasant children, Brynhild was expected to perform a variety of chores from an early age: milking, churning, drawing water, watching over the cattle to ensure that they did not wander off or, even worse, fall prey to the malicious hill-spirits who shrink cows to the size of mice and drive them away to a mysterious subterranean realm.[17] Because her family could not afford hardwood for its hearth fire, she was also sent out daily to collect *Snurkvist*, the tiny, dried-up twigs of the spruce tree normally used for kindling—a task that earned her the demeaning nickname *Snurkvistpåla* (roughly translated as "Paul's twig-daughter") among her less charitable neighbors.[18]

In June 1874, at the age of fourteen, she was confirmed at the Evangelical Lutheran Church. Her religious instructor, Pastor Agaton Hansteen, evaluated her as "good in religious knowledge and diligence," a ranking that "only one half of the girls obtained." That same year, she was hired out as a dairymaid to a neighbor named Rødde, who would later describe her as a "diligent human being that in all ways behaved well."[19]

After a full day of toiling the fields, she would often sit by the firelight, knitting mittens, caps, and other woolen goods adorned with the traditional "star rose" pattern for which Selbu was renowned. Diversion was provided by the family storyteller, who would regale the household with magical tales of clever country lads who win the hands of haughty princesses, giant trolls with an unquenchable hunger for human flesh and blood, and the sirenlike creatures known as *Hulder*: sinister females with hollowed-out backs and long cows' tails who lure mortal men to their doom.[20]

Not all of Brynhild's neighbors shared her pastor's and employer's high opinions of her. "Here in Selbu," the local newspaper, *Selbyggen*, editorialized, "she is remembered by many [as] a very bad human being, capricious and extremely malicious. She had unpretty habits, always in the mood for dirty tricks, talked little and was a liar already as a child . . . As a grownup she was still little respected and was a scum of society."[21]

Stories would also circulate that, at seventeen, she was impregnated by the son of a wealthy landowner who, having no intention of marrying her, lured her to a lonely spot and beat her so severely that she miscarried. According to this account, her assailant died soon afterward of an intestinal ailment whose symptoms were suspiciously like those of arsenic poisoning.[22]

There are good reasons, however, to doubt the truth of this anecdote, for which no documentation exists. Her neighbors' exceptionally harsh judgments of her character are likewise open to question, since they were offered many years after her departure from Norway and were almost certainly colored by subsequent events. By the time the *Selbyggen* editorial appeared, the young dairymaid from Selbu had metamorphosed into a creature as evil as any mythical *Hulder*: "a woman," as one historian puts it, "whose malevolence seemed to match that of the unseen beings peopling Norwegian folk tradition."[23]

2.

COMING TO AMERICA

The Norwegian emigrants who made the exodus to the New World in the latter decades of the nineteenth century left copious accounts of their arduous journey. It began for many of them, as it did for Brynhild Paulsdatter Størset, with a voyage from Trondheim to the English port city of Hull aboard the steamship *Tasso*. During the four-day crossing of the North Sea, the bulk of the travelers remained belowdecks in steerage, huddling in groups or stretched out, fully clothed, on the narrow wooden shelves that served as bunks. Even in good weather, the ship tended to roll about on the waves, and—as various letters and journal entries attest—seasickness was so common that even passengers accustomed to sailing were often made ill by the pervasive stench of vomit.

For those who could hold down their food, three daily meals were offered. Though promotional brochures described the menu in glowing terms, the testimony of one passenger tells a very different story:

> For breakfast there was always sweet tea without milk and dry hard biscuits, and the same for supper. There was butter, but it was so rancid that we could not digest it. For dinner, soup with meat, but there was no taste to the soup and the meat was as salty as herring. One day we had salted fish with a dash of soup, but it was inedible for most of us, and we just ended up dumping our portions into the sea.

The privies, located on the upper deck, were particularly vile: "small, cramped, dark spaces without water," as one observer wrote, "those for men and women being close together, the entrance in no way protected from the weather. Altogether more evil-smelling unsatisfactory places it is difficult to imagine."[1]

Upon their arrival at Hull, the emigrants were herded to various dockside lodging houses and given a simple meal of soup, coffee, and bread and butter while their baggage was being unloaded. They were then hurried to the station of the North Eastern Railway Company for the train ride to Liverpool, where they would board a steamer to America.

For the vast bulk of emigrants who traveled in steerage, the transatlantic crossing had improved considerably by the late 1800s. Advertisements for the new steamers touted the between-decks living area as "high, light, and spacey" with "different compartments for families, for unmarried males, and for unmarried females," and with a crew "specially employed" to maintain "order and cleanliness." The food was "fresh and rich, made of first class supplies," and "served to the passengers by stewards." The reality proved somewhat different. The meals were often barely palatable (one traveler recalled an offering of pork that "from its appearance had made the trip across the Atlantic before"), the toilet facilities were execrable, the decks—despite the supposed attentions of the special cleaning crew—were a vile mess from the constant, wholesale seasickness. Even so, the sheer reduction in travel time made the trip a far more tolerable experience than it had been in the past. Whereas the sailing vessels of an earlier era—brigs, schooners, sloops, barks, clippers—might take up to sixty-five days to make the voyage, modern passenger ships like the *Thingvalla*, *Hekla*, and *Geiser* could complete the journey in as little as ten.[2]

Most of the steamers docked in Quebec, New York, or Boston. From there, the new arrivals from Norway would make their way by boat, rail, and wagon to their final destinations: Minnesota, Illinois, Wisconsin, the Dakotas, Washington State. Most settled in small farm communities, though others chose ethnic enclaves in cities like Minneapolis and Seattle. And in the case of Brynhild Paulsdatter Størset, Chicago.

Several years earlier, Brynhild's older sister, Olina—her senior by ten years—had moved to the United States and settled in Chicago, where she met and married a man named John R. Larson. It was Nellie, as she now called herself, who had invited Brynhild to come live with her and her husband, and who had paid her sister's passage to the New World. Shortly after arriving in Chicago and moving in with the Larsons, Brynhild, like Nellie and countless other immigrants, adopted a new American name: Bella Peterson.[3]

At the time Bella embarked on her new life, most unmarried Scandinavian women seeking employment in Chicago chose domestic occupations over factory work. According to one eminent historian, "In 1880, about three quarters of Norwegian-born women working outside the home became servants, housekeepers, or laundresses."[4] Bella Peterson did likewise, taking in laundry, doing piecework sewing, and cleaning homes for meager wages that she handed over to the Larsons for her upkeep.

This type of labor was nothing new to the former farm maid, who had spent her hardscrabble girlhood performing precisely such menial tasks. But she hadn't come to America to slave her life away in drudge work. There were riches to be had here, and—as any stroll through the commercial heart of Gilded Age Chicago made tantalizingly clear—a world of glittering merchandise for sale. In his classic novel *Sister Carrie*, set in the late 1880s, Theodore Dreiser offers a portrait of another provincial young woman, newly arrived in Chicago, whose most covetous longings are aroused as she wanders for the first time through one of the city's great "palaces of consumption," a downtown department store:

> Carrie passed along the busy aisles, much affected by the remarkable display of trinkets, dress goods, stationery, and jewelry. Each separate counter was a show place of dazzling interest and attraction. She could not help feeling the claim of each trinket and valuable upon her personally, and yet she did not stop. There was nothing there which she could not have used—nothing which she did not long to own. The dainty slippers and stockings, the delicately frilled skirts and petticoats, the laces, hair ribbons, hair-combs, purses, all touched her with individual desire, and she felt keenly the fact that not any of these things were in the range of her purchase.[5]

The material desires aflame in Carrie Meeber's breast burned even more fiercely in Bella Peterson's. The deprivations of her youth had left her with a lust for wealth. "My sister was insane on the subject of money," Nellie Larson would later remark. "She would do anything to get it."[6] As for marriage, Bella made no secret of what she wanted in a mate. "She never seemed to care for a man for his own self, only for the money or luxury he was able to give her," Nellie observed. Years afterward, Bella would say of her first husband—the father of her children and, by all accounts, a kind and loving man—that she had stayed with him only because he provided her with "a nice house."[7]

His name was Mads Ditlev Anton Sorenson. The only extant photograph of him shows a powerfully built, bullnecked fellow with strong Nordic features, a handlebar mustache of the kind fashionable in those days, and a high balding dome. Five years older than Bella, he was one of the eight hundred employees of the Mandel Brothers department store on State and Madison streets, where he worked as the night watchman.[8]

They were married in March 1884 at the Evangelical Lutheran Bethania Church on Grand Avenue and Carpenter Street. Officiating at the ceremony was the Reverend John Z. Torgersen, a venerable figure among his fellow Norwegians who, at the time of his death in 1905, would be eulogized as "Cupid's Noted Aid," having performed over fifteen thousand weddings in the course of his thirty-six-year ministry, more than any other clergyman in the country.[9] In her wedding photograph, the twenty-four-year-old Bella poses proudly in a formal black dress, "perhaps taffeta or silk moire, with lace ruffles and a triple strand of pearls around her neck," her left hand crossed over her right so as to display her "double wedding bands."[10]

The historical record of the Sorensons' life is a virtual blank for the first decade of their marriage. Still, it is possible to draw some inferences from the few documented facts.

By most accounts, Bella seemed possessed of powerfully maternal impulses. "She had great love for children," her sister Nellie recalled. "Almost every Norwegian Sunday school child in Chicago knew her for her kindness." She appeared especially touched by the plight of the orphaned or abandoned. Attending "the children's picnics at Humboldt Park, she would get out on the platform and offer to take care of children" who needed a home.[11]

Indeed, it was her eagerness to raise a child that led to a bitter break with her sister. Unable to conceive during the early years of her marriage, Bella directed much of her maternal feeling toward her four-year-old niece, Olga, the youngest of Nellie's five children. "She was an awfully cute little girl," Nellie later explained, "and my sister demanded to have her to rear." Though Olga was permitted to stay with her aunt for an extended visit of six weeks, Nellie, quite understandably, "refused to let [Mrs. Sorenson] adopt my little daughter, and from that day, my sister would hardly speak to me."[12]

In 1891, Bella Sorenson realized her dream of taking in a child, an infant girl named Jennie. Living close to the Sorensons at the time was a couple named Olson, who became close friends with Bella and Mads. As Anton Olson, the child's father, later explained: "When Jennie was eight months old her mother was dying. [Mrs. Sorenson] begged the dying woman to bequeath the child to her. My wife put the baby in Bella's arms and called on her to swear that she would guard the little one as her own, rear and care for her. Bella swore that she would regard the pledge as sacred. My wife died soon afterward . . . After Bella took the child, I saw her frequently. She brought Jennie to me often and kept her well dressed. The child was happy."[13]

Years later, after he had remarried, Olson tried to regain custody of his daughter. Bella fought him in court and won.[14]

Though Mads never brought home more than fifteen dollars in weekly wages (equivalent to roughly $450 today), he and Bella somehow managed to acquire enough money by 1894 to purchase a small candy store at Grand Avenue and Edward Street. Occupying the street-level floor of a two-story wood frame building, the store (as a newspaper photograph makes clear) sold tobacco and cigars, newspapers and magazines, stationery, and some grocery staples, along with the popular confections of the time.[15] Despite its location in a busy commercial district, however, the shop failed to prosper, and Bella watched with growing consternation as her cherished money drained away.

Less than a year after she and Mads bought the place, a fire broke out in the store. At the time, no one was present except Bella and her foster daughter, Jennie, then a three-year-old toddler. "The first known of the fire," reported the *Chicago Tribune*, "was when Mrs. Sorenson, with her child, came running out onto the sidewalk, crying 'Fire!' at the top of her voice."[16] By the time the blaze was extinguished, the interior of the store had been completely destroyed. Though Bella claimed that "a small kerosene lamp had exploded," insurance investigators, sifting through the debris, could find "no trace . . . of glass fragments or other evidence of a broken lamp." Despite suspicions of arson, the insurance company ultimately paid up. Soon afterward, the Sorensons divested themselves of the store, selling it to the brother of its original owner.[17]

Having recouped their investment, Bella and Mads moved out to the "blue-collar fringe of the well-to-do suburb" of Austin, where they purchased a three-story, bay-windowed house on Alma Street.[18] Over the next two years—between 1896 and 1898—they became the parents of four more children: Caroline, Myrtle, Axel, and Lucy.[19] Whether these were babies born in rapid succession to Bella (then in her late thirties) or, as seems more probable, orphaned or unwanted infants that she took in (perhaps, according to later accounts, "for a monetary consideration")—remains, even today, a matter of dispute.[20] One fact is certain. Soon after their births, two of them died: Caroline at five months old, Axel at three months. At a time when the US infant mortality rate was shockingly high—approximately one hundred deaths per one thousand live births—no suspicions were aroused by the sudden passing of the little ones, whose causes of death were given, respectively, as enterocolitis (acute inflammation of the bowels) and hydrocephalus (commonly called "water in the brain").[21]

Mads, who had found work with the Chicago & Northwestern Railroad, was bringing home wages of twelve dollars a week, when a seemingly golden opportunity came his way.

On the evening of Friday, October 1, 1897, the Sorensons were visited at home by a gentleman named Angus Ralston, who presented himself as the agent and chief engineer for an enterprise known as the Yukon Mining & Trading Company. Ralston explained that Yukon Mining was "a corporation of great financial resources that had been incorporated with a capital stock of $3,500,000, owned mines in New Mexico, and had great and extensive interests in Alaska and the Klondike regions." The company was presently hiring miners willing to endure the rigors of a yearlong stretch in the Alaskan wilderness for the chance to strike it rich. At Bella's urging, Mads quickly signed on, entering into a formal agreement with the company that was signed, sealed, and witnessed on October 27.

According to its terms, Mads agreed to "go to Alaska in the employ of [the company] and prospect for gold, locate same, and do any other kind of work that the manager in charge of the expedition requires done, for one year, beginning April 1, 1898." In return, he would not only be paid "the same wages as other men in the camps where the mines are located" but also receive "one-fourth interest on all mines located by him," along with twenty-eight hundred shares of stock in the corporation. Since the Sorenson family would be without their breadwinner for a full year, the company also agreed "to pay Bella Sorenson, his wife, thirty-five dollars each month while he is in their employ and to charge same to his account for salary."[22]

Bella—who, as her sister observed, cared little for Mads as a person—was happy to send him off for a year to prospect for gold. Blinded by the promise of dazzling wealth, she and Mads also agreed to invest a considerable sum of their own money to cover his "supplies for one year." On the same day that Mads entered into his agreement with the company, he and Bella signed over a joint promissory note for seven hundred dollars (equivalent to over twenty thousand today), putting up the deed to their Alma Street property as collateral security.

What happened next is detailed in a lawsuit Bella and Mads subsequently launched against the Yukon Mining & Trading Company. "In compliance with said contract," reads the document, Mads "made all preparations and at great sacrifice and expense to himself to go to Alaska, and presented himself to said corporation on or about the first day of April, 1898, and informed the officers of said corporation that he was then ready to fulfill his contract and would hold himself in readiness to go to Alaska." When two months passed with no word from any representative of the company, he and Bella, their suspicions aroused, contacted a lawyer who "demanded the right to examine the books of said corporation." His investigation confirmed the Sorensons' worst fears.

Far from the booming gold-mining operation it purported to be, the Yukon Mining & Trading Company had "absolutely no financial resources." According to the bill in chancery filed by Bella and Mads in June 1898,

> said corporation had not and has not any interest of any value in any mines in New Mexico, Alaska, or elsewhere. [It is] absolutely without means, and it has given away large blocks of stock, to wit: five hundred and twenty-five thousand shares. [Its] officers and promoters are men without means and men who are not financially responsible. [It] was formed for the sole purpose of defrauding innocent investors, and never at any time intended to fulfill its contract . . . [It] is now entirely defunct, insolvent, and abeyant [with] no assets or means to pay its legitimate debts or to continue in business.

Like others whose greed gets the better of their judgment, Bella and Mads had fallen victim to a scam. Their promissory note, along with the accompanying trust deed on their property, had been sold to a real estate salesman and mortgage broker named Emanuel Hogenson for five hundred dollars.[23] When that note came due in two years, the Sorensons would be required to pay him seven hundred dollars plus interest or risk losing their home.

Though the Sorensons ultimately prevailed in their lawsuit, preventing Hogenson from cashing in on their note, their get-rich-quick dream had come to a mortifying end.[24] Mads returned to his earlier job as night watchman at the Mandel Brothers department store, while Bella seemed destined to spend the rest of her days as the wife of a low-earning workingman. But as events would soon prove, she had other plans.

On the evening of Tuesday, April 10, 1900, a fire, reportedly caused by a "defective heating apparatus," broke out in the Sorensons' Alma Street home. Though firefighters arrived in time to save the building, Bella and Mads suffered the loss of roughly $650 worth of "household goods." Fortunately, as the *Chicago Tribune* reported, "all the property destroyed was insured," and the couple received another hefty settlement.[25]

For Bella, there was still more to come.

At the time of the fire, Mads belonged to a mutual benefits association that provided him with a $2,000 life insurance policy, set to expire on Monday, July 30, 1900. He had decided to let that policy lapse and take out a new one for $3,000 that would become operative on the same day.

That very Monday afternoon, Dr. J. C. Miller, a young physician who had once boarded with the Sorensons, received an urgent summons from Bella. Hurrying to the Alma Street address, he found Mads, fully clothed, lying dead atop his bed. By then, another doctor—Charles E. Jones, the Sorensons' family physician—had arrived. Questioning Bella, they learned that her husband, who was suffering from a bad cold, had come home from work that morning complaining of a "fearful headache." She had given him a dose of quinine powder, then gone down to the kitchen to prepare dinner for the children. When she went back upstairs a short while later to check on her husband, she had found him dead.

Thinking, as he later explained, that "the druggist had made a mistake and [given] her morphine instead of quinine," Miller asked to see the paper in which the powder had been wrapped. Bella replied that she had thrown it away. With no other evidence to go on beyond the symptoms as Bella described them, the two doctors concluded that Mads had died of a cerebral hemorrhage.[26]

For Bella—the sole beneficiary of her husband's two life insurance policies—the timing of his sudden death could not have been more fortuitous. "Had Sorenson died a day earlier," one newspaper later explained, "his wife would have been able to collect only on the first policy for $2,000, or if a day later, only on the second for $3,000. Dying as he did, she collected on both the old and new policies, a total of $5,000." Translated into today's dollars, the widow Sorenson was richer by $150,000.[27]

Three days later, on the morning of Thursday, August 2, 1900, Mads Ditlev Anton Sorenson was laid to rest beside his two infant children at the Forest Home Cemetery. Among those attending the funeral was Bella's estranged sister, Nellie. Exactly what transpired between them is unknown, though—according to Nellie's testimony—she was gripped at one point with a dark premonition.

"While I was there," she would later recount, "a terrible feeling came over me. I felt just like something was going to happen." The sensation hit her with such force that she grew dizzy and "could not stand up." Another eight years would pass before she understood the meaning of the dread that seized her that day.[28]

3.

THE GRINDER

Situated on McClung Road on the outskirts of La Porte, the property known locally as "Mattie Altic's Place" had a checkered history. The original owner of the land was John C. Walker, one of La Porte's founding fathers, who, in 1846, erected an imposing house for his daughter, Harriet, and her husband, John W. Holcomb. Nearly twenty years later, in 1864, the Holcombs—whose Southern sympathies made them pariahs in a county that sent more than twenty-five hundred men to fight for the Union cause—left La Porte for good.[1]

Not long after they absconded, the house was reportedly sold to one B. R. Car, a local coal and lumber merchant whose son, G. Hile Car, became the leader of an outlaw band that "terrorized that section of Indiana." When things got too hot for the gang, the younger Car headed west to Denver, where he was eventually shot to death during an attempted bank holdup. Soon after his son's body was shipped back home, the elder Car sold the place and disappeared from La Porte, leaving behind a bundle of unpaid debts.[2] In the following years, the house passed through the hands of several more reputedly ill-fated owners, including two brothers who "died so suddenly that the coroner was called in to investigate," a farmer who hanged himself in an upstairs bedroom, and, in 1892, the individual who would briefly hold the title of "the most notorious woman in northern Indiana," Mattie Altic.[3]

A transplanted big-city madam, the flamboyant Mattie—a statuesque woman in the Gibson Girl mold who sported a hat with an enormous ostrich plume when she went shopping downtown—transformed the place into the region's classiest whorehouse, complete with a marble-topped bar in the front "entertaining room," a fancy carriage house, and a flashy, fringe-topped surrey used to pick up her clients when they arrived by train from Chicago. When she died suddenly a few years later, the cause was officially given as heart disease, though stories persisted that she had either taken her own life after being jilted by a lover or been poisoned by her sister, a rival brothel keeper named Eva Ruppert, who ran a competing "resort" (as the newspapers euphemistically described it) in South Bend.[4]

Despite its "sordid reputation," the Altic place had no trouble attracting buyers.[5] In the eight years after it ceased to operate as a bordello, it would have a succession of owners before being purchased by the woman whose infamy would so vastly surpass that of its earlier proprietress that, by comparison, Mattie Altic would seem as respectable as a midwestern schoolmarm.

Exactly how Bella Sorenson learned that the Altic place was for sale is unclear. Following the death of her husband, she paid a visit to a relative on a farm in Fergus Falls, Minnesota, and the idea of resettling on a farmstead of her own seems to have taken hold of her then. Back in Chicago—according to certain historians of the case—she placed a classified advertisement in the *Tribune*, seeking a suitable property. The ad caught the eye of the then-current owner of the Altic place, who contacted Bella. An agreement was struck, and in November 1901, after selling her Alma Street property, Bella Sorenson and her three children, Jennie, Myrtle, and Lucy, moved to La Porte.

The people of her new community would know her by a different name. Though she continued to sign herself "Bella" in her private correspondence, she adopted the plainer, more typically American "Belle" in her dealings with her neighbors. And within a few months of her arrival in La Porte, her last name was no longer Sorenson.

During their first decade of marriage, Belle and Mads had briefly taken in a boarder named Peter Gunness. Surviving photographs of Peter confirm one writer's description of him as a "fine-looking blond Viking of a man with clear blue eyes and a pointed yellow beard and mustache."[6] An emigrant from Oslo who arrived in this country in 1885, he joined his brother, Gust, in Minneapolis before moving to Chicago in 1893—the year of the great World's Fair—where he rented a room from the Sorensons while working in the stockyards. After a brief visit back to Norway, he returned to Minneapolis, where, in June 1895, he married a young woman named Jennie Sophia Simpson. They lived in a house on Hennepin Street while Peter worked as "an order man for a grocery house." Their first child, a girl they christened Swanhild, was born in 1897. Four years later, Jennie Gunness died while giving birth to their second child, another girl.[7]

During her visit to her cousin in Minnesota following Mads's death, the widow Sorenson made it her business to take a trip to Minneapolis and become reacquainted with her handsome—and suddenly available—former boarder. The years had not been kind to Belle. Hardly a beauty to begin with, she had aged into a coarse and mannish figure, described, in the particularly harsh words of one of her contemporaries, as a "fat, heavy-featured woman with a big head covered with a mop of mud-colored hair, small eyes, huge hands and arms, and a gross body supported by feet grotesquely small."[8] That she had so little trouble attracting men, even one as handsome as Peter Gunness, says much about the seductive appeal of her forty-eight-acre Indiana farmstead. On April 1, 1902, the physically incongruous couple were married in the First Baptist Church of La Porte, the Reverend George C. Moor officiating.

Five days after the nuptials, Peter's seven-month-old daughter died. "Edema of the lungs" was given as the official cause of death. Her body was shipped to Chicago, where it was interred in the Forest Home Cemetery beside the remains of the two other infants who had died in Belle's care.[9]

Eight months later, at around 3:00 a.m. on Tuesday, December 16, Swan Nicholson and his family—the Gunnesses' nearest neighbors—were startled awake by a sharp banging on the front door, as though someone were striking it with an iron rod. Hurrying downstairs in their bedclothes, they found Belle's foster daughter, Jennie, standing on their porch, a stove poker clutched in one hand.

"Mamma wants you to come up," said the twelve-year-old girl. "Papa's burned himself."

When they arrived at the Gunness farmhouse a few minutes later, Swan and his young son Albert found Belle seated in the kitchen, so overwrought that she could barely speak coherently. Her husband, dressed in his long white nightshirt, was sprawled facedown in the parlor—"laying on his nose and blood on the floor," as Nicholson later testified. Squatting by the body, Nicholson "took hold of his arms to feel the pulse and tried to talk to him. But he wouldn't give me no answer."

Ordered to go fetch a physician, young Albert ran all the way into town and roused Dr. Bo Bowell, then serving as the county coroner. While the doctor got dressed, Albert hurried over to the barn where Bowell stabled his rig. Then the two quickly drove to the Gunness place.

Striding into the parlor, Bowell got to his knees and made a close examination of the body, while the others—Swan, Albert, Jennie, and a sobbing Belle—stood around in a circle. Bowell could tell at once that Gunness had been dead for some time. The body was already growing rigid. The back of his head bore an ugly wound, thickly caked with blood, and his nose was broken and bent to one side. Bowell's immediate impression was that the man had been murdered.

Belle, whose "condition bordered on hysteria," was led back into the kitchen and seated in a chair. Bowell did his best to find out what had happened, though the story he managed to extract from the inconsolable woman raised more questions than it answered. From what he could gather, her husband had gone into the kitchen to get his shoes, which he kept near the stove to stay warm. As he stooped to retrieve them, a meat grinder had tumbled from a shelf above his head, striking the back of his skull and overturning a bowl of hot brine that scalded his neck. Despite his injuries, he'd assured her that he was all right and had lain down to rest. A few hours later, she'd discovered him dead on the parlor floor.

Though Bowell found this story highly suspect, he decided to reserve judgment until a postmortem could be performed the next day. Young Albert Nicholson, however, harbored no such doubts. As he and his father headed back home, he "remarked that he thought Mr. Gunness had been murdered. His father cautioned him not to say anything of the sort, or there might be trouble for Mrs. Gunness."[10]

Reporting on Peter Gunness's death the following day, newspapers exhibited little of the caution that Swan Nicholson had urged on his son. "Crime of High Degree," blared a headline in the *Fort Wayne Daily News*. During the past few weeks, so the paper declared, murder had been "running rampant in La Porte County." Residents were still mourning the death of the heroic young Wesley Reynolds, killed in a shoot-out with two would-be bank robbers. The three "negro footpads" who had murdered grocer John Koonsman remained at large, despite a five-hundred-dollar reward offered for their capture by the local Retail Merchants' Association. Police were attempting to track down the person who had sent a box of arsenic-laced bonbons to young servant girl Matilda Baker who, "unsuspecting the poison in the candy, partook freely of it." And the mother of seventeen-year-old George Shearer barely escaped death when the youth "suddenly became demented and tried to kill [her] with a carving knife."

This string of tragedies had culminated with the sudden death of Peter Gunness in a "mysterious manner" that gave "strong indications of foul play."[11]

On the afternoon of December 16, Dr. Bowell, assisted by another local physician, Dr. H. H. Martin, conducted a postmortem on Gunness's body. As detailed in his official report, Bowell found "no evidence of scalds or burns on the entire body." Gunness's "nose was lacerated and broken, showing evidence of severe blows (or the result of falling upon a blunt article such as the edge of a board)." The most significant wound was "a laceration through the scalp and external layer of skull about an inch long, situated just above and to the left of the occipital protuberance. Upon removing the pericranium, there showed a fracture and depression of the inner plate of the skull at a point corresponding to the external laceration. There was also marked inter-cranial hemorrhage." Bowell concluded that "Death was due to shock and pressure caused by fracture and said hemorrhage."[12]

Far from shedding light on the mysterious circumstances of Gunness's death, as Bowell had hoped, the autopsy only exacerbated his doubts about the story he had gotten from Belle. Determined to get at the truth, he announced his intention to impanel a jury and conduct an inquest.

The inquest was held on Thursday, December 18, 1902, at the Gunness farmhouse, in the room where Peter died. Belle, the primary witness, underwent a lengthy and at times quite pointed interrogation by Dr. Bowell, while his clerk, Louis H. Oberreich, transcribed the exchange.

Asked to describe the events of that fateful night, Belle explained that, after putting her children to bed, she had gone into the kitchen to stuff sausage casings with the freshly butchered pork Peter had ground for her that afternoon. After completing the task, she had washed the meat grinder, then retired to the parlor, where Peter was reading the newspapers.

"We were sitting here looking at them, I think it was after eleven o'clock," she recalled. "I said to him, 'I guess it's pretty near time to go to bed.' He thought so, too, and he picked up his pipe and went out into the kitchen. He always used to lock the door before we went upstairs to sleep. And I heard him make some little noise out there, and he always put his shoes back of the stove to warm, and I guess he must have been back to get hold of a pair of shoes, and all at once I heard a terrible noise and I dropped my paper and went and when I came out there, he was raising up from the floor and putting both hands on his head. I had a big bowl with some brine on the back of the stove, and I was going to put it on some head cheese I left there, and the bowl was full and hot and I thought I couldn't use it until tomorrow morning and thought I might as well leave it there until morning."

"Where was that?" asked Bowell. "On the stove or the shelf?"

"On the back part of the stove. I had washed the meat grinder and wiped it off and put it on a shelf of the stove to dry. I generally put my iron things up there to dry. 'Mamma,' he says, 'I burned me so terrible.' I was so scared I didn't know what to do, all his clothes were wet. I said, 'You had better take your clothes off.' He said, 'My head burns terribly.' I heard baking soda and water was good to put on so it would not get blistered, so I put that on. I bathed a towel in it and put it on his neck."

"Was all this brine spilt?" Bowell asked.

"Yes," said Belle. "I think the bowl was nearly empty."

"Was that brine boiling hot?"

"Well, it had been boiling," said Belle, "but it had stood for some time on the stove, so it was not so warm but it was warm enough to burn. I rubbed him with Vaseline and liniment."

When Bowell asked if she had noticed the wound on the back of his head while she was ministering to him, Belle acknowledged that she had.

"Was it bleeding?" asked Bowell.

"Not very much," she replied. "The bleeding seemed all to be stopped."

Told to continue, Belle explained that they sat in the kitchen while she rubbed Vaseline on her husband's scalded neck. "He said he was afraid he was going to lose some of his hair on account of that burning, and he was complaining terribly." They then returned to the parlor and "sat there a couple of hours anyway." By then, "he was beginning to get a little better and I said, 'Don't you think you had better lay down?' And he said, 'Probably I will,' and I said, 'You had better not go upstairs to bed but lay down on the lounge and I will fix that up there, for it is warmer.' He thought so, and I went and fixed the lounge for him and took off his clothes and put on his nightshirt. I told him, 'I think I'll go up and lay down with the girls, and if there is anything you want call me down.' So I went up and went to sleep. I was tired."

In dramatic terms, Belle narrated the grievous denouement. "All at once, I heard him calling. He was over by the door and calling 'Mamma' as fast as he could and so that the children waked up and I was trying to think and said they should keep quiet, that I had to go to Papa, that Papa was burned. I tried to put on my clothes because it was cold. I went down the steps and when I came down he was walking around the room and saying, 'O Mamma, Mamma, my head. I don't know what is the matter with my head.' I asked what the matter was. 'My head, my head,' he says. 'It's like something going on in my head.' 'Papa,' I said, 'what are you talking about? Let me see what it is, I suppose you rubbed off the skin.' 'O my head, my head.' 'Well, if you think it is best, I had better send for the doctor,' I said, and I went upstairs and I got the girl up and she went over to the Nicholsons. And when I came from upstairs he was holding his head and said, 'O Mamma, I guess I am going to die.' I asked him what was paining him so terrible and took him some water and he said not to touch his head. When Nicholson came to the door I was rubbing his head, and I opened the door, I think, and they come in and he then thought he was gone but I did not think he was gone before you came, I think he was only unconscious."

"About how long do you think it was from the time that he was hurt out there before he died?" asked Bowell.

"Well, I guess it must have been after eleven o'clock he was hurt, and I didn't think he was gone until after you come here."

"You sat up with him two hours after he was hurt?"

"Yes," said Belle. "Of course I wasn't upstairs long. I said good night and went upstairs and was there a short time when he called me."

"Did you say that he was burned bad?"

Belle nodded. "He was red on the neck and the skin was blistered by the ear here."

"How do you think he got that hurt on his head?"

"I don't know, Doctor. I picked up the meat grinder from the floor, and I think that must have tumbled on him one way or another, that's what I think but I didn't see it."

"Did he say anything about it?" asked Bowell.

"He didn't say anything about the hurt on his head."

"When you found that cut, did you tell him his head was cut?"

"I asked him where he had been with his head because it was sore in the back but he didn't tell me."

In response to Bowell's further inquiries, Belle averred that her husband never explained how the bowl of hot brine "came to tip over on him" beyond saying that he "must have got against it in some way." When asked how he broke his nose, she professed ignorance. "I can't say. I didn't notice the nose before they told me."

"Didn't he complain of that?" asked Bowell. "Didn't he bleed from the nose?"

"He didn't bleed from the nose at all," said Belle.

Bowell wondered if Belle "thought it possible that somebody may have come in here and killed him, hit him with that sausage grinder, and you not hear him?"

She was emphatic in her denial. "If anybody had come in, I would have heard them some way or another."

Bowell had a final question regarding Belle's relationship with Peter, whose dreadful death in her presence just two days earlier had seemingly sent her into a wild paroxysm of grief.

"You always lived happily together, you and him?" Bowell asked.

"As far as I know," a dry-eyed Belle said with a shrug.

Jennie Gunness, six months shy of her thirteenth birthday, testified next. Her account of what happened on the night of her stepfather's death jibed precisely with Belle's. Her parents, she said, "had been butchering a pig and they were fixing the meat and they were going to make sausage." After completing the work, "Mamma washed everything and put it on the stove . . . to dry." She then joined her husband in the parlor, where they sat "reading the paper and then I guess he was just going to go out and get his shoes." Moments later, after hearing a startling noise, Belle hurried into the kitchen to find that Peter "had burned himself . . . she didn't know it was anything else and thought he had better take a little rest."

After getting him settled on the couch, Belle had gone upstairs to sleep beside her children. A short time later, she "heard him call, 'Mamma, Mamma.' He told her his head hurt and she should come down to him."

Asked what happened then, Jennie replied that she had "gotten right up" and come downstairs, where she found her stepfather lying on the parlor floor. While her mother tended to his burns, Jennie "went right out to the Nicholsons," taking "the stove poker to rap on the door to get them up." When she returned with Swan and his son, Belle, who seemed beside herself, "told them to go right for the doctor."

"Did she tell you he scalded himself?" asked Bowell.

"She said he had burned himself," Jennie answered. "She didn't know it was anything serious."

"When she was bathing his head, did she find he was cut?" Bowell asked.

"I don't know, I guess she only thought it was just a little place, for it didn't show."

"How do you think he got hurt on his head?"

"Well, I couldn't tell you, or Mamma either," said Jennie, "but when she came out there that thing was on the floor."

"Didn't he tell her?"

"Not that I know of."

"Don't you suppose he knew his head was cut?"

"Well, I suppose he did, but I don't know."

Suspecting that the girl was merely repeating what her mother had told her to say, Bowell asked if the two of them had "talked about how he got hurt." Jennie shook her head vigorously, insisting that "we haven't talked at all." At the same time, she admitted that she had been asleep when the purported accident occurred. Given how exactly her story matched her mother's, it seemed inescapably clear that, despite her denials, she had been carefully coached.

As Bowell certainly recognized, there were deeply troubling aspects to the story related by Belle and echoed by her foster daughter. Even conceding its weight, could a meat grinder, knocked off a shelf by a stooping man, really strike his head so hard as to fracture his skull? How could Belle and Peter sit together in the parlor for two hours without once discussing the cause of the accident? Why didn't he mention his head wound? How could she not notice his broken, bloody nose? Why hadn't the autopsy revealed any evidence of burns?

Some of Bowell's questions to Jennie made it unmistakably clear that he not only harbored serious doubts about Belle's version of events but suspected that she might be what future criminologists would call a "Black Widow" killer—the type of female psychopath who murders a series of mates for their money. Did Jennie's stepfather have life insurance? Did he leave a will? Had he brought "any money with him" when he moved to La Porte? To each of these questions, the twelve-year-old girl gave the same answer: "I don't know."

She had more to say when Bowell suddenly asked if she had been "in the house" when her mother's first husband, Mads Sorenson, died.

Acknowledging that she had, Jennie poured out a breathless account of that day. "He worked during the night for the Mandel brothers," she said, "and he came home generally at eight o'clock in the morning, and then he slept through the day and every morning we would always sit on the porch and he would play with us, and that morning I went down and sat down on the front porch with some chums of mine and then he said he would go up to bed, and he went there and there were some other people living there by us and Mamma went in the laundry and was washing out some clothes and Mrs. S called to her and told her that Papa was calling her and she ran up and asked him what he wanted and he just told her to lock the door and then she brought him some water but he didn't drink it, and all at once we heard a scream but I don't know where Mamma was then, she came downstairs and they said he took hold of his bedclothes and gave a scream and died."

"Did he leave you any life insurance?" asked Bowell, revealing once again his forebodings about the now twice-widowed woman who had lost both her husbands under such peculiar circumstances.

"I don't know."

"Didn't he leave any money at all?"

"I don't know. I think he did, but I don't know anything about that."

Where, asked Bowell, did her mother get the money to "buy this place"?

"Why, I don't know," said Jennie.

The inquest concluded with the testimony of Swan Nicholson, who stated that he "didn't see no burns" on Peter Gunness's body. Nor had he observed any blood on the couch where the severely wounded Gunness had supposedly gone to lie down. Asked if he thought that the "sausage grinder falling from where it did, hitting [Gunness] on the head, could have broken his skull," he gave a somewhat equivocal answer. "I think it could have possibly but I never thought there was anything else but the way she told me."

Bowell ended his brief interrogation by asking directly if Nicholson thought it "possible that [Mrs. Gunness] might have killed him." This time, Nicholson was more emphatic. "No, I never thought that, no sir. They be like a couple of children, and the same as the day they were married." Just a few minutes earlier, however, at the start of his deposition, Nicholson had testified that he knew virtually nothing about his new neighbors. Asked about his impressions of Belle, he had replied: "So far as I knew I found her to be all right, but we had so little dealing with her, we were up there, my wife was up there once last winter, but I wasn't up there but once."

By the time Bowell conducted his inquest, the community was aswirl with "rumors regarding foul play," as one local newspaper reported.[13] Residents scoffed at Belle's explanation for her husband's death. "Peter Gunness was killed with a meat grinder *dropping* on his head," sneered one farmwife. "A very likely story!"[14] Belle's reported behavior at her husband's funeral also raised eyebrows. The service took place in the parlor of the Gunness farmhouse on Friday, December 19. The rites were conducted by the Reverend George C. Moor, the same minister who had united Belle and Peter in marriage just eight months earlier. "During the preaching," writes one chronicler of the case, "Belle sat moaning with her fingers before her eyes. Albert Nicholson could see, however, that she was peering alertly between them to check the effect she was making."[15]

Young Albert remained so convinced of her guilt that, following the funeral, he wouldn't stop sharing that opinion with other attendees until "Pa told me to shut up."[16] He was hardly alone in his view. It came as a shock, then, to many La Porteans when Dr. Bowell issued his findings on the same day that Peter Gunness was buried in the Patton Cemetery.

"After having examined the body and heard the evidence," it read, "[we] so find that the deceased came to his death by the accidental falling of the augur part of a sausage mill falling from the heating shelf of cook stove in his kitchen and striking him on back of head: the impact of said augur part of sausage mill causing fracture of skull & inter-cranial hemorrhage resulting in death."[17]

If Bowell's report officially put an end to the case, it did little to quell the rumors. One of these would come to be widely accepted as unquestioned truth. It concerned little Myrtle Sorenson, five years old at the time of her stepfather's death. Just a week before her own death, so tradition has it, "she whispered in the ear of a small schoolmate, 'My mamma killed my papa. She hit him with a meat cleaver and he died. Don't tell a soul.'"[18]

4.

THE FARM WIDOW

A few months after Belle's second husband was consigned to his grave, another child was added to her household, a boy she named Phillip. Mysterious circumstances attended the infant's arrival. The midwife who came to assist with the delivery was bewildered to find that the baby had already "been born, bathed, and dressed."

Later that morning, after being notified by young Jennie Gunness that her mother had "gotten a little baby boy," a neighbor named Catherine Lapham went over to lend a hand. Much to her amazement, Belle was at the cistern out back, washing clothes.

"You shouldn't be up!" exclaimed Mrs. Lapham.

"Ah," said Belle, "in the old country they never go to bed after they get a baby."

Another farmwife, Mrs. Louisa Diesslin, was similarly astonished when she visited the following day and found Belle "in the yard chasing pigs and running around." When Mrs. Diesslin expressed her shock—"How can you do that, a new mother?"—Belle, once again, shrugged off her neighbor's concerns.

Besides the seemingly miraculous recuperative powers of the forty-three-year-old new mother, there was something else that struck each of these women as strange. As one of them put it, the baby "looked too old to be a newborn." Rumors quickly spread that the widow Gunness hadn't given birth at all. The boy, neighbors speculated, must have been adopted.

In later years, other, far more sinister theories about the child's origins would circulate among the people of La Porte.[1]

Among those least persuaded by the official verdict on Peter Gunness's death was his brother, Gust. Suspecting that foul play was involved not only in his brother's case but in the sudden death of seven-month-old Jennie Gunness—the infant who had died less than a week after Peter's marriage to Belle—he had reason to be concerned about the well-being of his surviving niece, five-year-old Swanhild, who remained in her stepmother's care. He also knew that, prior to the marriage, Peter had taken out a $2,500 life insurance policy, naming Swanhild as the beneficiary. Gust wanted to make sure that the payout ended up where it belonged.

In the early months of 1903—the exact date is uncertain—Gust traveled to La Porte from his home in Minneapolis. He was reassured to find that, though occasionally lonely for her family members back in Minneapolis, Swanhild appeared to be doing well. He was less satisfied when he inquired about the $2,500 she was owed. Before her late husband's unfortunate demise—so Belle explained—Peter "had turned the insurance policy over to a mining company for the purchase of stock, and if the stock ever amounted to anything, Swanhild would be a rich girl." When Gust asked to see the stock certificates, however, Belle could not produce them. Instead, she made him a proposition: that he "stay with her and manage the farm." Given the doubts he harbored about the manner of his brother's death, it is hardly surprising that he declined the offer. Belle reacted with a baleful look. "I didn't like her eyes," Gust would say later. He stayed at the farm for several days with a growing sense of unease. One morning, less than a week after his arrival, Belle awoke to find that Gust was gone—and that he had taken Swanhild with him.[2]

The friendly relations Belle enjoyed with her neighbors when she first came to La Porte were not fated to last. "No one was a friend of hers," Louisa Diesslin's daughter, Dora, later recalled. "You didn't want to have nothing to do with her. All the neighbors, not just us."

Belle's break with the Diesslins was provoked by a conflict over some stray cows. As Dora explained, Belle's two heifer calves kept wandering onto the Diesslins' property to graze in their fields. Infuriated by this gross "violation of small-town codes," Dora's father warned Belle that, unless she kept her cattle fenced in, he would demand payment for the use of his pasture. The next time he found the calves on his property, he made good on his threat, locking the cows in his barnyard and refusing to return them until Belle paid him a dollar. Shortly afterward, she retaliated. Spotting some of Diesslin's cows grazing along the road, she drove them into her yard. When William hurried over to retrieve them, she demanded a dollar for their return.

"But you run them in here off the road!" Diesslin shouted.

Belle coolly insisted that the cows were "trespassing" and repeated her demand.

When the outraged Diesslin reached for the gate to free his cows, Belle turned to her foster daughter, Jennie. "Go in and get the revolver," Belle ordered. Moments later, the girl ran back out with the gun.

"Don't touch that gate," said Belle, leveling the weapon at Diesslin.

"And so he had to pay her a dollar!" Dora recounted. "*That's* the kind of neighbor she was!"[3]

A similar clash over livestock led to her rupture with the Nicholson family, until then her closest friends in the community. As Albert Nicholson told the story, a bunch of Belle's pigs kept roaming onto his family's farm and getting "into the corn." Tired of driving them home, his father, Swan, finally shooed them into his own pigpen, then hitched up his buggy and headed into town to lodge a complaint with the constable. Belle was forced to pay a fine to retrieve them: eleven dollars, "a dollar a head for damages."

The following Monday, Albert's mother was in town when she ran into Belle. Though Swan Nicholson's testimony at the coroner's inquest over Peter Gunness's death had been instrumental in keeping Belle from being indicted for murder, he had now—in the warped view of the "money-mad" woman—committed an ultimate offense. Her broad face reddening with fury, Belle turned on Swan's wife and spat: "That's all Mr. Nicholson has been trying to do all these years is get my money. Well, now he has got it. I don't want nothing more to do with any of you!"

From that time forward, the Nicholsons and Belle Gunness never spoke or set foot on each other's farmsteads again.[4]

With Peter gone, Belle assumed the work that would normally have been performed by a man. She did her own planting and harvesting, pitched her own hay, milked her own cows. Wearing a sealskin cap, a man's leather coat, and a pair of her husband's old shoes, she would join the men at farm auctions, "tramping around in the mud . . . looking at farm machinery, while the rest of the women stayed up near the stove." At livestock sales, she would buy a two-hundred-pound hog, then lift it up and toss it into her wagon as easily as if it were a sack of laundry. When the time came to butcher the animal, she handled the business herself—"shot it, bled it, scalded it, gutted it, and saved the head for head cheese."⁵

Like other local farmers, she earned extra money by selling some of her produce in town. One La Porte native, Mabel Carpenter, would always recall the day in her childhood when Belle Gunness drove up to her house in a ramshackle buckboard, hopped off the seat, then lifted "up this great big basket of potatoes, [put] it on her shoulders . . . and marched right into the house."⁶

An inventory of Belle's farm property would eventually include "sows, a boar, stoats, heifers, calves, a bull, chickens, horses, a foal, a Shetland pony . . . wagons, a cultivator, planter, harrow, binder, plow, harnesses and saddles, saws, ladders, wheelbarrows, buggy, pony cart, bales of wire, and all sorts of buckets and rope."⁷ Even for a woman of Belle's exceptional strength and abilities, such a substantial operation was more than she could manage on her own. By the winter of 1904, she was in pressing need of a man—and not just to help out with the farmwork.

In February of that year, thirty-year-old Olaf Lindboe—a Norwegian immigrant who had arrived in Chicago three years earlier—came upon a "help wanted" ad in the Norwegian-language newspaper *Skandinaven*. The job was for a laborer on a farm in La Porte, Indiana. Packing his worldly belongings—including his life savings of $600—he headed for Indiana, where he was promptly hired by the proprietress of the farm, the widow Gunness.

Within a short time of his arrival, neighbors began to notice that he and Mrs. Gunness seemed to enjoy an unusually close relationship—so much so that, as one newspaper reported, it was "generally accepted that he was her fiancé."[8] Lindboe himself did nothing to dispel that notion. Writing to his father back in Norway just two months after coming to work for Mrs. Gunness, he rhapsodized about the "exquisite location" of the farm and "mentioned that he might be getting married soon." To the other immigrants he befriended, including Swan Nicholson, he was even more direct. As Nicholson later testified, Mrs. Gunness was "very kind to [Olaf]—so kind that he became imbued with the notion of marrying her. Olaf began to look upon himself as master of the farm."[9]

Not long after Lindboe posted the letter to his father, one of Belle's neighbors, Chris Christofferson, received word from Mrs. Gunness that "she needed help [because] her hired hand, Olaf, had left in the middle of a major job." Belle was in the field plowing corn when he arrived. When Christofferson asked about Olaf's disappearance, she explained that he had gone to St. Louis to see the World's Fair "and that he was going to buy some land" there. Swan Nicholson heard a different story: that his friend Olaf had gone "home to see the new king of Norway crowned." And when Olaf's father, after receiving no communication from his son for many months, wrote to ask about his whereabouts, Belle sent a letter saying that, from what she understood, he "went west and took up a homestead someplace."[10]

In truth, he was still on her farm. Four years would pass, however, before Olaf Lindboe—or what remained of him—was seen again.

During the second week of April 1905, just months after Lindboe's disappearance, neighbor Chris Christofferson was at the Gunness place when a stranger arrived from town. Introducing himself to Christofferson as Henry Gurholt, he explained that he had "come there to work for Mrs. Gunness." He had a heavy trunk with him, and Christofferson helped him carry it up to the room recently vacated by Lindboe. Gurholt was very pleased with the accommodations and conveyed his appreciation to his new employer.

"Oh yes," said Mrs. Gunness, "I always like to have it neat and nice for a person who works for me."

Everything about his new situation was to Gurholt's liking. In a letter to his mother written a week after his arrival, he described the farm as "one of the nicest places in the neighborhood," with a handsome, thirteen-room brick house surrounded by "a grove of nice green trees." "I am being treated almost the same as one of the family," he declared.[11]

Chris Christofferson saw Gurholt repeatedly over the following weeks, often in Mrs. Gunness's company. One day in August 1905, during harvesttime, Belle appeared at the Christofferson home and asked if he could help her stack oats. Gurholt, she explained, had suddenly quit.

"Did he leave you at such a time, when he had just cut the oats?" Christofferson exclaimed.

"He said he was sick and couldn't do the work," answered Belle. He had gone to Chicago, she said, taking only "a satchel with some clothes." His trunk and the bulk of his garments, including a heavy fur coat, he had left behind.

That winter, as he later testified, Christofferson saw Mrs. Gunness wearing "the fur coat which Gurholt had left." Puzzled as to why a man would move to Chicago without his coat, Christofferson asked Belle "if Gurholt didn't want it"—if "he hadn't written to her for it."

No, Belle replied, she "had not heard a word from him."[12]

5.

THE MISSING

In the late summer of 1905—shortly after Henry Gurholt disappeared—a classified advertisement began appearing in Norwegian-language newspapers throughout the Midwest, including the *Minneapolis Tidende*, the *Decorah-Posten* in Iowa, and the *Skandinaven*. Translated into English, it read:

> WANTED—A woman who owns a beautifully located and valuable farm in first class condition, wants a good and reliable man as partner in same. Some little cash is required and will be furnished first class security.[1]

Interested parties were invited to write to "B. G." care of the newspaper.

Precisely how many replies this ad elicited is unknown, though D. J. Hunter, the postman who delivered mail to Belle Gunness's farm, later reported that she typically received "from one to four" letters every morning, and sometimes as many as "eight or ten letters a day."[2] Among the first to respond was a middle-aged Norwegian immigrant named George Berry, who left his home in Tuscola, Illinois, with $1,500 in cash—roughly $40,000 in today's money—after informing acquaintances that he was moving to La Porte "for a job and possibly marriage."[3] A few weeks later, a subscriber to the *Decorah-Posten*, Christian Hilkven of Dover, Wisconsin, sold his farm for $2,000 and bid farewell to his friends after arranging to have the paper forwarded to his new address in La Porte.[4]

Informing his boss that he was going "to marry a rich widow," Emil Tell, a Swedish bachelor from Osage, Kansas, quit his job at the Howard-Massey Furniture Company and traveled to La Porte "with $2,000 in his pocket."[5] Fifty-year-old widower Ole Budsberg of Iola, Wisconsin, sold his farm to his grown sons and—explaining that "he was going to La Porte to get married"—set out for Indiana with $1,000 in cash.[6] In December 1905, John Moe, a forty-year-old bachelor from Elbow Lake, Minnesota, and a *Skandinaven* subscriber, visited his local bank to cash $1,000 in checks, explaining to the teller that "he was going to La Porte, Indiana, where he would use the money."[7]

And there were more. Many more.

According to the subsequent testimony of Emil Greening—"a square-cut, commonsensical, happy" nineteen-year-old hired as a farmhand—"Mrs. Gunness received men visitors all the time. A different man came nearly every week to stay at the house. She introduced them as cousins from Kansas, South Dakota, Wisconsin, and Chicago. Most of the men that came brought trunks with them. Mrs. Gunness kept the cousins with her all the time in the parlor and her bedroom. She was always careful to make the children stay away from her cousins."

None of these men stayed around very long, though neither Greening nor anyone else ever witnessed their departure. Strangely, every one of them left his trunk behind. Eventually, Greening recalled, "there were about fifteen trunks, and one room was packed full of all kinds of men's clothing. Mrs. Gunness said that the cousins had left their clothes, and she wasn't certain that they'd be back for them."[8]

In the summer of 1906—during one of the intervals between visits from her many male "cousins"—Belle hired a local man, a Polish immigrant named William Brogiski, to dig a couple of holes in the muck of her fenced-off hog pen. She was very exact about their dimensions: six feet long, three feet wide, and four feet deep.

"They are to be rubbish pits," Belle explained.

The following week, Brogiski had occasion to return to the farm. The holes, he noticed, still lay empty. As he later testified, he "never saw what went into the bottom of these pits, nor when they were filled."

Several years would pass before Brogiski, along with the rest of a horror-struck world, discovered their true purpose.[9]

By the fall of 1906 Belle's foster daughter, Jennie, had blossomed into a strikingly pretty sixteen-year-old. A photographic portrait taken around that time shows a fresh-faced, full-lipped young woman with thick blond hair, mild eyes, and flawless skin: the very picture of a fetching, milk-fed farm girl. Unsurprisingly, she had attracted several male admirers.

One of these was Emil Greening, Belle's young farmhand. Over the course of his lengthy employment at the farm, he and Jennie had become confidants. "She told me a good deal about herself when we were alone," Greening would later explain. Sometime in the winter of 1906, she informed him that her mother had decided to send her to college in California and had arranged for one of the professors to come to La Porte and escort her to the school.

Shortly before Christmas, Greening heard that the professor had arrived. Early the next morning, he was sent on an errand. When he returned, he asked to see Jennie so that he could bid her goodbye. He was nonplussed by Belle's response.

"Mrs. Gunness told me that Jennie had left that same morning," Greening said. "But no one saw her leave. And no one about the place ever saw the professor."[10]

John Weidner, a young carriage shop worker who was paying court to Jennie, had a similar experience. During a visit to her home about ten days before Christmas, Jennie told him that she was going off to Los Angeles to attend college. Her mother had made all the arrangements. Weidner was crestfallen. Jennie herself did not seem especially happy about leaving and made him promise that he would return the following Sunday to say goodbye.

When Sunday came, Weidner hired a buggy and went out to the farm. "It was snowing. Blowing," Weidner later recalled. "When I got there, I rapped on the door and asked for Jennie. Mrs. Gunness said, 'Why, Jennie has gone to Los

Angeles.' I said, 'Is that so? How funny. She asked me to come see her before she went.' Mrs. Gunness said, 'Yes, she went Wednesday.'"

Over the course of the next half year, Weidner sent several letters to Jennie in California but received no reply. Encountering Mrs. Gunness in town one day in October 1907, he told her of his failed efforts to communicate with her daughter.

"Oh, that's all right," Belle said with a laugh. "I heard that you had gotten married and wrote to tell Jennie."

Weidner explained that it was his brother who had gotten married and "asked her to write and tell Jennie that I was still single." Mrs. Gunness promised that she would.

But Jennie never wrote to him.[11]

6.

RAY

With Jennie gone, life on the Gunness farm lost whatever charm it possessed for Emil Greening. In June 1907, six months after her abrupt departure, he quit his job and headed west. One month later, he was replaced by Ray Lamphere.[1]

Newspaper photographs of Lamphere show a thin-faced, long-nosed man with a thatch of dark curly hair, a bushy unkempt mustache, and eyes with the look of a wild, cornered animal. Thirty-seven years old at the time he became involved with Belle Gunness, he was the son of a once-prominent member of the community, William W. Lamphere, a former schoolteacher, politician, and justice of the peace who "had drunk away his money, his respectable social position, and his happy home."[2]

Like his father, Ray was overly fond of the bottle. Though a skilled carpenter when sober, he was generally regarded as a "weak, worthless, no account man" whose wages—when he earned any—were squandered on liquor, whores, and gambling, and who was reputed to have lost fifty dollars in a single night on a backroom saloon slot machine.[3]

Accounts of how he came to be hired by Belle differ. Several chroniclers claim that—having had her eyes on him for a while—she stopped him on the street one day in June and proposed that he come live at the farm and work for her. Others, more convincingly, say that, as a member of the local Carpenters' Union, Ray heard about some "work that needed to be done at the Gunness farm from a fellow carpenter and met up with Belle for an interview in La Porte. She hired him on the spot."[4]

Whatever the case, it is certain that, by early July, Lamphere was living at the Gunness place, occupying the room on the second floor of the farmhouse recently vacated by Emil Greening. He had also—as he regularly boasted to his drinking companions—become her lover. The notion of the slightly built young man throwing himself into a sexual affair with the coarse-featured, 280-pound female nearly eleven years his senior has led at least one student of the case to indulge in some armchair psychoanalysis, speculating that it was Belle's "very maturity" that made her irresistible to Lamphere. "To a lonely man with an urge to be mothered, to return to the security of the womb, such a woman may have represented the safety of fulfillment without any of its responsibilities."[5]

Perhaps. It is also true, however, that other employees of Belle's had become her bedmates. One of them, Peter Colson, who worked on her farm for two years, would later describe in titillating detail how she would come to his room at night and make "love to him with sweet words and caresses." She "purred like a cat," Colson testified. "She was soft and gentle in her ways. I never saw such a woman."[6]

Throughout the fall of 1907, Ray and Mrs. Gunness were often seen together. Looking much like Jack Sprat and his wife, they rode into town in her wagon and strolled side by side along the streets. To his cronies, he would crow that she had begged him to marry her, and he flaunted the gifts she had lavished on him, including a handsome silver watch. From a town laughingstock—a "shiftless loafer and bum," as one newspaper described him—he was to become master of a fine, sprawling farm.[7]

And then Andrew Helgelien showed up.

7.

HELGELIEN

Beginning in the summer of 1906, even while other respondents to her ad were arriving regularly at her farm, Belle embarked on a correspondence with Andrew Helgelien,[1] a forty-nine-year-old wheat farmer from South Dakota, who had seen her advertisement in the *Minneapolis Titende.* Over the course of the next eighteen months, she would send dozens of letters to him—between seventy-five and eighty, according to the most reliable sources.[2]

All were written in Norwegian and were so sloppy in their diction, spelling, and penmanship that the translator who later provided English versions for the court described them "as extremely faulty and evidently the work of an ignorant person."[3] Crudely composed as they were, however, these "siren missives" (as one contemporary newspaper called them) worked their sinister spell, luring their recipient, like the parade of eager suitors who preceded him, to the place soon to be known throughout the nation as the "murder farm."[4]

That Belle spent a year and a half setting her snare says a good deal not only about her malevolent cunning but about Helgelien himself. Unlike most of her earlier victims, he was no easy prey. Among the few surviving photographs of him are a full-face view and accompanying profile: his prison mug shot. A burly, thick-necked Norwegian of somewhat porcine appearance, he had spent ten years in the Minnesota Correctional Facility for robbing the village post office in Red Wing, Minnesota, then burning down the building in an attempt to destroy any evidence. At the time he responded to Belle's ad in 1906—twelve years after his release—he was farming in Abderdeen, South Dakota, not far from his brother, Asle, a homesteader in nearby Mansfield and a sister, Anna, in Lebanon.[5]

Addressing him as "Dear Sir" and signing herself as "Mrs. P. S. Gunness," Belle wrote back to Helgelien on August 8, 1906, describing herself as the owner of "a beautiful home right in the midst of where the rich people have their fine summer homes . . . All kinds of fruit trees abound here and good new houses with all improvements and fine boulevard roads." She claimed to "have 74 acres of land"—50 percent more than the actual size of her spread—with an estimated value of "$12,000 to $14,000" (roughly equivalent to $400,000 today). To see if he was a worthy candidate for her attentions, she closed by asking him "to tell me a little further respecting yourself" and, most crucially, "how much cash you intend to invest."[6]

Though Helgelien's half of their correspondence no longer exists, it is clear from Belle's next letter to him, dated August 20, that he wrote back at once and that his response more than satisfied her of his assets. Her tone conveys the barely suppressed excitement of an angler who has felt an enormous catch take the hook and must summon every bit of skill to reel it in.

"Dear Friend," the letter began. "You impress me with being a good man with a strong and honest character. A real genuine Norwegian in every respect, and it is difficult to find such a man and not every woman appreciates. There are plenty of these American 'dudes' around here but I would not even look at them, no matter how often they asked me." She presented an idyllic picture of her adopted state, describing Indiana's climate as "mild in the winter and not so very warm [as South Dakota] in the summer, with plenty rain and no storms and the land is all good so we can raise everything."

La Porte, in her telling, was a place of golden opportunity. "There is a good market for everything because it is so near Chicago, and the land is going up all the time," she wrote. "There are very many who are almost millionaires now by having bought pieces of land a few years ago and have doubled the price many times and sold out the land in small lots to business people in Chicago for summer homes . . . You will have a much better chance to make use of your capital here, and it will probably make you independent for the rest of your life." Declaring that she had chosen him to be her partner "out over a hundred applicants," she urged him not to delay. "Take all your money out of the bank," she advised, "and come as soon as possible."

By September—just a month after they first made contact—Bella (as she would spell her name in all succeeding letters) was already treating Helgelien not as a mere business partner but as a potential mate. "I long so to know you better but I will try to wait with patience until you get [here]," she wrote in the fervent tone of a lovesick woman yearning to be reunited with her absent sweetheart. "I have now thrown away all the other answers I got and keep all of yours in a secret place by themselves . . . You truly do not know how highly I prize them as I have not found anything so genuine[ly] Norwegian and real in all the 20 years I have been in America."

In her enamored eyes, Helgelien towered above the common run of men, and she could hardly wait to devote herself entirely to his needs. "I do not think a queen could be good enough for you," she gushed, "and in my thoughts you stand highest above all high and I will not let anything stand in the way of my doing anything for you."

She sketched an enticing portrait of the blissful domestic life they would share. "We shall be so happy when you once get here," she vowed, "then I will make a cream pudding and many other good things . . . How lonesome it must seem for you to be up there all alone, but you must hurry and come to me as soon as you can . . . You have been there long enough and worked hard for many a day and now you must take it easier for the rest of your days."

There was one thing, she stressed, that would make their new life together even sweeter. Helgelien must tell no one of his plans to join Belle in La Porte, especially his family members. "When we get all settled we will have your dear sister Anna in Lebanon visit us," she promised. "But my dear, do not say anything about coming here, then the surprise will be so much greater when she finds it out . . . It is so much pleasure to keep this secret to ourselves and to see how surprised everyone will be when they find it out."

Before signing off, she made sure to emphasize the practical advice she would repeat many times in the following months. "Now sell all that you can get cash for, and if you have much left you can easily take it with you, as we will soon sell it here and get a good price on everything. Leave neither money or stock up there but make yourself free from Dakota so you will have nothing more to bother with up there.

"Now my dearest friend," she closed, "come soon."

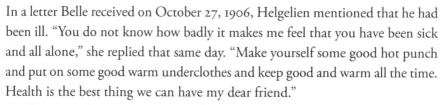

In a letter Belle received on October 27, 1906, Helgelien mentioned that he had been ill. "You do not know how badly it makes me feel that you have been sick and all alone," she replied that same day. "Make yourself some good hot punch and put on some good warm underclothes and keep good and warm all the time. Health is the best thing we can have my dear friend."

Expecting his imminent arrival, she promised to meet him at the train depot. He would have no trouble recognizing her: "I am a rather stout woman," she said with considerable understatement, "a genuine Norwegian with brown Norwegian hair and blue eyes." Helgelien could expect the warmest of welcomes. "You must remember that you will get a meeting that comes from the heart. Even if the world has been a little hard with me, I have just the same kept my good nature."

It was important, she repeated, that no one else be privy to his travel plans, delivering her advice with a flirtatious wink. "Come alone," she said. "Do not take anyone from up there with you before we become a little acquainted . . . Do you not think that would be best if we were alone, especially at the beginning?"

She ended with the kind of farewell that lovers exchange during long separations. "Now I must close because I am getting sleepy. I will now go to bed and think about you."

With winter approaching and no indication that he had made his travel arrangements, Belle's tone became more urgent. She pleaded with her "dearest best friend" to settle his affairs as quickly as possible and hurry to her side. "Why must you stay so long up there where it is so bad? I am now so afraid that you will become ill if you stay any longer. If only you were here, we could have it so much better, both you and I . . . You do not need to stay up there and work yourself to death, dear friend, but, as you say, live in peace and get a little good out of life."

Conveying a wifely concern with his well-being, she admonished him to bundle up for the journey: "Procure some good woolen underclothing and a good big bearskin coat so you will not take cold on the trip." His health, however, was not her sole concern. "You talk of leaving some of your money up there. This I would not do if I was you," she counseled. "Take all your money and bring it with you when you come, as you can get high interest for your money here . . . My dear friend, have all the money changed into bills, into as large a denomination as possible, and sew them real good, first on the inside of your underwear and put a thin piece of cloth under so it would not be noticed and sew it good."

Once again, she reminded him of the importance of maintaining absolute secrecy. "Do not say one word about it to anyone, not even your nearest relative." Here, as before, Belle's words take on a distinctly suggestive quality, "implying between the lines what could happen between the sheets," as one historian puts it.[7] "So dear friend," she wrote, "this is a secret between us and no one else. Probably we will have many other secrets between us, not so, dear friend? . . . We will have many things between us which no one else will know which we will enjoy, won't we, my dearest friend? I will surely see to it that you will enjoy yourself."

She ended with a word of caution that, in light of what she truly had planned for Helgelien, reveals much about the depravity of her character, the sadistic pleasure she clearly derived from toying, catlike, with an intended victim. Reminding him again of the need to protect his money during the journey, she urged him to be on his guard. "I know now that you are a man with knowledge of many things and have seen how smooth and evil so many people are and how much fraud and tricks they are up to, and would take all one had and do not want to work but live on others and do not care what evil they do . . . My friend, just keep away from such people."

In early December 1906, Belle received word from Helgelien that he would be unable to make the move to La Porte as soon as they had hoped. "My dearest best friend," she wrote back on the fourteenth. "You do not know how downhearted I became when I read that you could not come for Christmas and that you have decided to remain up there all winter. Who will eat all this Norwegian codfish, cream pudding, etc. and enjoy all the pleasures I have planned?"

Disappointed as she was, however, she assured him that she would continue to wait patiently for him. "I place you higher in my affections than any one on this earth," she declared, "and will remain true until you come." With her usual calculation, she ended with a picture of shared domestic contentment that must have been irresistibly tantalizing to a lonely bachelor fending for himself on a harsh Dakota farmstead. "If only you were here with me and were sitting in a rocking chair talking to me. Then I would go and get you a glass of fruit wine which I made myself, but you will get it when you do come, my dear friend."

Shortly after the new year, Helgelien received word from Norway that his mother had died. On January 12, 1907, Belle sent a consoling letter, urging him to take comfort from the knowledge that his mother had gone to her reward—that "the Lord has called her home.

"It is hard when the bond breaks between which keep together the parents and children," Belle conceded. "But we must all bow down to our God's wise guidance and we know that sometime we shall meet again. We must try and make the best of our lives as long as we live in this wicked world and we will not grieve over the dead, they have received their rest and we must hope they are with God in heaven, joyous and happy."

The best remedy for bereavement, she asserted, was to put aside thoughts of the departed and "live for the ones who are here with us and do the best we can for them." In Helgelien's case, that meant hastening to the side of the person so eagerly awaiting his arrival. "Now, my dear friend," she closed, "I hope you will do all you can to get here as soon as possible."

With the coming of spring, Belle—who clearly saw no excuse for any further delay—intensified her pressure on Helgelien. Addressing him not merely as her "dearest best friend" but as her "very best and faithfullest friend in the whole wide world," she filled her letters with relentlessly rosy pictures of their future life together.

"I wait so for you," she wrote to him in April. "When you come, then we will have many calves, little pigs, chickens and kittens. This will be fine and lots of fun, won't it? All these animals I have, I make such pets of them and they all like me so well."

Several weeks later, she reported excitedly that she was "fixing up inside the house" in preparation for his arrival. "It will be real comfortable and pleasant when it is all ready and then I hope you will be here and everything is all right," she exclaimed. "Then we will be so cozy and have some good homemade cake and some good coffee and cream pudding and many other good things. Then we will also sit and talk and talk until we get so tired we cannot talk any more. Yes, my dear friend, we will make up for this long waiting, that you can be sure of . . . Oh, if only you knew how I would love to talk with you about everything, my good friend . . . Yes, my dear friend, it will be so pleasant."

Though Helgelien had evidently given Belle good reason to believe that he would finally join her in the summer of 1907, he postponed his departure again. That fall, for the first time, she gave vent to her frustration.

"Now it is already the 25th of September and last year at this time I waited for you and yet you haven't come to me," she chided. "I know you are a man I can trust and therefore I have waited so faithful but it is so tiresome and lonely to wait so much longer and the fall is here again and I have the whole year managed the best I could without steady help because I have waited for you from one time to another as you have promised and promised and it seems as if you will never get your belongings in order up there."

Though assuring him that he remained her "dearest, faithfullest, and only friend in the whole world," she ended with a thinly veiled ultimatum. "Make up your mind as soon as possible as to what you really intend to do . . . In your next letter let me have the great happiness to hear that you are soon on your way here as then I will be the happiest and will know that I have found the best friend in the world."

Helgelien's reply, like all his other correspondence, no longer exists. From Belle's last surviving letter to him, however, it seems clear that he took her message to heart, assuring her that her long wait would soon be over.

"Dear one, make all haste, I beg of you," she wrote on December 2. "I am so anxious about you, my only and very best friend in all things. I wait every day to hear that you are coming, and be sure to arrange all matters so that you will not have to go back any more."

Another month would pass before he made good on his promise. In early January 1908, Andrew Helgelien finally came to La Porte.

8.

THE RIVAL

Having happily settled into the role of Belle Gunness's paramour, carpenter, and farmhand, Ray Lamphere received a cruel jolt on the morning of Friday, January 3, 1908, when a burly stranger in a shaggy fur coat that hung down below his knees arrived at the farm. Later that day, Belle informed Ray that she was turning over his bedroom to her guest. Ray, she said, could "go sleep in the barn."[1]

At daybreak the next morning, Ray returned to the house and, following his usual morning routine, started building a fire in the parlor stove to warm up the room before breakfast. He was just finishing when the new man came downstairs. The two struck up a conversation that was interrupted when Belle appeared and angrily motioned Ray aside. "She gave me the dickens," Ray would testify, "and told me to leave him alone."

With the arrival of the big Norwegian farmer from South Dakota, it seemed to Ray that his whole relationship with Belle had changed overnight. "We got along all right before that and she used to come to my room at night," he said later. "But after he came, she had no use for me."[2]

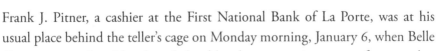

Frank J. Pitner, a cashier at the First National Bank of La Porte, was at his usual place behind the teller's cage on Monday morning, January 6, when Belle Gunness came in with a broad-shouldered man wearing a gray fur coat that reached to his shins. Introducing himself as Mr. Helgelien, he presented three certificates of deposit from the First National Bank of Aberdeen, South Dakota, and announced that he wished to redeem them for their full value. When Pitner explained that he would have to send them to the issuing bank for collection, Mrs. Gunness asked how long that would take.

"Four or five days," Pitner estimated.

Though Helgelien accepted the delay without complaint, Mrs. Gunness couldn't conceal her annoyance. "She argued and urged," writes one historian, "but no cash was forthcoming, and at last they went away moneyless."[3]

A draft for the full amount arrived at the La Porte bank on January 11, but three more days elapsed before Mrs. Gunness and Helgelien showed up again. When Pitner lightly remarked that they seemed in less of a hurry for the money now, he was told that Helgelien had been sick for the past few days.

Given the amount—$2,839 (nearly $75,000 in today's dollars)—Pitner suggested that he write a cashier's check. Helgelien seemed willing, but Mrs. Gunness insisted that he take the entire sum in cash. As Pitner counted out the money—half in gold coins, half in currency—he asked Helgelien what he meant to do with it all.

"Mind your own business!" Mrs. Gunness snapped, then took her companion by the arm and led him from the bank.[4]

Later that same day—Tuesday, January 14—Belle sent Ray Lamphere off on an errand. She had arranged a horse trade with a cousin of hers, she explained. John Moe was his name. Lamphere was to meet him in Michigan City, where the transaction would take place. If, for some reason, Moe failed to show up that evening, Lamphere was to spend the night there and await her cousin's arrival the next morning.

At around 5:00 that evening, Lamphere set out for Michigan City, about twelve miles away from La Porte. He brought along a friend for company, a brewery-wagon driver named John Rye. There was no sign of Moe at the livery barn where the swap was supposed to take place, so Lamphere and his pal killed a few hours, first at an oyster house, then at a five-cent vaudeville show.

At around 8:00, after checking again at the livery barn, Lamphere, in defiance of his employer's express orders, told Rye that he was heading back to La Porte. They caught the 8:15 interurban car, pulling into La Porte about an hour later.

Saying that he wanted "to see what the old lady was up to," Lamphere promised to meet Rye later at Smith's saloon, then strode off in the dark toward the Gunness farm. Rye waited at the bar for an hour but Lamphere never showed up.[5]

As for Andrew Helgelien, no one ever saw him alive again.

9.

ENDGAME

In preparing for his trip to La Porte, Helgelien had ignored some of the suggestions so lovingly proffered by his dearest best friend in the whole wide world. He had not, for example, withdrawn all his cash from the local bank and brought it with him sewn inside his underwear. In other regards, however, he had gone along with her proposals. Evidently, he agreed with her that it was best to tell no one about their relationship—that his plan to start a new life with Belle should remain a delicious secret between the two of them. As a result, before setting off for Indiana on January 2, he had said nothing to his brother, Asle, about his destination—only that "he would be back home in a week surely."[1]

When ten days passed with no sign of his brother, Asle grew concerned. Thinking that Andrew might have gone to see a family friend named Minnie Kohn in Minneapolis, Asle sent her a letter. She confirmed that Andrew had paid her a visit but said that he had stayed only "about one hour."[2] "I am surprised to hear that Andrew is not home," she wrote.

John Hulth, the farmhand Andrew had hired to look after his livestock, had also begun to wonder about his employer's absence. Looking around Andrew's cabin for a clue to his whereabouts, he came upon dozens of letters, which he promptly turned over to Asle. All were signed "Bella Gunness."[3]

Precisely what happened between Belle and Ray Lamphere on February 3, 1908, is unclear. Some newspaper accounts claim that she fired him; others that he quit following a dispute over some unpaid wages.[4] It is certain, however, that a bitter break occurred between them on that date. So abrupt was Ray's departure from the farm that he left his clothes and carpenter's tools behind. Less than a week later, she hired a replacement, Joseph Maxson, who took up residence in the second-floor bedroom reserved for Belle's hired hands.

In the meantime, Lamphere had consulted a local attorney, who counseled him to return to the farm, demand his money and belongings, and, if refused, inform Mrs. Gunness that he was prepared to file a replevin suit, an action to recover unlawfully taken personal property. Lamphere did as advised. Far from being cowed by his threat, however, Belle not only drove him from her property but immediately wrote several letters to the county sheriff, Albert Smutzer, complaining that she was being harassed by her former handyman. The following month, after spotting Lamphere skulking around her farm, she had him arrested for trespassing. Tried on March 13 before Justice of the Peace S. E. Grover, Lamphere, with no legal representation, pleaded guilty and was fined one dollar plus costs.[5]

In mid-March, after writing to the La Porte postmaster and confirming that Mrs. Gunness was a resident of the city, Asle Helgelien sent Belle a letter. She responded on March 27. "You wish to know where your brother keeps himself," she wrote. "Well this is just what I would like to know but it almost seems impossible for me to give a definite answer." According to her highly dubious account, Andrew had left home to search for another of his brothers, a professional gambler who had absconded from Aberdeen in January. After failing to find him in Minneapolis, Andrew had briefly stopped off in La Porte before continuing on his quest. "He was going to make a thorough search for him in Chicago and N[ew] York," she wrote. "He always thought he, the Bro., had gone to Norway and he would go after him."

Belle claimed that, after arriving in Chicago, Andrew sent her a letter "saying that he was to look for his brother the next day & he said I shouldn't write until I again heard from him. Since then I have neither heard or seen anything of him."

"Now this is all I can say to you about the matter," she said in closing. "I have waited every day to hear something of him."[6]

On March 28, one day after writing her letter to Asle Helgelien, Belle filed an affidavit alleging that Ray Lamphere was insane.

According to the document—a printed questionnaire on which her responses were recorded by hand—she noticed "the first signs of insanity" in Lamphere in December 1907 when "he told me things that I knew were not true and unreasonable." Asked if he had "shown any extraordinary propensities of feeling or conduct," she replied with an emphatic "Yes. He comes to my house every night, at all times of night, and looks in the windows, commits misdemeanors." Though he had already been found guilty and fined for this harassing behavior, he "continues same," generally while "intoxicated." Presented with a checklist of behavioral traits that best described Lamphere, Belle indicated that he was "silent, melancholy, restless, seclusive, dull, profane, filthy, intemperate, sleepless, and criminal."

Appended to Belle's affidavit was a statement from Ray's physician, Dr. Bo Bowell, who testified that he had "prescribed for Lamphere at different times during past five years. Have never treated him for any mental disturbance. I do not consider him insane."

The three-member insanity commission appointed to examine Lamphere and rule on Belle's allegation came to the same conclusion. "We find patient quiet, clean, and neat," they wrote. "He is slightly nervous. His memory is good for recent and remote events. Speech is intelligent and coherent. Ray Lamphere is not insane."[7]

Thwarted in her effort to have Lamphere declared insane, Belle had him arrested again for trespassing in early April. His trial was set for the fifteenth. Shortly before it took place, Asle Helgelien wrote to her again, asking to see the letter she had referred to in their previous exchange, the one ostensibly sent to her by Andrew from Chicago.

Belle replied that she was unable to do so, because the letter had been stolen by "a man named Lamphere, who worked for me for a while . . . This Lamphere began to find so many wrong things to talk about until at last they arrested him, and they had three doctors examine him and see if he was sane. They found him not crazy enough to put in a hospital. But perfectly sane he is not. He is now out under bonds and is going to have a trial next week . . . but one thing I am sure of is that in one way or another he has taken the letter from Andrew he had sent me. Others have told me that Lamphere was jealous of Andrew and for that reason troubled me this way."

To represent him at his second trial, Lamphere retained the services of local attorney Wirt Worden, who requested a change of venue to the nearby town of Stillwell. The proceedings took place as scheduled on Wednesday, April 15, Justice Robert C. Kincaid presiding.

During his cross-examination of Belle, Worden, seeking to undercut her credibility, launched into an increasingly combative interrogation of her past.

"Peter Gunness, your husband, died very suddenly, didn't he?" he inquired.

Instantly, the state's attorney, Ralph N. Smith, was on his feet. "Objection!"

"He carried considerable life insurance, didn't he?"

"Objection!"

"You collected that life insurance, didn't you?"

Smith, growing angrier by the moment, told the witness "that she did not need to reply."

"Mrs. Gunness," said Worden, "how did that sausage grinder and crock of hot brine come to drop on Mr. Gunness' head, anyway?"

Springing to his feet, Smith, his face flushed with indignation, "protested in strong language against the practice of browbeating a witness and insulting a defenseless woman."

Undeterred, Worden proceeded to question Belle about the sudden death of her first husband, Mads Sorenson—"how he happened to die, whether he had any life insurance, and whether she got the life insurance." Smith's heated objection to each of these questions was sustained by Justice Kincaid. When Worden then pressed Belle about the suspicious circumstances of Mads's death—"Wasn't there some talk about taking up his body to see if he had been poisoned?"—Smith gave full vent to his outrage. "I object to these questions!" he cried. "They have nothing to do with this case. I demand that they be stopped." Then, turning to the witness stand, he said: "Mrs. Gunness, you would be justified in waylaying this man on his way home!"

Justice Kincaid concurred. "I think these questions have gone a little too far," he told Worden.

Worden, seemingly chastened, indicated that he was ready to dismiss the witness. As Belle was getting to her feet, however, he said: "Oh, just a moment. When will your daughter, Jennie Olson, return, Mrs. Gunness?"

This question brought a sharp response from Justice Kincaid, who rebuked Worden "for wasting the court's time by asking such questions."

By the time she left the stand, Belle, who had been perfectly composed at the start of Worden's interrogation, was visibly agitated. To Kincaid, there was nothing surprising about her reaction: it was that of "any decent woman resenting such insinuations." Soon enough, he would arrive at a very different conclusion: that Worden's pointed questions had been deeply unsettling to Mrs. Gunness, reinforcing her fear—already aroused by Asle Helgelien's inquiries into his brother's whereabouts—that her crimes were catching up with her.[8]

Lamphere was found guilty and ordered to pay a fine of five dollars plus costs—a total of $19.01, which was covered by his current employer, a farmer named John Wheatbrook. But Belle wasn't done with her former farmhand and lover. Less than a week later, she had him arrested again for trespassing.[9]

He was lodged in the county jail when Belle received another anxious letter from Asle Helgelien. In Belle's reply, dated April 24, she expressed her "wonder . . . "as to where Andrew keeps himself." Promising to "tell you all I know," she repeated her earlier story, adding a few minor details. "I cannot remember the accurate date he left La Porte, but it was either the 15th or 16th of January," she began.

> My little daughter . . . took him to the street car station. He
> went by way of Michigan City as he had a desire to see that

little town about 12 miles from LaP[orte]. He didn't stay there more than a day and he left here at one o'clock in the afternoon.

Two or three days afterwards I had a letter from him from Chicago saying that he had hunted for his brother, but did not find him . . . If he couldn't find him, he would go to New York and find out if he had gone to Norway. If such was the case I think he would go to Norway too. As I said before he told me not to answer his letter until I had one from him telling where he would stop for a little while so he could get an answer. This is all I can tell, and I haven't his letter. I got the letter in the morning and read it and laid it in a china closet in the kitchen and went to milk & when I came back the letter was gone. That Lamphere was here and he had probably taken it . . .

I don't understand what keeps [Andrew] away so long unless as you say he has gotten into some trouble and does not want any of us to know about it. I for my part thought it was strange I didn't hear from him but I was pretty sure Lamphere had taken his letter but I don't see why he hasn't written to you.

Responding to Asle's proposal that he come to La Porte and initiate a search for his brother, Belle assured that she would be happy to assist him in any way she could, though "I don't know what we could do to find him."

The day after Belle composed this letter, Ray Lamphere was brought once more to trial. On the witness stand, both Belle and her eleven-year-old daughter, Myrtle, claimed that Lamphere "was back to his prowling." Just a few days earlier, they had "spotted him by the pig pen, and hurried out to chase him away. They were within fifteen feet of him when he coolly cut the wire fence, pulled out the fence post, and carried it away."[10]

This time, however, Ray's defense lawyer Wirt Worden was able to call a pair of witnesses—"two substantial citizens of the county"—who swore that, on the day his client was allegedly vandalizing her property, "Lamphere was at the home of . . . John Wheatbrook, about six miles out of town, and could not possibly been at the home of Mrs. Gunness." Lamphere was acquitted, leaving Belle to foot the bill for the costs.

Miss Bertha Schultz—a clerk in the Chicago Leader dry goods store on Main Street "who frequently waited on Mrs. Gunness"—later reported that, during the last week in April, Belle had come in looking very distressed. When Miss Schultz asked what was the matter, Belle recounted her troubles with Lamphere, describing "the things which . . . he did to harass her" and declaring that he "acted as if he knew something about her and that he was bold and annoyed her repeatedly."

The next day she was back in the store, once again giving vent to her worries over Lamphere. "She told me that she feared he would some day set fire to her home and buildings," Miss Schultz would say afterward, "and that he would murder her and her children."[11]

10.

MONDAY, APRIL 27, 1908

Joseph Maxson, Ray Lamphere's replacement, would later testify that Belle had kept her daughters home from school that day. Their teacher at the Quaker school, however—Miss Carrie Garwood—told a different story. As Miss Garwood recounted:

> On the morning of April 27, I noticed that the two little girls of Miss Gunness came into the schoolroom crying. Their cheeks were swollen from weeping, and they seemed in great distress.
>
> I called Myrtle to me and asked if she was in trouble. She replied that she and her sister had been given a terrible beating by their mother that morning. It was the first time I had ever seen the children behaving so, and I was surprised. I pursued the questioning and Myrtle told me that she and her sister had started in play toward the cellar of the Gunness house. Mrs. Gunness rushed after them before they reached the bottom of the stairway and dragging them back had given them both a terrible beating.
>
> "You keep out of there," she told the oldest girl. "Don't you poke your faces where they are not wanted."
>
> I asked the children if they had been forbidden to go down into the cellar and they said they had, but they had forgotten the injunction.[1]

Later that day, Belle hitched up her buggy and drove into town. Her first stop was the office of her lawyer, Melvin E. Leliter. Tearfully she informed him that she was living in fear of Ray Lamphere, who was threatening to "burn the house down over my ears."

Leliter advised that the simplest way to deal with Lamphere was to "fill him full of buckshot" the next time he showed up at her farm uninvited. Dismissing the suggestion, Belle told the lawyer that she wished to make out her last will and testament. She "wanted to leave everything in good shape in case something happened."

Leliter proceeded to write out the document according to Belle's instructions. She left all "her property both real and personal to her three children, Myrtle Adolphine Sorenson, Lucy Bergliat Sorenson, and Phillip Alexander Gunness, providing that in the case of the death of any of said children without issue before her death, the survivor is to inherit the whole of the property, and provided also, that in the case of the death of all three of said children without issue, the whole of the property should go to the Norwegian Children's Home of Chicago."[2]

Once her will was completed and signed, Belle took it to the State Bank, where she placed it in a safe-deposit box and made a cash deposit of $730.[3]

Her next errand was at a store where she purchased candy, cake, and a toy train, telling the clerk, Marie Farnheim, that she was "going to give the children a little treat."

"Is it a birthday party?" asked Miss Farnheim.

"No," said Belle. "I am just going to give them a little surprise."[4]

Belle's trip to town that afternoon ended at John Minich's general store, where, as clerk George Wase recalled, she purchased "a large quantity of groceries." She bought something else, too—two gallons of kerosene in a five-gallon can that she borrowed from the proprietor, explaining that she had searched for her own oil can before leaving home but had been unable to find it.

She had been in the store about fifteen minutes when Ray Lamphere entered and asked for a five-cent plug of chewing tobacco. According to Wase, "No words passed between Lamphere and Mrs. Gunness . . . not even a nod of recognition." Lamphere just stood by the counter and glared at her while she finished up her shopping. He then followed her outside and watched as she untied her horse from the hitching post and drove off in her buggy.[5]

⇒ •((◉))• ⇐

Belle arrived home at around 5:30 p.m. Joe Maxson helped her with her purchases, carrying the oil can into the house and stowing it in the entry under the back stairs.

An hour later, he and the family sat down to a supper of "bread and butter, dried beef, salmon, beefsteak, and potatoes. Everyone showed a fine appetite," Maxson said later. "We all had a couple of helpings of beefsteak and lots of cookies and jam."

When the meal was done and the dishes cleared from the table, the five of them—Maxson, Belle, Lucy, Myrtle, and Phillip—repaired to the parlor and "played all kinds of games, the main one being 'Little Red Riding Hood and the Fox.'" According to Maxson's recollections, Mrs. Gunness "loved to play this game and almost cried if the bad fox chanced to catch Red Riding Hood."

By 8:30 Maxson was having trouble staying awake. Bidding the others good night, he headed for the stairway. "The last I saw of Mrs. Gunness," he recalled, "she was sitting on the floor with her daughters and son, playing with the toy engine and passenger coaches" she had bought earlier that day for the children.[6]

PART TWO

THE MURDER FARM

11.

CONFLAGRATION

Mrs. Gunness was already up and cooking breakfast: that was Maxson's first thought as he surfaced from his sleep. From the smell of it, though, the hotcakes were burning. Suddenly, he was fully awake, choking and coughing. His room was filled with smoke.

Leaping from his bed in his long johns, he threw open the window and stuck his head outside. The house was ablaze. He yanked on his boots and started kicking and pounding the door that separated his room from the main part of the house where Mrs. Gunness and her children slept. He tried yelling "Fire!" but the smoke was so dense that he could hardly breathe.

Pulling on his overalls, he grabbed a small satchel and a handful of belongings, then raced down the rear stairs and made for the carriage shed about fifty feet away, where he left his stuff before running back to the burning house. He tried reaching his room again but got only as far as the second-floor landing before the flames drove him back outside.

After trying to kick in the front door, he grabbed an ax from the toolshed and chopped out a panel. All at once, there was a great crackling sound overhead. Looking up, he saw the flaming roof collapse into the bedroom where, just a few minutes earlier, he had lain sound asleep.[1]

Not far away, Mrs. Ella Clifford arose as usual at around 4:00 a.m. to prepare breakfast for her husband, Michael, who went off to work before daybreak. Looking out the kitchen window, she saw her neighbor's house ablaze. She called to her teenage son, William, rousing him from sleep. Within minutes, he was on his bicycle and pedaling furiously to the Gunness place "in order to wake the people, if there was any chance," as he later testified.

He arrived just as Joe Maxson was taking his ax to the front door. Running to his side, the teenager peered through the broken-in panel. All he could see was fire.[2]

By then, Mrs. Clifford had alerted both her husband, Michael, and her brother-in-law, William Humphrey. They arrived at the Gunness place to find Joe Maxson standing helplessly by the front door, ax in hand.

"Where do they sleep?" said Humphrey, yelling to be heard over the roar of the flames.

Maxson pointed to the two upstairs windows on the west side of the house. Searching around, Humphrey found some bricks and flung one at each of the windows. The glass shattered, flames spurted out, but no one responded from inside.

"Is there a ladder around here?" Humphrey shouted to Maxson, who immediately made for the woodshed.

He returned a moment later, dragging a ladder. With Michael Clifford and his son supporting it on either side, Humphrey scaled the rungs and peered through one broken window. There was an empty bed in one corner of the room—"no bodies, just a mattress on the bed, no body or sheets," Humphrey said afterward. Fire was coming through the floor.

Hurrying down, he and the Cliffords moved the ladder to the second window. Again Humphrey climbed to the top, peered inside the other room, and saw nothing but an empty bed. He "thought of going into the room," he testified, "but as the flames were coming through the floor, I was afraid to risk going in."[3]

Humphrey sent Michael Clifford to alert Daniel Hutson, who lived with his family a short distance away. Roused from bed by Clifford's insistent pounding—"I thought someone was going to break the door in," he commented afterward—Hutson, still dressed in his nightshirt, groggily asked what was wrong.

"Are you going to let your neighbors all burn up while you sleep?" cried Clifford, jabbing a finger toward the Gunness place. Looking in that direction, Hutson "saw a constant blaze from every window. Everything was alight with fire."

As Clifford hurried back to the burning house, Hutson threw on his clothes—"I didn't even stop to tie my shoes," he related—and "went over there as fast as I could, half dressed. I got over there and everything was alight with fire. The only place that I saw that wasn't burning was the southwest corner—the wind blowed right hard against that. The east side was ready to drop, and the whole thing was a solid blaze."

Hutson saw at once that there was nothing he and the others could do. "You better notify Sheriff Smutzer," he said to Maxson, who immediately ran to the barn and led out one of the four stabled horses.

"The horse was afraid," Hutson remembered, "but, between the three of us, we got him hitched to the buggy, and Mr. Maxson started for La Porte, the horse going at a good jump."[4]

The courthouse clock read five o'clock when Joe Maxson reached the jail. Manning the desk was Deputy Sheriff William Antiss, who—after hearing Maxson's story—accompanied him to Sheriff Smutzer's house a few blocks away.

Despite the six-shooter he wore cowboy style on his hip, there was something almost dandyish about Albert F. Smutzer. His best-known newspaper photograph shows a round-faced fellow with a large, neatly trimmed mustache and an incongruously snazzy outfit: knitted turtleneck sweater beneath a nicely tailored wool jacket, with a peaked leather cap riding jauntily on his head. He liked to travel in style, too. In stark contrast to his neighbors' horse-drawn modes of transportation, he tooled around town in a snappy red Ford runabout.[5]

With Antiss in the passenger seat, Smutzer drove his automobile out to the Gunness place, while Maxson followed in the buggy. By the time they arrived at the home, only parts of three walls were still standing. "There was nothing to do but watch until the flames died down," one chronicler records. Smutzer summoned the members of the volunteer fire company, who "went to work throwing water by the pailful over the glowing embers and pulling down the tottering fragments of brick wall."[6]

By then, at least fifty spectators had gathered at the scene—a number that would soon grow into the hundreds. Among them was Harry Burr Darling, editor of the *Argus-Bulletin*, one of La Porte's two dailies. That afternoon, his newspaper carried the first of what would quickly become a nationwide deluge of sensationalistic, page-one stories that would not subside for months.

"The house of mystery has become a house of horror," his article began in fine melodramatic style:

> Several years ago this house was associated with a mystery. Today it is a funeral pyre. The tragedy of the husband and father, whose mysterious taking out of the world proved a mystery on which little light was ever thrown, was followed this morning by a holocaust in which the wife and children were tortured to death by flames . . . The fire raged for an hour until nothing remained but three brick walls, which stand as grim evidence of the devastating work of the holocaust.[7]

Though the blaze had burned itself out by daybreak, the heat from the smoldering ruins kept Smutzer and the others at a distance. Setting up a bucket brigade to carry water from nearby Clear Lake, volunteers doused the rubble until it was cool enough to approach. By the cellar door, the men "perceived signs of a blaze so concentrated that it must have been man-made"—the work of an arsonist (or "incendiary," in the terminology of the time). Among the crowd of rubberneckers, a rumor spread that Mrs. Gunness herself, suffering from a "weakened mentality" over her recent troubles, had started the fire—that, as Darling reported, her "despondency . . . caused her to plan and execute the harrowing tragedy."[8]

Sheriff Smutzer and others, however, who knew the details of her ugly feud with Ray Lamphere, believed otherwise. As Darling informed his readers, the officers were firmly convinced that the "former hired hand . . . had set fire to the house through a motive of revenge." Smutzer immediately assigned his two deputies to track down the suspect. At the time the *Argus-Bulletin* went to press that afternoon, however, Ray Lamphere's whereabouts remained unknown. "No trace has been found of the man upon whom suspicion rests," Darling wrote. "He has disappeared."

In the meantime, another hunt was about to commence. Arming themselves with picks and shovels, a dozen men, Smutzer among them, made ready to dig through the ruins of the fire-ravaged house in search of any sign of its missing residents: "evidence," wrote Darling, "of the four lives which were snuffed out."[9]

12.

DISCOVERY

About two miles away from the Gunness farm, beside the tracks of the Lake Shore Railroad, stood the Interlaken School, a progressive institution founded by one of La Porte's most eminent citizens, Dr. Edward A. Rumely. Opened in September 1907 with an enrollment of thirteen male students between the ages of nine and eighteen, its purpose—as Dr. Rumely explained to an interviewer—was to produce young men "of initiative, courage, and self-reliance—men who will dare to do great things, who will not bow before precedent, and who will have the power to become fit leaders of men in this great industrial Republic."[1]

Among the first students to attend the school was Carter Hugh Manny, who, fulfilling Dr. Rumely's ambitions, would go on to have a distinguished career as a businessman, civic leader, and supporter of the arts. At around four o'clock on the morning of April 28, 1908—so he recalls in an unpublished memoir—Manny, then just a few months shy of his seventeenth birthday, was awakened by a schoolmate, "Tubby" Washburne, who occupied a room with a window that faced north: the "exact direction" of the Gunness place. Washburne had "come to tell me that there was a big farm fire a couple of miles away." A few moments later, Dr. Rumely himself made the rounds of the bedrooms, telling "us to stay up and watch if we wished but please not to leave the school grounds."

While Rumely went off to use the school telephone to see what he could learn, Manny accompanied Washburne to his room, where they pulled up chairs before the big open window and watched the conflagration. "The fire was obviously a fair-sized farmhouse," Manny observed, "because it burned for nearly two hours. Had it been a barn, the fire would have consumed it rather quickly."

When daylight came, Rumely informed the boys that the fire had consumed the home of the widow Gunness. "It was the first time we had ever heard the name," Manny reports. There would be no classes that morning, Rumely announced. After breakfast, the boys were free to visit the farm "but should be back by noon."

"Thus," Manny writes,

> after breakfast we all trotted down the tracks and when we reached the site were surprised to see all the things that had developed. There were uniformed men from the sheriff's office, including himself, and a couple of policemen from La Porte. Firefighters were there from volunteer groups, aided by a water tank wagon from La Porte's equipment. One shed building had been set aside for newspapermen and already there were a half dozen or so of these from Michigan City, La Porte and South Bend. Others would soon arrive from Chicago, Indianapolis and other places, for already word had gone out over the railroad telegraph keys telling of the fire and indicating that it was not an ordinary farm fire.

All that remained of "what was once a beautiful country home" were three "ghastly and blackened walls." As Manny watched, a corps of firemen under the direction of Chief Thomas Whorwell, using ladders, ropes, and hooks, tore down the walls, so that searchers could work in the ruins without worrying about falling bricks. By the time they were done, nothing was left but the cellar—"a sort of open well," as Manny described it.[2] With Smutzer leading the way, the searchers began digging through the cellar, while firemen did their best to cool off the still-smoldering debris with bucketfuls of water.

Following a brief midmorning respite, when he went back home for breakfast, William Humphrey returned to the Gunness place and joined in the digging. "The work was conducted under great difficulties," one observer recorded, "for the ruins were a hotbed of coals, from which smoke and steam constantly poured." After hours of labor, however, the men had brought to light nothing but "pieces of bedding, bedsteads, an old pistol, and articles of that kind." By midafternoon, after excavating nearly the entire cellar, they were "becoming mystified, for they began to think that the bodies were not in the ruins."[3]

Only one area—the southeast corner—remained unexplored. William Humphrey was shoveling through the charred wreckage there at around 3:45 p.m., when, as he later put it, his shovel "hit something soft."

He called to Sheriff Smutzer, who was working nearby, "and we commenced to dig carefully." Other men quickly gathered around them. A moment later, Humphrey paused and said, "Here they are."[4]

La Porteans learned of this grisly development just a few hours after it happened, Harry Burr Darling having managed to insert a two-sentence bulletin into his page-one story before his paper went to press. "The bodies of the mother and her children were found . . . piled up together," he announced, "indicating that the mother had evidently made an effort to escape from the house with the children clinging to her."[5]

The following day, a far more extensive account dominated the front page. According to Darling, the condition of little Phillip Gunness—"the youngest of the trio of little innocents [and] the least burned of the four" bodies—told a heart-rending story of his mother's "heroic, but futile effort . . . to save her offspring":

> The mother, aroused from her sleep by the crackling of the flames and the fumes of suffocating smoke, true to the maternal instinct, had thrown a quilt about the child, evidently with the idea of protecting its little body from the cold after they had gained the open. The quilt served to protect in a measure the body of the child.

Catering to his readers' appetite for morbid titillation, Darling did not stint on the ghastly details in picturing the remains of the boy, "whose face was black, with a hole in the forehead evidently from a falling brick. Its limbs below the knees had been burned away. The child's mouth was open, silent testimony to the agony of death."

His description of Phillip's two sisters was an equally shameless blend of mawkish sentimentality and rank sensationalism: "The little girls who the night previous had breathed a tender prayer, lisping the words, 'Now I lay me down to sleep, I pray the Lord my soul to keep,' were but a semblance of human beings who a few hours previous lived in the smile of their Master."

Hideous as these "blackened and dismembered" bodies were, however, it was Mrs. Gunness who "presented the most ghastly appearance." Her body was "an unrecognizable mass, with the bones protruding through the naked flesh." Rendering her remains even more appalling was the absence of her head. Evidently—so Darling surmised—the corpse had been decapitated "by the ruthless and torturing flames." The "diggers in the ruins have yet to find the skull," he reported, "for this would be all that remained of the missing head."

The four corpses were carefully removed from the debris and placed on boards, where they remained until the town undertaker, Austin Cutler, arrived in his hack wagon. The bodies were then loaded on board and driven to the funeral home morgue.[6]

Only one member of the doomed family had escaped the "holocaust," noted Harry Burr Darling: Mrs. Gunness's stepdaughter, Jennie. Even at that moment, the young woman was "on her way from California to this city. She is expected to arrive here in a day or two, and it is thought that she will be able to throw some light on the mystery."[7]

13.

ARREST

Though initial reports claimed that he had "disappeared," Ray Lamphere had, in fact, gone off to work at John Wheatbrook's farm that morning. He was still there when Deputies Leroy Marr and William Antiss drove out in the late afternoon. About a mile from the farm, the road grew so muddy that Marr got out and walked the rest of the way. Just as he reached the front gate, Lamphere—who must have been watching through a window—opened the front door of the house.

"Ray," said Marr, "get on your coat and come to town with me."

If Marr had any doubts that the wiry little handyman had some involvement in the tragedy, they were dispelled by the first words out of Ray's mouth: "Did those three children and the woman get out of the building?"

Asked how he knew about the fire, he told Marr that, after rising at three that morning, he'd set out on the six-mile hike to John Wheatbrook's farm. As he passed near the Gunness farm, he'd seen "smoke coming out of the windows and around the roof."

"Why didn't you yell?" asked Marr.

"I didn't think it was any of my business," said Ray.[1]

Brought to the county jail, Ray was subjected to the first of what would be a string of third-degree grillings—"sweatings," as they were commonly called at the time. The interrogation was conducted by Sheriff Smutzer, Deputies Antiss and Marr, and State's Attorney Ralph N. Smith, who had hurried to the jailhouse when he heard of Lamphere's arrest.

Though Ray stuck to the essentials of his original story, he offered a different explanation for his failure to sound the alarm. "I was afraid I'd be blamed for starting the fire," he said. He also provided a detail he had omitted from his initial account, one that he begged his interrogators not to make public: he had spent the night of the fire in bed with Elizabeth Smith.[2]

The pervasive, everyday racism of American culture in the early decades of the twentieth century—an era of "Mammy" songs, "pickaninny" jokes, and blackface vaudevillians—requires no documentation. It might also be noted that, within twenty years of the Gunness fire, Indiana would be home to the largest branch of the Ku Klux Klan in the nation, with a membership of 250,000— roughly one-quarter of the native-born white male population of the state.[3] It is not surprising, then, that, in referring to Elizabeth Smith, the local newspapers routinely used the name by which she was known among her neighbors: "Nigger Liz."

The daughter of Virginia slaves who migrated to Indiana after the Civil War, Smith was said to have been a beauty in her youth—"the handsomest black girl in Indiana." According to local rumor, she had won the hearts of "many of the young men of the time, not all of whom had black faces." One of her reputed lovers was "a brilliant La Porte lawyer" with whom she bore an illegitimate, half-white daughter. A half century later, stories were still being told of the sensational climax of that affair, "when the man gave her a note for $600 to educate their child and then became converted at a revival, in which he arose and confessed his misdeeds. For thus publicly drawing attention to their affair, the negro girl horsewhipped the lawyer on the public square before a great crowd, the man finally breaking away and finding refuge in a nearby drug store."[4]

By the time of Ray Lamphere's arrest, no vestige of her former loveliness remained. With her bony frame, wrinkled face, tattered black shawl, and "musty, old Mother Hubbard dress," Smith—now in her seventies—cut a scarecrowish figure. Among neighborhood children, her ramshackle, refuse-crammed hovel was believed to be the habitation of a witch. Long into adulthood, many remembered "running past her place as youngsters, filled with terror."[5]

Her advanced age and physical deficiencies appeared to make no difference to Ray Lamphere, a man evidently blessed with highly flexible standards of female beauty. Cast out by his nearly 300-pound lover, Belle Gunness, he had found comfort in the bed of the spindle-shanked Elizabeth Smith.

Visiting the jail on the morning following Ray's arrest, Smith spoke to a local reporter, confirming Lamphere's alibi while discreetly omitting the more scandalous detail that the latter had confessed to officials the evening before.

"That man Lamphere came to my house Monday night and asked for a room," she explained.

> "He said he was sick and had no money. 'If I ever get any money, I'll pay you,' he told me, and then he sat down a while. He fell asleep in the chair and slept about half an hour. Then he woke up and said, 'Are you going to let me have the room?' I told him I thought so, and he went over to Smith's saloon and got something to eat. I had my clock set for 4:30 and he turned it back to 3:30. I heard the alarm go off and went in to wake him up. He was snoring like a good fellow and I told him it was after 4 o'clock. He said, 'My God, I ought to be over to Wheatbrook's by this time' and started out. I didn't see him after he left my house until this morning. I can sure say, though, that he was at my house at 4 o'clock that morning."[6]

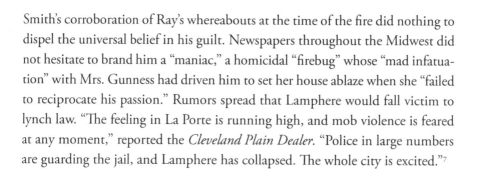

Smith's corroboration of Ray's whereabouts at the time of the fire did nothing to dispel the universal belief in his guilt. Newspapers throughout the Midwest did not hesitate to brand him a "maniac," a homicidal "firebug" whose "mad infatuation" with Mrs. Gunness had driven him to set her house ablaze when she "failed to reciprocate his passion." Rumors spread that Lamphere would fall victim to lynch law. "The feeling in La Porte is running high, and mob violence is feared at any moment," reported the *Cleveland Plain Dealer*. "Police in large numbers are guarding the jail, and Lamphere has collapsed. The whole city is excited."[7]

At the inquest that evening, conducted by Coroner Charles Mack, five witnesses testified: Joe Maxson, Michael and William Clifford, William Humphrey, and Daniel Hutson. Attending the proceedings were State's Attorney Smith; Sheriff Smutzer; Deputies Antiss and Marr; clerk J. Roy Morrison, who transcribed the evidence; and a handful of newspapermen.

Between them, the five witnesses offered a vivid account of the events of that fateful morning. Maxson, asked about the evening before the tragedy, stated that by the time he went to bed, the fire in the woodstove had died out, and that the kerosene lamps in the house were never left burning during the night. "His evidence was important in bearing out the . . . the belief that an incendiary started the fire," one reporter noted.[8]

It was Daniel Hutson, however, who offered what the newspapermen deemed the most dramatic testimony of the inquest. Asked by Sheriff Smutzer about the discovery of the four bodies in the cellar, Hutson—who had been one of the men who had helped lift the corpses from the rubble—declared that "the whole head of Mrs. Gunness was gone from the neck back." Looking at what remained of her after she was placed on a board, he "could see her heart from where her head should be. I could look right on from her shoulders to the heart." At least, that's what he thought he was seeing. "She was burned so," Hutson said, "that I cannot say what it was."[9]

Repeated "sweatings" of Lamphere having failed to produce a confession, Sheriff Smutzer resorted to another time-honored technique for trying to break down a suspect. Early Thursday morning, Ray was taken from his cell in handcuffs, escorted to Smutzer's jaunty little automobile, and told he was going for a ride. Unbeknownst to him, his destination was the morgue in the Cutler funeral home, where—as Harry Burr Darling would report in his typically overwrought way—"he was to look upon all that was mortal of the woman he had hounded in life and the three little innocents who, but a few days ago, played about the home which was even then fated to become their funeral pyre."

Confronted with the hideously charred remains of Belle and her children, Lamphere trembled and paled. "My God," he gasped.

"Now, Lamphere," said Smutzer, "there is some of your work. What do you think of it?"

"Isn't that awful," stammered Ray, who seemed on the brink of collapse.

Deeply shaken, he was hustled back out to Smutzer's car and driven directly to court for his arraignment. Before Justice Grover, State's Attorney Smith read aloud the affidavit, charging

> that on the 28th day of April, 1908, one Ray Lamphere did then and there unlawfully and feloniously kill and murder one Belle Gunness in the perpetration of arson and did then and there feloniously, willfully, and maliciously set fire to the house of the said Belle Gunness . . . and by reason and means of said burning by said Ray Lamphere, as aforesaid, said Belle Gunness was then and there mortally burned, and then and there died, contrary to the form of the statute in such case made and provided and against the peace and dignity of the state of Indiana.

After pleading not guilty, Ray was ordered held without bond. He was then returned to his cell to await the action of the circuit court grand jury, scheduled to meet Monday, May 11.[10]

In the meantime, a score of men continued to dig through the rubble in search of the dead woman's missing skull. "Where Is the Head of Belle Gunness?" ran a headline in the *Chicago Tribune*. According to Dr. Lucius Gray and other La Porte physicians, "no heat could have been severe enough to have wholly cremated the woman's skull." Failure to find it in the ruins of the cellar would therefore lend credence to a theory that many had come to believe in recent days: that Ray Lamphere wasn't merely an arsonist but a fiendish killer who had "stolen into [Mrs. Gunness'] room in the dark, decapitated her, and then set fire to the house to cover the evidence of his crime."[11]

14.

SIBLINGS

Stories about the missing head continued to swirl. According to one, Mrs. Gunness had been murdered and decapitated for the gold in her teeth. Sheriff Smutzer, however, scoffed at this theory, arguing that no one would perpetrate such an atrocity for "several hundred dollars' worth" of gold fillings—and besides, "it would have been rather cumbersome for anybody to carry off a head."[1]

The postmortem examination of Mrs. Gunness confirmed his opinion. A team of physicians, led by Dr. J. Lucius Gray, concluded that "the head of Mrs. Gunness was not cut from the body before death. All agree[d] that it was burned off . . . They found no evidence of violence . . . nothing to indicate that death had been caused by anything other than suffocation and fire."[2]

The head was not the only missing part of the body. Though cast in cool, clinical terms, the final autopsy report vividly conveyed the sheer ghastliness of the woman's remains: "Left arm burned off to the upper third of humerus. Right arm burned off at the shoulder. Right leg burned off at the knee. Left foot burned off at ankle . . . All muscular tissue was thoroughly burned and charred." The entire right side of the torso, from chest to abdomen, had been burned away, leaving the internal organs completely exposed. The lungs, intestines, liver, and pancreas all "appeared normal," the report noted, "except cooked."[3]

On Friday, May 1, the alleged perpetrator of the atrocity was reported to be "seeking the consolation of religion." Summoning Dr. Edwin A. Schell, pastor of the La Porte Methodist Church, to his cell, Ray Lamphere requested and received a copy of the Bible. On the front page of the following day's *Argus-Bulletin*, editor Harry Burr Darling interpreted the prisoner's sudden interest in scripture as a sign that he might be on the brink of confessing—that, as Burr put it in his typically turgid way, Lamphere "wanted to read the sacred word hoping that he might find therein some message of the Master which would cause a penitent heart to unfold a tale."[4]

Among the passengers who arrived by train from Chicago that same Friday morning was a stout, white-haired matron with wire-framed granny glasses who looked to be in her seventies, though her actual age was fifty-four. This was Mrs. Nellie Larson. Eight years had passed since she had last seen her younger sister, then known as Bella Sorenson. It had come as a dreadful shock to her when, while reading Wednesday's newspaper, she found herself looking at a photograph of her estranged sibling and learned of the inferno in which Bella and her three children had died.

Her dismay was compounded when a subsequent article reported that, according to the provisions of the will Bella had made one day before the fire, her entire estate, estimated to be worth $15,000, would go to the Norwegian Children's Home of Chicago. Accompanied by her adult children, John R. Larson and Mrs. Edward Howard, Nellie had hastened to La Porte.[5]

Alighting from the train, the trio proceeded directly to the Cutler morgue. Unable to bring herself to view the awful remains, Mrs. Larson consigned that solemn duty to her son. Afterward, the three conferred with undertaker Cutler about arrangements to transport the bodies to Chicago, where, in accordance with Belle's final wishes, they would be laid to rest in the Forest Home Cemetery.

Their next stop was the office of Belle's attorney, Melvin Leliter. There, Mrs. Larson and her children made it known that they intended to contest Belle's will and, as the closest living relatives of the deceased, claim their share of the estate.[6]

Another interested party who had read of the tragedy in the papers arrived by train that morning: Jennie Olson's older sister, Mrs. George Olander of 2818 South Park Avenue, Chicago. Though separated since childhood, when Jennie was given over to Belle's care, the sisters had kept up a regular correspondence. Mrs. Olander, however, had not heard from the younger woman in two years, when Jennie wrote to say that she was being sent to a Norwegian seminary in California. Mrs. Olander had made efforts to discover the exact name and location of the school but without success.

Like Nellie Larson, Mrs. Olander had hurried to La Porte after reading accounts of the tragedy in the Chicago papers. Stories had begun to circulate that Jennie had gotten married in California and was on her wedding tour. "She is now supposed to be on her way to this city with her husband," the *Argus-Bulletin* reported, "and is doubtful in ignorance of the tragic fate of the woman who guided her steps in childhood." Mrs. Olander was worried, however, that Jennie might have reached home the day before the fire and met the same awful death as her foster mother and siblings.

There was something else troubling Mrs. Olander. She, too, had read the newspaper stories about Mrs. Gunness's will. She could not understand why Belle had bequeathed everything to Myrtle, Lucy, and Phillip—or, in the event of their deaths, to the orphanage in Chicago—and left nothing at all to Jennie.[7]

In his efforts to locate his missing brother, Asle Helgelien had communicated not only with Belle Gunness but with La Porte police chief Clinton Cochrane, who confirmed that a man matching Andrew's description had been seen in the city. After learning that Andrew had arranged to have his savings wired to the First National Bank of La Porte, Asle also sent a query, along with a photograph of his brother, to Frank J. Pitner, the clerk who had handled the transaction. Pitner promptly wrote back to say that "Andrew was without doubt" the man who had come to the bank with Belle Gunness to cash in his certificates of deposit.

On May 1—the same day that Mrs. Larson, her two children, and Mrs. Olander all arrived in La Porte—Asle received an envelope from Pitner. Inside was the front page of the *La Porte Daily Herald* of April 28, reporting on the fiery destruction of the Gunness house and the death of its occupants.[8]

The following day, Asle Helgelien was on his way to La Porte.

15.

HORROR

He arrived late Sunday, May 3, and stayed overnight at the Hotel Teegarden.

Early the next day, he made his way to the office of the *La Porte Herald*, purchased back issues of all the daily papers from the date of the fire on, and spent the next hour or so poring over them. He then proceeded to the sheriff's office and introduced himself to Al Smutzer, who listened to his tale, then drove him out to the Gunness farm.

By then only two men were still engaged in digging through the rubble: Belle's hired hand, Joe Maxson, and her neighbor, Daniel Hutson. Hoping to find some clue to his brother's fate, Asle joined in the work, while Maxson and Hutson kept an eye out for Mrs. Gunness's still-missing head.

The cellar yielded nothing but charred household debris. That night, Asle accepted the hospitality of Belle's neighbors, the Swan Nicholson family, who were happy to open their home to a fellow Norwegian. When he returned to the Gunness farm early the next day, Maxson and Hutson were already at work, shoveling through the ruins of the cellar.

Asle spent some time hiking around the property, searching for anything suspicious. Seeing the big lake nearby, he returned to the two diggers and—as he later testified—"asked some questions, whether there were any holes in the ice on the lake in the winter, how deep the water was." If his brother had met with foul play, Fishtrap Lake would have been a handy place to dispose of the body. But as far as Maxson and Hutson recalled, the lake had been a solid sheet of ice all winter.[1]

It seemed to Asle that there was no point in hanging around the Gunness place any longer. He would have to look elsewhere for some trace of Andrew. "I told the boys goodbye," he recalled afterward, "and I started down to the road." He hadn't gone far, however, when he stopped and swiveled on his heels. "I was not satisfied," he would explain, "and I went back to the cellar and asked Maxson whether he knew of any hole or dirt having been dug up there about the place in spring."

As a matter of fact, Maxson did. Sometime back in March—he couldn't remember the exact date—he had helped Mrs. Gunness load up a wheelbarrow with "old cans, shoes, and other rubbish," then hauled it to a pit that had been dug in a fenced-off portion of the barnyard used as a hog lot, about fifty feet south of the house. At his employer's direction, he had then dumped in the refuse and filled in the hole.

Asle asked Maxson to show him the spot, and the three men, shovels in hand, headed for the yard and began to dig.

It wasn't long before their nostrils were assaulted with "an awful bad smell. Mr. Maxson told me that Mrs. Gunness had put a lot of tomato cans and fish cans there. Maybe it was they made it stink," Asle would say. But the fetor that arose from the pit smelled nothing like rotting tomatoes and fish.

Their shovels struck the source of the stench about four feet down: "something hard, covered with a gunny sack." There was a tear in the fabric. Through it they could see a human neck. In the dirt beside the sack lay a man's severed arm.

Within minutes, Maxson was at the reins of Mrs. Gunness's buggy and racing to town. Looking around the yard, Asle found an old coat and a few gunnysacks and laid them over the grisly find. Then he and Hutson picked up their shovels and carefully cleared away more of the dirt from the fetid grave.

They had just finished when Sheriff Smutzer drove up. Beside him was Coroner Charles S. Mack, an imposing, white-bearded fellow, garbed in a rumpled three-piece suit with a wing-collared shirt, black bow tie, and fob chain strung across his vest. Under Mack's watchful eye, Smutzer and the others soon brought the rotted body parts to the surface.

Coroner Mack would later depose that it was impossible to provide a "particular and minute description" of the corpse, "owing to the fact that . . . the head was separate from the torso, as was each arm from the shoulder down, and each leg from about three inches above the knee down; and to the further fact that putrefaction had set in."[2] The face, moreover—or what remained of it—was, in the words of one chronicler, "a thing of horror": sunken holes for eyes, a leering gash for a mouth, a zigzag crack running from the top of the skull to the forehead.[3]

Certain deductions could be drawn from the putrid remains despite their appalling condition. It seemed clear, for example, that the victim "had fought for his life. Across his left wrist, as if he had lifted it to ward off a slashing blow, were two deep cuts laying it open to the bone. Another savage blow had chopped off the first joints of every finger of his right hand. In a death grip the mutilated hand held a tuft of short brown curly hair torn from the head of his murderer."[4]

The ghastly face—though resembling a Halloween horror mask more than anything human—also retained enough of its features to make an identification possible. "I recognize it by the form of the face—across the eye—the forehead—across the cheeks," Asle Helgelien would later testify. "When you have been with your brother every day for fifteen years, you know him."[5]

Asle's long search for his brother Andrew had come to an end in a trash pit in Belle Gunness's barnyard.

A drizzling rain had begun to fall. As Coroner Mack squatted on his haunches for a nearer look at the unearthed remains, Sheriff Smutzer asked Joe Maxson if he knew of any other "soft spots" on the property—places where holes had been dug, then loosely covered over with dirt. Maxson pointed to a spot a short distance away.

By then, a small crowd of curiosity seekers had gathered at the farm. As they pressed their faces to the wire mesh fence, Maxson, Hutson, and Smutzer began to dig. Three feet down, beneath a pile of rubbish, they uncovered a jumble of putrefied body parts: naked torsos wrapped in burlap, heads, arms, and legs scattered around.

The buggy shed was turned into a makeshift morgue for the hideous trove. There were four victims in all: two men, one woman, one female adolescent, each divided into six pieces. As with Andrew Helgelien's corpse, few firm conclusions could be drawn from the dismembered and badly decomposed relics. The difficulty faced by medical investigators can be seen in the deposition of Dr.

Franklin T. Wilcox of La Porte, brought in by Coroner Mack to conduct the autopsy on the adult female:

> With the exception of the uterus, none of the viscera could be recognized. The right arm was severed by a chopping instrument an inch below the head of the humerus. Both arms were detached from the body. The two femora were cut off through the lower third. There were found four arms and four forearms with hands with the body, but it is impossible to say which, if any, belong to this body. There were found two skulls and two lower maxillary bones with this body, but it is impossible to say which, if any, belong to this body. There were also two sets of fibula but they could not be positively identified as belonging to this body. From the examination it is impossible to determine the cause of death.[6]

Though in equally appalling condition, the remains of the younger female did retain one distinguishing feature: a matted tress of long blond hair sprouting from the fleshless skull. From this unmistakable evidence, witnesses who knew her in life were able to positively identify the butchered young woman.

Jennie Olson had not been sent away to a seminary in California two years earlier. She had not gotten married and was not on her honeymoon journey. Chopped into a half-dozen pieces, she had been dumped into a corpse-filled hole and covered with rubbish in her foster mother's hog pen. And—as newspapers around the nation would soon report—the date on which her butchered remains were brought to light, May 5, 1908, would have been her eighteenth birthday.[7]

16.

MURDERESS

There had, of course, been notorious murders in Indiana before. Perhaps the most sensational was the 1895 case of Reverend William E. Hinshaw. A much-admired figure in the village of Belleville, Hinshaw was accused of killing his wife, Thirza—who had discovered his affair with a pretty young parishioner—then inflicting nearly twenty flesh wounds on himself with pistol and razor and claiming that he had sustained the injuries while grappling heroically with a pair of intruders who had snuck into his bedroom at night and murdered his wife. His trial in September of that year (which climaxed with his conviction) became a courtroom sensation, the "one absorbing topic of public interest" for its two-month duration.[1]

For all the titillated fascination it generated, however, the "Belleville Tragedy," as it became known, remained a local story, little known beyond the Hoosier state. By contrast, the Gunness case would be front-page news throughout the country, and even overseas.[2] "Big-time newspapermen from all over converged on La Porte," writes one historian of the crime. "Seven Chicago papers had a total of twenty-two reporters on the ground. Others arrived from New York, St. Louis, Detroit. There were thirty-five in all. They set up headquarters at the Hotel Teegarden . . . In ten days they would put out an estimated million words of sensational copy."[3]

Overnight, Belle Gunness—formerly lauded in the press for her "heroic, but futile effort . . . to save her offspring"—was transformed into a demon. In its earliest report on the gruesome discoveries of May 5, the *Chicago American*, within the space of a few paragraphs, branded her as both "the most fiendish murderer of the age" and "the most fiendish murderess in history." The same paper was also the first to raise a possibility that would haunt the case forever. Given her diabolical cunning, it now seemed conceivable that the headless body found in the ruins of the cellar was not Belle Gunness at all but another of her victims, whose decapitated corpse had been substituted for the "arch-murderess."

Mrs. Gunness, the paper declared, was "now thought to be still alive."[4]

Ray Lamphere was reading his Bible and chewing meditatively on a wad of tobacco when Sheriff Smutzer returned from the Gunness farm and informed him of the day's horrific developments.

"My God," gasped Lamphere.

"Five bodies. I knew that woman was bad but nothing like this."

Led from his cell, he was brought before a group of reporters, who peppered him with questions about the unearthed corpses. He insisted he knew "nothing about it," though he admitted that he had harbored some suspicions.

"There were things I noticed," he said. "I guess they were more serious than I thought."

Asked to elaborate, he told of the time, immediately after Helgelien's arrival, that Mrs. Gunness instructed him to go to town and buy a container of Rough on Rats, a popular pesticide compounded of 10 percent soot and 90 percent arsenic. "Another time she wanted chloroform," Lamphere said.

"Anything else?" one of the reporters pressed.

"Well, about a year ago," said Ray, "there was a man with a black mustache who came to the farm, and Mrs. Gunness told me he was a friend of Jennie's. He had a big trunk with him. A long while after he went away, the trunk was still at the house. It used to stand upstairs. It still had the man's clothes in it, which seemed to me kind of funny."

Speaking of Jennie, did Lamphere think the dead girl dug up that afternoon might be her? someone asked.

Lamphere nodded gravely. "It must be Jennie," he said. "I never believed she was in California. I never heard of any letters coming from her."

Before being taken back to his cell, Lamphere was asked again about Andrew Helgelien.

"Look here," he answered. "I don't know anything about that, and I don't know anything about the fire, except what I told a long time ago. She used to tell me not to talk to Helgelien. One time, she found us together in the sitting room when she came in. She was angry and told me to get out and never speak to him again. I told her I'd speak to him if I felt like it. Well, a few days later, I came home from town and Helgelien was gone. I asked about him and she said, 'I told you you'd never talk to him again.'

"I didn't know what she meant," Lamphere said as Smutzer took him by the arm and led him away. "But now I understand."[5]

That same day, a letter arrived at the La Porte post office addressed to Mrs. Gunness. Like all her mail since the fire, it was handed over to Wesley Fogle, a local "implement dealer," appointed by Belle as her executor.

The letter was from a Waupaca, Wisconsin, man named Carl Peterson, writing to say that he was "sorry he could not meet Mrs. Gunness' requirements as to his financial condition" but assuring her that he was "respectable and worthy in every way." Tracked down by reporters, Peterson explained that he had initially contacted Belle after seeing her ad in the *Skandinaven*. In her response, which he had received just the previous week, she had described her farm in glowing terms and explained that she was looking for a man to share it with. She was perfectly willing to consider Peterson as a partner, as long as was "able to put up $1000 cash." If not, there was no point in pursuing the matter.

As papers throughout the country would report, Peterson had good cause to "congratulate himself on his narrow escape." As recently as the week before the fire, Belle Gunness was still trolling for victims.[6]

17.

THE GRAVEYARD

The road leading to the Gunness place was so choked with buggies, buckboards, and bicycles on the morning of Wednesday, May 6, that Sheriff Smutzer had trouble maneuvering his own vehicle through the traffic as he drove up to the farm. A massive crowd of men, women, and children—whose number that day would eventually swell to the thousands—was pressed against the wire mesh fence surrounding the hog lot, eager for a glimpse of the latest horrors.[1]

They didn't have long to wait. Smutzer, Joe Maxson, and a few other men recruited for the grim task began digging in the northeast corner of the lot, about five feet from the spot where the four decayed corpses had been found the day before. Almost immediately, their spades struck a patch of loose soil that gave off a nauseous smell. About three feet down, they turned up the butchered bones of another victim. Rotting burlap—the remnants of the sack in which the torso had been stuffed—clung to the rib cage, pelvis, and spine. The skull—which bore a three-inch gash, "as if made by some cutting instrument"—lay nearby, along with the sawed-off leg bones. The stink of the corpse was made even worse by the grave in which it lay, the body parts having been dumped into an abandoned privy vault.[2]

The ghoulish work did not deter Smutzer and his team from taking a break for their lunch. They resumed their digging about thirty minutes later. Just a few feet from the excavated latrine, their shovels uncovered more than a dozen pairs of men's shoes. Under the shoes lay a heap of human bones.

"One of the men dug into the pile and his spade brought out parts of the legs of two bodies," one Chicago newspaper reported:

> A second spadeful of dirt and bones revealed the fact that three bodies were hidden in the hole. All of the bodies were wrapped in gunny sacks. Quicklime had been placed in the sacks, but it had been poorly applied to the bodies. Many pieces of flesh clung to the bones where the lime had not eaten.
>
> As the leg bones were drawn out, the marks on them revealed for the first time the horrible insane anger with which the woman worked over her victims. About the joints she had hacked them with an ax. The bones had been crushed on the ends, as though they had been . . . struck with hammers after they were dismembered. Two of the skulls were near each other; they had been buried face up. Quicklime had been scattered over the faces and stuffed in the ears. In one of the heads, a sufficient quantity had not been placed and the brain remained intact . . . The lower parts of the bodies were decomposed, and it was impossible to tell whether they were men or women.[3]

The noisome relics were placed in tin pails and transferred to the buggy shed serving as a temporary morgue, from which, as one reporter observed, "there proceeded a stench that daunts even the most resolute curiosity seeker."[4]

Added to the five bodies dug up the previous day, the latest discoveries brought the total of butchered corpses buried in Mrs. Gunness's hog lot to nine. Across the country, from the *New York Times* to the *San Francisco Chronicle*, newspapers trumpeted the latest ghastly findings, branding Belle with a variety of lurid nicknames: "a modern Lady Macbeth who poured blood into her coffers and turned it into gold," the "La Porte Ghoul," the "Indiana Ogress," the "Human Vampire," the "Female Bluebeard," the "High-Priestess of Murder," the "Mistress of the Castle of Death," the "Queen of Crime," and "Hell's Princess." In the view of the *Pittsburgh Press*, "The murders in the Rue Morgue pale into insignificance when compared to this case," while a writer for the *Chicago Evening American* opined that if Poe were to "come back to life, he might write a new and more thrilling story of 'The Fall of the House of Usher.' Mrs. Belle Gunness, the grim widow of La Porte, Indiana, with her castle of death and her yard filled with graves, would afford him material for a new 'weird tale' more thrilling than any he conceived."[5]

Given a variety of factors—the proximity of La Porte to Chicago, Belle's former residence in that city, and the shameless sensationalism of its yellow press—it was hardly surprising that the Chicago papers had a field day with the story. The Wednesday edition of William Randolph Hearst's *Examiner* made an especially startling claim. "Belle Gunness a Member of Band of Chicago Thugs," the headline blared. "Police Seeking Her Here."[6]

According to Assistant Police Chief Herman F. Schuettler, Chicago was home to "a gang of murderers organized for the purpose of collecting insurance on their victims." Mrs. Gunness, he asserted, was "a member of this gang of murderers . . . who received the bodies of the victims done to death in Chicago and disposed of them in her La Porte home." Schuettler's theory was largely based on the testimony of several local liverymen, who revealed that, in 1906 and 1907, they had delivered at least nine heavy trunks to the Gunness farm. It was the belief of the Chicago police, the newspaper declared, "that this and the other trunks contained human bodies."

One of these liverymen, Claude Sturgis, offered a dramatic account of his own experience in the fall of 1907. After carting a large, "tightly corded" trunk up on the porch of the Gunness farmhouse and rolling it into the front parlor, he had begun to remove the ropes. At that instant, Mrs. Gunness had "rushed madly at him and asked what he was doing. 'I always untie the trunks for the ladies,' Sturgis replied. In a fit of rage, she grabbed him by the arm and, pushing him out the front door, told him to mind his own business."

Receiving a tip that "two mysterious trunks" were currently awaiting shipment to the Gunness farm, Captain O'Brien of the Chicago City Detective Bureau, immediately instituted a search of all railroad baggage rooms and local express companies. According to the informant who contacted the police, the trunks "contain[ed] the corpses of murder victims."[7]

Picking up on this story, newspapers throughout the country declared that Mrs. Gunness was part of what was variously described as a "crime bureau," "criminal conspiracy," "murder syndicate," and "man-killing trust." Her role was that of "fence" or "clearinghouse" for this sinister organization, which used her farm as a graveyard for its victims.

Stories began to circulate of a "secret death chamber" in Belle's "house of horrors" that had served a ghastly function in this diabolical racket. "There was a room of the Gunness home that was used exclusively by the woman," one paper reported. "No one was allowed to enter there, not even her children. The door was a heavy oaken affair and the windows were tightly shaded. It was in this room the bodies were stored after they were shipped from Chicago. The woman piled them in there until they were old enough, so there was no danger of their bleeding. Then she hacked them to pieces."[8]

Dr. J. H. William Meyer—former member of the Cook County Hospital staff and president of the Alumni Association of Rush Medical College—suggested a somewhat different possibility. After taking part in the postmortem examinations of several of the unearthed corpses, including the one identified as Andrew Helgelien, Meyer declared to reporters that "the decapitation and severance of limbs from the bodies was done by an anatomical expert . . . someone familiar with the dissecting room."

The "disarticulation of the ball and socket joints of the shoulder," Meyer explained, was especially telling. "This cannot be done by an amateur with an ordinary instrument," he insisted. "Every one of these operations was clean cut. It was done by a strong hand with nothing less sharp than a surgeon's knife."[9] The clear implication was that the victims had been dismembered in Chicago by a killer with medical expertise, then shipped in pieces to La Porte.[10] With the memory of Dr. H. H. Holmes still fresh in their minds—the infamous serial killer who had purportedly dispatched and dissected an indeterminate number of victims in the dungeon of his so-called horror castle—Chicagoans could easily believe in the existence of a medical monster involved in a murder-for-profit scheme.[11]

The notion that Belle had accomplices in Chicago also lent credence to the widespread conviction that she was still alive, particularly after an unnamed witness came forward to say that he had spotted a "cloaked figure" boarding the Chicago train from La Porte on the morning of April 28, the day of the fire at the Gunness farmhouse. Based on this intelligence, Schuettler speculated that Belle "had been met in Chicago by a confederate and was now hiding" while awaiting a chance to "escape to Norway."

A massive search was launched for the archmurderess.

"Every depot in Chicago is being watched by the police," the *Examiner* reported. "The post office is under the eye of the police. So are numerous other places at which it might be supposed that the woman would appear. Express warehouses and baggage rooms are being winnowed for traces of trunks to or from the woman. A dragnet is out that encompasses the city."[12]

While police conducted their manhunt for the supposed fugitive, reporters tracked down Dr. J. C. Miller, who had been called to the bedside of the stricken Mads Sorenson eight years earlier. Recent developments had compelled Dr. Miller to reevaluate his original diagnosis.

"When I arrived at Sorenson's home," Miller told the newsmen, "he was clutching the bedpost and was in great agony. He died within half an hour. Sorenson was apparently in the best of health before he died. At the time, I believed that his death was probably due to hemorrhage of the brain. As I think of it now, however, I can see that the symptoms may have been those of strychnine poisoning."[13]

Convinced that Belle's connection to "an organized gang of trunk murderers" dated back to her days in Chicago, Assistant Chief Schuettler ordered an immediate investigation into the records of all missing persons who had disappeared from the Austin area at the time she lived there. Meeting with reporters late Wednesday, he also announced that, at sunrise the following day, his men would "begin to spade up the backyard" of the home she and Mads had shared on Alma Street.

"We confidently expect to find bodies in this yard," Schuettler told the newspapermen.

Moreover, he had reason to believe that not all those bodies were those of adults. In addition to her other monstrous activities, Belle Gunness, according to Schuettler, was in the business of "baby farming."[14]

In the late-nineteenth and early-twentieth centuries, mothers of unwanted infants—typically unwed women, prostitutes, or destitute females already overburdened with children—would consign the luckless newborns to paid caregivers who, for a flat or monthly fee, would agree to provide a home for the babies or find them suitable families for adoption. While some of these so-called baby farmers treated their charges with warm maternal care, a sizable number proved to be utterly callous females who sought to maximize their profits by supplying the children with the barest of necessities.

When a social worker named Arthur Alden Guild conducted an investigation into Chicago's baby farms for the Juvenile Protection Agency, he found hundreds of diseased, malnourished children living in appalling conditions.[15] So high was the mortality rate among these unregulated operations that, to many observers, they were little more than death traps. Some of the women involved in this sordid business, moreover, were guilty of far worse than criminal neglect. Perhaps the most notorious was the British baby farmer Amelia Dyer, believed to have murdered several hundred infants in her care.[16]

Chicago authorities were now firmly convinced that Mrs. Gunness had engaged in the same gruesome business—"taking in babies for a sum of money until they could be conveniently put out of the way." While they did not believe she had matched Amelia Dyer's record, they thought it likely that—as Lieutenant Matthew Zimmer of the Austin police station told reporters—"she may have murdered children by the score." Indeed, said Zimmer, it was her "success in hiding her crimes with the bodies of children [that] may have encouraged her to continue her crimes along bigger lines."

The awful career of the La Porte ghoul, Zimmer speculated, had "begun by murdering babies."[17]

In La Porte, authorities waved off the theories of the Chicago police. Informed of Schuettler's belief that the bodies dug up on Mrs. Gunness's farm had been shipped there by her cohorts in a Chicago crimes syndicate, La Porte mayor Lemuel Darrow was emphatic in his response.

"There is only one solution to the mystery," he declared to reporters. "Mrs. Gunness enticed all these people here for the purpose of getting their money and then murdered them.

"She carried on a correspondence with countrymen of hers when she knew they were single men or widowers with money," Darrow continued, "and after making offers of marriage or other inducements, such as having a suitable farm for sale, she would request a visit. After she got her men to the farm, she would entertain them so hospitably that their visits were prolonged. When the time was opportune, she would administer some kind of poison, probably arsenic or chloroform, and when death resulted, take her time in dismembering them and burying the remains in the yard.

"I believe she has been carrying on this extraordinary means of securing for several years," said Darrow as the newspapermen scribbled his words in their notepads. "I believe further investigation will reveal more bodies of the woman's inhuman traffic."

Asked by one of the reporters how many more bodies he expected to find, Darrow replied without hesitation. "I would not be surprised," he said, "to have the list of victims reach a score of men, women and children."[18]

18.

BUDSBERG

A drenching rain on Thursday, May 7, put the digging on hold. With the grim work suspended, Sheriff Smutzer traveled to Chicago early that morning to confer with his counterparts.

He was still away when a messenger arrived at the jail to inform Deputy Antiss that a pair of men had broken into the locked buggy shed on the Gunness farm, where the exhumed piles of rotted flesh and bone lay on wooden planks.

Hurrying out to the farm, Antiss was met by Joe Maxson, who told him that, while walking in the yard, he had spotted the two men climbing out of the shed's rear window.

"One was a tall man with dark hair and other was heavyset, not quite so tall," said Maxson. "It was raining heavily, and I could not see much of their faces because their hats were pulled down low and their coat collars were up. I told them that the sheriff's orders forbade anybody entering the shed, and one of them said, 'Mind your own affairs. We're doctors and have a right to go in.'"

Maxson immediately sent one of the neighbor boys into town to notify Antiss. By then, however, the two men had already gotten away, hightailing it through the woods to a rig they had left nearby. Rumors quickly spread through town that "accomplices of Mrs. Gunness had smashed the lock of the shed and broken in to destroy evidence against her . . . They stole several bottles said to contain poison and attempted to mix up the bones of the skeletons to prevent identification."[1]

The truth turned out to be more mundane: The two men, later identified as residents of Michigan City, had snuck in through the window of the temporary morgue for no more sinister reason than to satisfy their morbid curiosity with a close-up look at the charnel remains of Mrs. Gunness's victims.[2]

At around 1:30 that afternoon, before Smutzer's return, two young men arrived by train from Iola, Wisconsin, in the company of an older acquaintance, a hardware dealer named Edwin Chapin. They were met at the depot by James Buck, president of the La Porte Savings Bank, who escorted them to the courthouse, where Deputy Antiss took charge of them. The two young men were brothers Mathias and Oscar Budsberg, ages twenty-seven and twenty-nine, respectively: "simple, ingenuous young farmers," as one newspaper patronizingly reported, "slow of thought and utterance."[3] They were there on a somber mission: to view a human skull thought to be that of their father, Ole Budsberg.

Fourteen months earlier, Budsberg—a fifty-one-year old widower and subscriber to both the *Skandinaven* and the *Decorah-Posten*—informed his sons that he was taking a trip to La Porte, Indiana, to see about managing a farm there. To his brother, Budsberg told a different story: that he was going there to marry a wealthy widow.

He left Iola in the third week of March 1907, returning a week later to settle his affairs before moving permanently to his new home. He sold his farm to Mathias for $1,000. On April 5, with the cash from the sale plus a mortgage note for an additional $1,000 secured by some land that he owned, he departed by train, promising his sons that he would write as soon as he was settled.

The following day—as a cashier named J. W. Crumpacker later testified—Budsberg appeared at the First National Bank of La Porte in the company of Belle Gunness and requested that his mortgage note be sent to the Farmers State Bank in Iola for collection. He was back with Mrs. Gunness on April 16 to pick up the money. "That was the last time I saw him alive," Crumpacker would say.[4]

By late April, having received no word from their father, Mathias was sufficiently concerned to send him a letter at the Gunness farm. It was eventually
returned as undeliverable by the Dead Letter Office in Washington, D.C. In the
meantime, the mortgage note having come due, J. C. Swenson, a cashier at the
Farmers State Bank in Iola, sent a letter of inquiry to cashier Crumpacker, asking
as to whether he "had seen anything of Mr. Budsberg lately." Crumpacker passed
along the letter to his employer, bank president Buck, who took it upon himself
to drive out to the Gunness farm and see if Budsberg was there. At his knock,
Mrs. Gunness came to the door but did not invite him inside. To his question
about Budsberg, she replied that she did not know where he was. During a visit
to Chicago, she explained, he had been robbed of "most of his money." When
he got back to La Porte, he decided that "he would go out west and try to make
up what he had been robbed of before any of his relatives should learn of it." A
few days later—she could not remember the date—she had taken him to the
train depot where he set out on a trip to Oregon. That was the last she had seen
of him.[5]

Buck had Crumpacker notify the bank officers in Iola. Several months later,
following the conflagration at the Gunness farm and the discovery of the first
bodies in the hog lot, Crumpacker sent newspaper clippings to cashier Swenson,
who notified the Budsberg brothers. Fearing the worst, Mathias and Oscar had
set out at once for La Porte.[6]

At around 2:00 p.m., Deputy Antiss drove the Budsberg brothers out to the
Gunness farm. Despite the inclement weather, twenty or so men—drawn by
the fast-spreading stories of the supposedly sinister break-in that had taken place
earlier in the day—were gathered outside the buggy shed. Antiss led his two
charges into the foul-smelling outbuilding, the other men crowding in eagerly
behind them.

By the glow of an oil lamp, Mat and Oscar peered at the row of planks holding the rank remains dug out of the barnyard. Atop one mass of decayed bones
and skin sat the skull they had come to view, and they bent to take a closer look.

Though the head retained few recognizable features, there was no mistaking its distinctive facial hair: "a tangled red waterfall mustache," as one historian

describes it, "curling into the fleshless mouth."[7] After a moment, the brothers straightened up, exchanged a grim look, then pushed their way out of the shed and into the open air.

Withdrawing a ways, they engaged in a brief, whispered conversation before returning to the shed. By then, Antiss had emerged and stood waiting for them.

"It's him," said Mat. "I'm sure of it."

"It's what we feared," said Oscar.[8]

The Budsberg boys had found their father.

In a front-page story datelined May 7, the *New York Times* summed up for its readers the four main theories surrounding the Gunness case, "a series of crimes which have startled the whole country":

> Theory No. 1—That Mrs. Gunness, fearing exposure of her long murderous career, killed her three children and herself, setting fire to the house to conceal the crimes.

> Theory No. 2—That Mrs. Gunness, fearing exposure, fled after killing her children, putting the headless body of another woman in the house to mislead authorities.

> Theory No. 3—That Ray Lamphere, her farmhand, did the killing from a double motive of revenge and jealousy.

> Theory No. 4—That the quadruple crime was committed by a murderous gang with headquarters in Chicago who feared exposure by Mrs. Gunness of a long series of murders for insurance, she being used as their "clearinghouse" for corpses.[9]

Even as this edition of the paper was going to press, however, authorities in Chicago were discounting the last of these theories. Just one day after making his confident pronouncements about Mrs. Gunness's involvement with a "crime syndicate," Assistant Chief Schuettler did a complete about-face on the issue. His reversal was prompted partly by a talk with Sheriff Smutzer, who gave no credence to the notion that the rotted remains exhumed from Belle's barnyard had been shipped there from Chicago. Investigators had also determined that the information about the two "mysterious trunks" supposedly awaiting delivery to the "death farm" was a false lead, if not an outright hoax.

"I no longer believe that Mrs. Gunness was the agent of a gang of murderers or that she ran a baby farm," he told reporters:

> It appears certain that she herself killed the suitors whose bodies were found in the farmyard graves. That she could have lured and killed more than a dozen men in this way is entirely plausible. I believe she answered letters from men of her own nationality and invited them to her farm. There she showed them the abundant fields. The prospect was pleasing. So much accomplished, the rest was not so difficult as might be supposed. A little chloral in a glass of beer or coffee brings quick death. So does a well directed blow with a hammer or hatchet. There is no reason why she, a strong woman, could not have buried them as well. Her farm is far from the nearest neighbor.

At the same time, Schuettler clung to his conviction that the archmurderess was still alive. "I cannot believe that she is dead. She was too expert a criminal to be caught that way. She may well be in Chicago."[10]

His opinion seemed to be confirmed by an acquaintance of Belle's who notified the police that he had seen her board "a North Clark streetcar at Summerdale Avenue" just one day earlier, Wednesday the sixth.[11] Several other witnesses claimed to have encountered her in the vicinity of Wabash Avenue district south of the Loop within the past week. One of these was a pharmacist named Al Levi, proprietor of a drugstore in the Commercial Hotel Building on Wabash Avenue and Harrison Street. After coming upon a photograph of Belle in the *Chicago Tribune*, Levi contacted the newspaper, claiming to recognize her as "the same woman who attempted to buy morphine from him within four or five days *after* the Gunness house of horror had been burned."

"I am certain it is her," insisted Levi, who would not be the last to assert that he had come face-to-face with the living Belle Gunness. "The features—the nose, the mouth, the eyes—are the same."[12]

Persuaded now that Belle's atrocities had been confined to her remote farm in La Porte, Schuettler called off plans to search for other missing persons in the yard of her former residence in Austin. His decision did not prevent a group of enterprising reporters from showing up with shovels on Alma Street. Before they could begin to dig, however, they were confronted by the current owners, brothers John and Daniel Nellis, a pair of burly plumbers from Wisconsin, who had purchased the premises in November 1907 and who threatened to "get an injunction restraining any excavating here. We bought this property," said Daniel, "and all this sensational talk is injuring it."[13]

Schuettler's belief that Belle had staged her own death and made her way to Chicago was shared by La Porte's mayor, Lemuel Darrow, and his police chief, Clinton Cochrane. Sheriff Smutzer and Prosecutor Smith, on the other hand, were adamant that she had perished in the fire. Of course, as newspapers were quick to point out, Smutzer and Smith had good reason to insist on that point. To admit that she was still alive would—as the *Chicago Tribune* put it—"destroy the case they are building against Ray Lamphere."

On that same afternoon, Thursday, May 7, Smith appeared before a flock of reporters to make a dramatic announcement. So far as the state was concerned, the case against Lamphere was "complete." Mrs. Gunness's former handyman and lover would be indicted and tried not only for arson but for murder.

"I am satisfied we have collected testimony of such a character that Lamphere's responsibility for the deaths in the house will be established beyond all reasonable doubt," Smith declared. "We will produce witnesses to prove that Lamphere was seen around the Gunness house before the fire broke out and that he was seen running away later. We shall also prove that he set fire to the place in revenge for action taken against him by the woman after they had fallen out, and that this disagreement was due to a quarrel over the murder of Helgelien in which Lamphere was implicated, according to our evidence."[14]

Asked by one newspaperman if, as was widely reported, police had resorted to the third degree—"sweating"—to extract information from Lamphere, Smith bristled. "We don't sweat people here," he said. "La Porte is a civilized town. We're not like Chicago and New York."[15]

He concluded that he would "endeavor to have the case called for trial at the next term of court." Lamphere, Smith predicted, "will be on trial within three weeks."[16]

19.

THE WEB

Reporting on State Attorney Smith's announcement, Friday's *Chicago Tribune* ran a story headlined "Weave Web Around Lamphere." A web of a very different kind appeared prominently in the same issue: a front-page editorial cartoon depicting a swarm of insect-winged men, satchels in hand, flying into the clutches of a fat, female spider. Blazoned across the spider's back were the words "Matrimonial Bureau."[1]

According to one informed estimate, Chicago in the first decade of the twentieth century was home to no fewer than 125 matrimonial (or "affinity") agencies, the vast bulk of them fly-by-night operations designed to milk as much cash as possible from desperately lonely men and women. Typical was the scam conducted by a woman named E. L. Glinn, who snared victims by running phony newspaper advertisements ostensibly placed by prosperous businessmen and well-to-do widows in search of congenial mates. The dupes who responded to these come-ons were required to mail Miss Glinn a five-dollar "initiation fee" in her matchmaking club, in return for which they would receive more detailed information about the (nonexistent) marriage seekers, along with a list of other possible (and equally fictitious) candidates. Before she was arrested, tried, and convicted of mail fraud, Glinn managed to rope in more than six hundred suckers of both sexes, none of whom, it seems needless to say, ended up with a husband or wife.[2]

Decrying Glinn and her ilk as "a menace to the American people" who "debased the ideal of love and marriage" by reducing it to a matter of "tawdry commercialism," Chicago authorities went after the worst of the offenders.[3] One larger-than-life character, Detective Sergeant Clifton R. Wooldridge—the self-styled "American Sherlock Holmes" responsible for twenty thousand arrests during his two-decade career—waged relentless war on these con artists, regarding their chicanery as "one of the most insidious forms of crime," a "volcano belching forth fraud, swindling, bigamy, [and] desertion." In his bestselling memoir, *Twenty Years a Detective in the Wickedest City in the World*, Wooldridge proudly proclaims that he had put more than one hundred of these "get-rich-quick schemers" out of business, seizing and destroying "40 wagon loads" of their meretricious circulars and advertisements.[4]

The battle against Chicago's "love brokers" turned into an all-out crusade in the wake of the Gunness revelations. Conveniently ignoring the fact that Belle had never availed herself of a matrimonial agency, the district attorney's office issued immediate instructions "that every manager of an affinity bureau in the Chicago district be placed under immediate arrest."

"The revelations in La Porte have been such," Assistant D. A. Seward S. Shirer told reporters, "that we believe different alleged 'matcher-up' bureaus have sent men and women to murder establishments like the one run by Mrs. Gunness. This was probably done to rob them of the few cents they may have had in their pockets. These poor persons are an unintellectual set and could be murdered and put out of the way without much danger of exposure." While conceding that not all matrimonial agencies were in the business of "wholesale murder," he insisted that there was "no telling how far each manager will go in his efforts to wring a few pennies out of the poor persons who answer their alluring advertisements."[5]

Detective Wooldridge's memoir echoed these sentiments. Switching from a geological metaphor—the "belching" volcano—to a botanical one, he described the matrimonial bureau as a "plant of hell" whose most hideous "blossom" was the Gunness murder farm.

"This wholesale murderess," Wooldridge proclaimed in defiance of the facts, "lured her victims to their fate through advertisements in a 'matrimonial paper' or through a matrimonial agency . . . Through the aid of these fraudulent agencies, [this woman] murdered more people than any other human being who ever lived." Accompanying this passage was an illustration of a scythe-wielding Belle standing in her yard at night. All about her were graves sprouting skull-flowered plants. "The Death Harvester," read the caption.

"This, then, is the crowning work of the matrimonial agency," Wooldridge concluded. "This horrid burying ground of dismembered bodies, this ghastly charnel pit on an Indiana hillside. By their fruits shall ye know them. In the dread Gunness Farm behold the ripened fruit of the matrimonial agency!"[6]

20.

THE CORPSE HARVEST

On Friday morning, May 8, the flooding rain that had fallen for the past thirty-six hours subsided to an intermittent drizzle. At daylight, a great caravan of buggies, hacks, wagons, and assorted conveyances began making its way toward the "horror farm." By 8:00 a.m., more than a thousand men, women, and children—" farmers, merchants, clerks, residents of adjacent towns and villages"—had shown up to watch the grave-hunting resume.[1]

Locating a "soft spot" not far from the pits they had excavated on Wednesday, Sheriff Smutzer, Joe Maxson, and Daniel Hutson bent to their task. The saturated soil came up easily under their spades. Just a half hour after digging began, Hutson struck something solid: a rotting wooden box, which disintegrated into splinters as he poked it with the blade of his tool.

"As the fragments fell aside," one observer wrote, "they revealed a mass of lime from which ragged pieces of gunny sack were lifted. In the bottom of the hole a tangled heap of bones was exposed, to some of which masses of jelly-like flesh still clung." There was also a skull with some strands of dark hair sticking to it.[2]

The bones were brought to the surface and examined by Coroner Mack. Like all of Belle's victims, this one had been carved up prior to disposal—the legs neatly sawed off two inches above the knee joints, the arms severed near the shoulders. From the size of the bones and the dimension of the skull, Mack concluded that the remains were those of an adult male, despite the incongruous fact that two pairs of women's shoes had been tossed into the pit with the body.

As word of the find spread through the crowd, hundreds made a mad dash for the freshly opened grave. One newspaperman witnessed a scene that captured the frenzy of the moment. An "old man with a long gray beard" had just arrived at the farm, pulling two toddlers, evidently his grandchildren, in a little wooden wagon. As he approached the hog lot, "the little wagon toppled over, and the two children were thrown to the muddy ground. It was at this moment that the cry was raised, 'another body has been found,' and the old man ran to the excavation, leaving the children crying on the ground."[3]

The mystery of the women's shoes was solved a few minutes later. Continuing to dig in the same hole, Hutson soon turned up another mass of bones. Because there was only one skull in the grave, Smutzer initially theorized that all the remains belonged to a single victim. Coroner Mack quickly disabused him of that notion. "If all those bones belonged to one person," Mack declared, "you'd have a monstrosity—someone ten or twelve feet high."[4] To Mack's practiced eye, it was clear that this second skeleton was that of a woman.

Placed in separate tin buckets, the two butchered skeletons—the tenth and eleventh to be dug out of the "death garden"—were transferred to the improvised morgue to join the other fetid remnants of Belle Gunness's victims.

As a result of the nationwide coverage of the case, police officials in La Porte were flooded with inquiries from people who feared that their long-missing loved ones had ended up in the muck of Belle Gunness's hog lot. From Mrs. J. M. Canary of Pine Lakes, Indiana, came a letter about her nineteen-year-old son, Edward. A somewhat troubled, "not intellectually bright" youth who had "once burned an empty cottage for the pleasure of seeing it being destroyed," Edward had disappeared abruptly from his job as a local farmhand in July 1906 and had not been seen since.[5]

William Stern, a Philadelphia saloonkeeper, wrote to ask about his twenty-eight-year-old employee, Charles Neiburg. A recent immigrant from Sweden, Neiburg—whose "one ambition was to marry a woman of wealth" and who "spent all his free time answering matrimonial advertisements"—had vanished in June 1906, telling his boss that he was going to Indiana to marry a "widow with a large farm." He had left his bicycle and a trunkful of clothing behind, saying that he would send for them once he was married. But Stern had never heard from him.[6]

Another letter came from Mr. G. R. Burk of Tuscola, Illinois, asking about his former worker George Bradley. The previous October, the forty-year-old Bradley had announced that he intended to marry "a widow who owned a nice farm near La Porte." Selling "about $1,500 worth of property," he had departed for Indiana, "leaving his clothing with Mr. Burk and saying that he would come back for it, but he never returned."[7]

The wife of Benjamin Carling, an agent for the Prudential Life Insurance Company in Chicago, sent a pleading letter about her husband, who had left home for La Porte a year before, "telling her that he had secured a splendid investment through a rich widow. He was enthusiastic over the plan, having borrowed several thousand dollars from Chicago men whom he had interested in the scheme. At the same time, he had in his possession $1,000 belonging to an insurance company." That was the last anyone had seen of him.[8]

Mrs. Kulers of McKeesport, Pennsylvania, contacted Sheriff Smutzer about her missing father, John E. Hunter of Duquesne, who "left his home in November, 1907, for Northern Indiana to marry a wealthy widow, as he informed his family. He took with him a large sum of money, telling his daughters he did not know when he would return."[9]

Gustav Thuns, a resident of Washington, Pennsylvania, likewise told his family and friends that he had been "in communication with "a wealthy widow in La Porte." According to a letter sent by his former employer, Pat Schimmack, the last anyone had seen of Thuns was when he "started for the Indiana town last summer with $1,000."[10]

And there were letters and telegrams concerning dozens of other vanished men: Herman Konitzer of Chicago; Auguste Gunderson of Green Lake, Wisconsin; Lindner Nikkelson of Huron, South Dakota; Andrew Anderson of Lawrence, Kansas; E. F. Plato of Youngstown, Ohio; I. T. Striver of North Bend, Nebraska; Bert Chase of Mishawaka, Indiana; Emil Tell of Kansas City, Missouri; George Williams of Wapawallopen, Pennsylvania. And more.[11]

The physical descriptions that generally accompanied these inquiries were, for the most part, utterly useless. Given the condition of the exhumed bodies— piles of hacked, rotting skeletons with an occasional fleshless skull—it was impossible to put names to most of them. Circumstantial evidence, however, left little doubt as to some of their identities.

From the testimony of various witnesses, authorities concluded that Belle's hired hands Olaf Lindboe and Henry Gurholt—who had both disappeared under highly suspicious circumstances—were two of her earliest victims.[12] Another man named Olaf—Olaf Jensen—had written to relatives in Norway that he was leaving his home in Carroll, Indiana, to marry "a rich widow who owned a farm in La Porte." Jensen had been seen on the Gunness place, helping Belle with some chores. He disappeared shortly after cashing a large check at the First National Bank of La Porte. When neighbors asked of his whereabouts, Belle "claimed that he had gone west because he 'didn't like La Porte.'"[13]

Arthur Peglow, an assistant cashier at the First National Bank, was able to identify another victim who had been lured into Belle's clutches. This was forty-year-old bachelor John Moe, resident of Elbow Lake, Minnesota, and subscriber to the *Skandinaven*, who arrived in La Porte after informing relatives that he was "moving to a town in Indiana, not far from Chicago." In December 1906, Moe had come into the bank to cash two checks totaling $1,000. He was never seen again. Peglow clearly "remembered Moe when he was shown a photograph."[14]

In early 1906, fifty-five-year-old Christian Hilkven of Dover, Wisconsin, had abruptly departed after selling his farm for $2,000 in cash. His fate was established by Johannes B. Wist, editor of the Norwegian-language newspaper the *Decorah-Posten*. After reading of the Gunness atrocities, Wist notified authorities that, in the spring of 1906, he had received a letter from Hilkven—a longtime subscriber—asking that future issues be mailed to him in La Porte. The La Porte postmaster confirmed "that Hilkven's mail was delivered to Mrs. Gunness's farm."[15]

As is typically the case when a community discovers that a homicidal monster has been living in its midst, people immediately came forward with breathless tales of narrow escapes. Some of these were clearly the products of overheated imaginations. Eighteen-year-old Harriet Danielson of Austin, for example, one of Jennie Olson's former playmates, reported that, the previous September, she had been invited to spend a week with her childhood friend at La Porte. "She told me what a beautiful home they had down there, and what a delightful time we could have together," Harriet explained. "She said her mother urged me to come. It was just an accident that I did not go. A friend of mine did not want me to, there was some pretext or reason I could not go at the time. I wrote Jennie saying I could not visit her at that time. I got no reply.

"Had I gone down there, I am firmly convinced the woman would have murdered me," Harriet asserted. "I know the only reason she consented to Jennie inviting me down there was with the hope of killing us both. The thought of it—chopping my head open and sawing my arms off—has made me sick."[16]

A young man named Melvin Kanaga garnered a fair amount of publicity for himself with a story that, for all its wild improbability, was widely reported as fact. According to Kanaga, a resident of Elkhart, Indiana, he and his friend Delbert Landers had been riding the train home from work the previous August when a "strange woman" entered the car and seated herself beside them.

"She began talking to Delbert in a friendly way and relating how lonesome it was out there," Kanaga recounted. "Then she pretended as though she liked him very much. She told him she was single and had a nice farm just a short distance from La Porte. Finally in a roundabout way she suggested that Delbert pay her a visit, as she was wealthy and would be more than pleased to show him a good time. Then she asked him to come and make his home with her, that they could live peacefully and well contented. He spoke to her of me, at which she turned to me and told me she would be glad to have me come also."

The woman disembarked at La Porte, and Kanaga had never given her a second thought until the news broke of the Gunness death farm. "Had Kanaga complied with the requests of the woman, who no doubt was none other than Mrs. Gunness," the papers reported, "it is probable that he would have been lured into the clutches to suffer the same penalty as did many other victims. No doubt her intentions were to get him to her home, induce him to get an insurance policy, and take his life."[17]

That Belle lusted after Harriet Danielson's blood or made seductive advances to Melvin Kanaga and his friend was exceedingly unlikely. Other individuals, however, had legitimate reasons for believing that—as the newspapers put it—they had "escaped the clutches of the fiend." Besides Carl Peterson—the thirty-six-year-old Waupaca, Wisconsin, man rejected by Belle because he lacked $1,000—there was Alonzo "Lon" Townsend of Topeka, Kansas, a well-to-do farmer who had arranged to visit her home in early May but was delayed by late "spring rains which prevented him from putting in his crops as soon as he had desired." By the time he was ready to make the trip, the Gunness home was ashes.

"Had she gone on with her career of crime a few days longer, Townsend would probably have perished by her hand," the *Argus-Bulletin* observed. "As it is now, he is so pleased over his escape from his prospective bride that he left Topeka on an early morning train for Kansas City so that he could best celebrate his fortunate escape."[18]

If Townsend had been spared by a fortuitous spell of bad weather, another bachelor farmer, Olaf W. Catchousen of Opheim, Illinois, attributed his salvation to a family emergency. After an increasingly ardent exchange of letters with Belle not long before the fire, Catchousen had, in accordance with her wishes, withdrawn $2,000 from his bank and made plans to move to La Porte. Just before his scheduled departure, however, he "received a message to hurry to the home of his parents in Bishop, Illinois, and there he went. Had the message not come, the Opheim man would have been one of the victims of the human slaughterhouse."[19]

George Anderson—a thirty-nine-year-old Missourian who had responded to one of Belle's ads in 1906—had an especially close call. Satisfied with his financial qualifications, she had instructed him to convert his property into cash and join her in La Porte, where they would be married. On the night of his arrival, he repaired to his bedroom on the second floor of the farmhouse and quickly fell asleep.

Sometime around midnight, stirred from his slumbers by a dream "that something uncanny was hovering over him," he opened his eyes "to find Mrs. Gunness standing over his bed. She spoke and then ran out of the room. Greatly frightened, he did not close his eyes after that, and at daylight left the place." In light of the recent horrific revelations, Anderson had no doubt that, as one newspaper put it, "Murder was in the heart of Mrs. Gunness when she entered the death chamber that night and Anderson would have paid the penalty of her lust had he been asleep. But Providence watched over him and he escaped decapitation, dismemberment, and burial in her private cemetery."

Anderson was certain of something else, too. "I am convinced the woman is still alive," he told reporters, "and that she set fire to the farmhouse herself."[20]

Sightings of Belle continued to be reported in Chicago. She was spotted riding on streetcars, hurrying along the streets, eating in restaurants. May Wagner, a waitress at Buchbinder's café on Van Buren Street, told police that, at around nine o'clock on the morning of May 8, a woman precisely matching Mrs. Gunness's description entered "with a man, the couple having alighted from the Rock Island train a few minutes earlier. The man ordered two steaks and Miss Wagner, who took the order, handed them a newspaper containing the latest details of the La Porte tragedy with a portrait of Mrs. Gunness on the open page. The man, said the waitress, took one look at the paper, threw it on the floor, and then he and the woman left hurriedly before they'd taken more than a bite of steak and a sip of coffee. She wanted to know if there was anything wrong with the food and the man told her no, he wasn't feeling well." About an hour later, the same couple was seen eating a hurried breakfast at Heibel's restaurant on West Jackson Boulevard and Halstead Street, their furtive manner attracting the notice of the proprietor.[21]

As far as the *Chicago Tribune* was concerned, these and other eyewitness accounts left little doubt that the archmurderess was at large in the city. "Fleeing from place to place, haunted by her conscience and in constant dread that she will be seized by the hands of the law, Belle Gunness is . . . being sought by scores of detectives," the paper informed its readers.[22] It was one of the *Tribune's* competitors, however—the *Chicago Inter Ocean*—that made the most dramatic claim about the issue. Its correspondent in La Porte had somehow wangled his way into the embalming room of the Austin Cutler funeral home, where the charred remains removed from the cellar of the incinerated farmhouse had been brought. Before the mutilated trunk of the dead woman was sewn into its burial shroud, Cutler weighed and tape-measured it in the reporter's presence. Allowing for its missing head and feet, the undertaker calculated that, in life, the dead woman was five feet two inches in height and weighed around 130 pounds. By contrast, Mrs. Gunness, according to her neighbors, stood five feet seven inches tall and weighed around 280 pounds.

There was only one conclusion to be drawn from this "astounding revelation," the paper proclaimed. Mrs. Belle Gunness—"the siren who lured a score of men to their death"—was, "beyond a reasonable doubt," alive.[23]

21.

THE MIND OF MRS. GUNNESS

The members of the governing board of the Norwegian Lutheran Children's Home, West Irving Boulevard and Fifty-Eighth Avenue in Chicago, were faced with a quandary. They were in the midst of a drive to raise $25,000 for a new building in Norwood Park and had just been named the beneficiary of a large, wholly unexpected gift. Unfortunately, it had been left to their institution by one of the most infamous killers in the annals of American crime, who had evidently acquired much, if not all, of it from her many victims. The Reverend C. E. Solberg, president of the board, was in Minnesota on church-related business when the terms of Belle's will were made public, and immediately arranged to return to Chicago to confer with his colleagues. Even before he arrived, however, Miss Caroline Williams, superintendent of the Children's Home, announced that the orphanage had no intention of accepting Belle Gunness's "blood money."[1]

Since the precise number of Belle's victims would never be known, it is impossible to say exactly how much money she realized from her butcheries. One widely syndicated article, headlined "Small Fortune for Indiana Murderess," added together the insurance payouts from the deaths of her two husbands with "the amounts she is believed to have received from the inmates of her charnel house" and arrived at the figure of $46,900—the equivalent, in today's dollars, of over $1,200,000.[2]

Though the "money-mad" Mrs. Gunness clearly killed for financial gain, greed alone could not account for the sheer savagery of her crimes, the evident gusto with which she slaughtered her victims like farm animals. Various specialists in the human mind were promptly called upon to offer their analyses of Belle's bizarre mentality. In the view of one prominent alienist, she was "a woman of dual personality: a kind and indulgent mother at certain times and at others a demon without fear of God of man or of the law." Another diagnosed her as a "victim of an uncontrollable passion for taking lives, a mania for murdering."[3]

Dr. Hugo Munsterberg, professor of psychology at Harvard University and author of the book *On the Witness Stand: Essays on Psychology and Crime*, saw in Belle a total absence of empathy, characteristic of the criminal type soon to be known as a psychopath. "The scientific investigator, in seeking an explanation for Mrs. Gunness' unnatural crimes, would say that she was emotionally dead," Munsterberg wrote.

> When once the emotions, that make most women so sensitive to any cruelty, are deadened, then the path is opened for carrying crime to any extent. When the emotions are dead, a woman is not affected by any of the natural feminine feelings of horror, fright at the sight of blood, or pity that ordinarily influence a normal person. Because her emotions were dead, she could carve a body to pieces, gather up all the piteous dismembered parts, throw them into a gunny sack, carry them out on her back in a moonlit night, dig a grave in the yard, and throw the troublesome bundle into the hole without a tremor.[4]

Basing his analysis on a newspaper photograph of Belle's face, Dr. J. M. Fitzgerald, an "Expert in Character Study," judged her to be a "woman of selfish and domineering will," "masculine resolution and power of mind," and "an instinct for killing, as shown in the base of her brain, which is remarkably expanded." To Dr. S. V. Rehart of Washington, D.C., the same photograph served as "a practical illustration of the truth of Phrenology. It shows a . . . practical, matter-of-fact intellect combined with ingenuity or Constructiveness, large Destructiveness, Secretiveness and Acquisitiveness, with a large development of the social nature and a small development of the moral and religious qualities. With her power to plan and devise, combined with her social nature to entrap her victims, and her executive nature to carry out her plans without moral restraint or sympathy, we have just the kind of character to commit the crimes with which she has been charged."[5]

A very different conclusion was reached by Dr. Charles Jones of Austin, Belle's family physician back when she was Mrs. Mads Sorensen. Though not an alienist by training, Jones claimed to be "a conscientious student of the psychology of crime." In his view, Belle was a religious fanatic, whose atrocities were motivated by the "same spirit as prompted tortures and burning at the stake in the name of religion in the middle ages.

"In my psychological studies," Jones explained, "I have observed that religion is not restraining in a moral see. Religion is not the same as ethics. Religion in its fanatic state may be a passion devoid of morality that will take any means to an end."

Already "unhinged by religious eccentricities," Belle was launched on her unparalleled career of crime after murdering Mads and collecting on his insurance. "The sudden wealth that came to her," Jones opined, "may have had an irresistible suggestion of the ease with which money might be obtained. In the incident of her husband's death, her temptation to commit the alleged atrocities may have had its birth."[6]

The most illustrious figure to weigh in on the issue of Belle's mental state was Cesare Lombroso, nowadays dismissed as a crackpot but, in his own time, the world's foremost criminologist. In his enormously influential book, *L'Uomo delinquente* (*Criminal Man*), Lombroso argued that violent criminals were not merely barbaric in their behavior but were literal atavisms: savage, apelike beings born by some hereditary glitch into the modern world. With their jutting brows, big jaws, thick necks, and other supposedly telltale features, violent criminals were evolutionary throwbacks: specimens of humanity in its most degenerate state.[7]

In a piece on the Gunness case widely reprinted in American newspapers, Lombroso argued that the La Porte murderess was a prime example of what he called the "born woman criminal." Such beings, he noted "generally commit fewer crimes than men, but when they *are* criminal, they are considerably more so than men. It is not enough for a woman to murder an enemy; she wants to make him suffer, and she enjoys his death."

Like others of her breed, "who always mix eroticism with crime," Mrs. Gunness "must have used the attraction of sensuality to obtain her victims . . . Her exaggerated and perverse sexual instincts manifested themselves in murdering the beings who should have been most dear to her, and she found in this a strange satisfaction." In the slaying of her children, Lombroso saw another element common to such criminals: in these unnatural females, "the maternal instinct, which is conspicuous in the normal woman, is not only suppressed but reversed, as it becomes in them a pleasure to torture their own offspring."

The explanation for such behavior offered by the great criminologist was breathtaking in its combination of rank misogyny, pseudoscientific blather, and fundamental incoherence:

> Woman has many traits in common with a child. Like it, she is vindictive and jealous, only in ordinary cases these defects are naturally neutralized by piety, by maternity, by less ardor in the passions, by weakness, and by undeveloped intelligence. But if there is diseased excitement of the psychic centers which intensifies the bad qualities and seeks a vent in evil, if pity and maternity are absent, if strong passions are also present, the desires derived from an intense eroticism, a sufficiently developed muscular force and a superior intelligence for doing evil and carrying it out are present, the born criminal appears and the woman will be more terrible than any male criminal.[8]

Far more persuasive were the insights offered by an unnamed specialist cited in a widely circulated article by noted journalist Arthur James Pegler. Placing her in the proper criminological category, this person saw Mrs. Gunness as "a maniac of the much-dreaded type that includes the White Chapel murderer." It is "not money" that drives such killers "but the constantly growing appetite for blood, to cut deep and watch the blood flow, to dabble the hands in it, to revel in the odor of it." One "distinguishing features of these criminals is their invariable use of the same methods in every case. Mrs. Gunness decapitated every one of her victims. In every case she severed the limbs. Always there was the maximum of mutilation."[9]

In comparing Belle to Jack the Ripper as a murderer driven by bloodlust and employing a signature MO, this anonymous expert accurately identified her as the type of homicidal maniac for which no name had yet been coined: what a later age would call a serial killer.

22.

JOHANN AND KATE

During the postmortem on Andrew Helgelien, his stomach, liver, and kidneys were removed, hermetically sealed in a jar, and sent to Dr. Walter S. Gaines of the Rush Medical College at the University of Chicago. Gaines would ultimately report that he had found nearly one and a half grains of strychnine in the stomach—"a quantity sufficient several times over to have produced death"—along with a "considerable amount" of arsenic.[1] It was, of course, impossible to say precisely how Belle dispatched her victims. Gaines's findings, however—combined with the condition of the various skeletal remains—suggested one plausible scenario.

After consuming a last, home-cooked, poison-laced meal, Belle's victim would soon be in the throes of an agonizing death. Wielding a hatchet or cleaver, she would put him out of his misery with several bone-splintering blows to the skull. She would then drag the body into her cellar abattoir for butchering. Once the head and limbs were removed from the trunk, she would package the separate parts in gunnysacks, haul them into her hog lot, dump them in a hole, and add quicklime to facilitate decomposition.

How many victims suffered this fate is another unanswerable question. Under the category of "Most Prolific Murderers," however, the first twelve editions of the *Guinness Book of World Records* estimated the total at twenty-eight—"the greatest number of murders ever ascribed to a modern murderess."[2]

Just two years before the Gunness horrors came to light, the country was riveted by the case of a serial killer every bit as diabolical as Belle. His birth name was Johann Schmidt, but he would assume many others in the course of his malevolent career: Albert Huschberg, Count Otto von Kein, Dr. L. G. Hart, Martin Dotz, Jacob Duss, Henry F. Hartman, Heinrich Valtzand, and at least a dozen more, including the one by which the world would come to know him: Johann Hoch.[3]

A native of Germany, he came to America in 1887 at the age of twenty-five, abandoning a wife and three children. In 1895, under the name Huff, he bigamously married a well-off widow named Martha Steinbucher. Four months later, she fell ill with a devastating intestinal ailment. As she writhed in agony, she told her physician that she had been poisoned but—attributing the remark to delirium—he paid her no heed. She died the next day. Immediately afterward, her husband sold her property for $4,000 and disappeared.

Huff's second murder victim was Caroline Hoch of Wheeling, West Virginia, who was hit with a violent illness shortly after their wedding. On a visit to the stricken woman, her minister surprised Huff in the act of giving his wife some white powder—presumably medicine. The next day, Caroline was dead. Huff immediately sold the house, claimed his wife's $900 insurance policy, then faked his own suicide and disappeared.

Now calling himself Johann Hoch, the killer made his way to Chicago. Along the way, he preyed on an indeterminate number of women, murdering some, merely fleecing and abandoning others. For a while, he worked in the Chicago stockyards, an occupation that would ultimately earn him his homicidal nickname, the "Stockyard Bluebeard."

In December 1904, Hoch placed a matrimonial ad in a German newspaper and, soon afterward, received a reply from a forty-six-year-old widow, Marie Walcker, who owned a small candy store. They were married a short time later. A week after the wedding, Marie was stricken with excruciating abdominal pains, a violent thirst, and a tingling in her extremities that felt, she said, like ants crawling over her flesh—all classic symptoms of arsenic poisoning. Her physician, however, diagnosed the problem as nephritis. She died two weeks later. No sooner had Marie exhaled her last, agonized breath than Hoch proposed to her sister, Julia, who had come to tend her dying sibling. Three days later, Hoch and Julia were married. Hoch soon disappeared with all of Julia's money.

While notifying the police, Julia learned that Hoch was already under suspicion for swindle and murder. Caroline Hoch's body had previously been exhumed, but examiners were unable to determine if there was poison in her stomach because Hoch had taken the precaution of eviscerating the corpse and dumping the organs into the Ohio River. Authorities had better luck with the body of Marie Walcker. A postmortem turned up lethal traces of arsenic in her viscera.

Police immediately distributed the fugitive's photograph. Hoch—who had fled to New York City—was arrested when his landlady recognized his picture in the papers. When police arrested him, they found a fountain pen in his possession. Instead of ink, the reservoir contained fifty-eight grains of a powdered substance that turned out to be arsenic. He was convicted of the murder of Marie Walcker and hanged on February 23, 1906. The number of his victims is unknown, though his most trustworthy chronicler estimates that Hoch "married between forty-three and fifty women, about a third of whom he murdered."[4]

As soon as the enormity of Belle's crimes became clear, stories comparing her to Johann Hoch began to appear in the papers. The strangest of these was a widely syndicated article headlined "If Their Paths Had Crossed," a piece of alternate history inspired by the speculations of Charles Peters, deputy chief sheriff of Chicago.

"It would have been interesting from a criminological point of view to watch a contest between Mrs. Gunness and Hoch," Peters mused to reporters. "Suppose that Hoch had seen one of her advertisements, answered it, and a meeting had been arranged. She would have been after Hoch's money, and he would have been after hers. Then would have come the contest, each plotting, scheming with all of his or her cleverness to get the better of the other. It would have beaten any drama of villainy ever produced on the stage."[5]

Elaborating on Peters's macabre what-if? scenario, the article described in lurid detail the imaginary encounter of the male and female Bluebeards. Replying to Mrs. Gunness's ad, Hoch "would have grinned in ghoulish glee" as he pictured the "rich farm" soon to come into his possession. Belle would have read Hoch's response with a "cruel smile" upon her face, then "glanced out of the back window into that graveyard of mutilated victims and figured out where she could bury one more."

At their first meeting, each would have sized the other up and decided, "This one will be easy." On the following day, Belle "would have carelessly held his hand or patted his cheek as she showed him over the acres. He would have returned the caress, believing that his appearance and winning mannerisms had already made an impression." Soon they would be discussing finances: "Hoch would have told the widow he had thousands of dollars with him to be put into the common fund. She would have smiled and answered that her farm would belong to him when they were married. Possibly, right there, they would have set the date for the wedding."

Once they had completed their nuptials and taken a brief honeymoon tour, the couple would have returned to the farm, where "the curtain on the last act would have been raised," and their "fiendish plotting" would reach its "tragical" climax.

As for the winner of this grim contest between the two matrimonial monsters, the writer could only speculate.

"Which would have outwitted the other? Who would have found the first opening to strike, either with poison at a meal, an ax in the darkness of night, or a dagger while in a loving embrace? Which of them would now be under the ground, the victim of the other's treachery, and which enjoying the money of the other?"[6]

If Belle's crimes resembled those of Johann Hoch, they also called up memories of another notorious case, that of the "Bloody Benders" of Kansas.

The Bender family consisted of the sixty-year-old patriarch, John, a hulking, heavily bearded man (generally referred to simply as "Old Man Bender" in historical accounts); his wife, known only as "Ma," a stout, homely female in her fifties with "a tallow-white" face and a temperament every bit as surly as her husband's; John Jr., a slender young man in his midtwenties, with a pleasant face, a trim mustache, and a way of breaking into sudden, nervous giggles that led some people to regard him as a simpleton; and a daughter named Kate, a young woman in her early twenties who, by default, was considered the brains of the operation. Though Kate has gone down in legend as a red-haired temptress, she appears to have been a ruddy-faced, mannish-looking female who held séances under the name "Professor Miss Kate Bender" and claimed to be a faith healer.

Sometime around 1870, the Bender family arrived in Labette County, Kansas, and built a home along a stretch of road a few miles south of the railway town of Cherryvale. The dwelling was little more than a one-room log box, sixteen by twenty feet in size. The interior was divided in half by canvas curtain. One side served as the family's living quarters. The other was turned into a rudimentary inn, where wayfarers could enjoy a home-cooked meal and a straw mattress on the floor for those who wished to bed down for the night.

No one knows how many guests the Benders entertained during the two years they ran their ghastly roadhouse, but at least nine of them were never seen alive again. Their dreadful fate was uncovered in the spring of 1873, following the mysterious disappearance of a prominent local physician named William York, last seen traveling by buggy along the Osage Trail. A search party led by the doctor's brother, Colonel A. M. York, traced his movements to the Bender homestead. Questioned by Colonel York, John Jr. confirmed that the doctor had, in fact, spent a night at the inn but insisted that he had departed in good health the following morning. Claiming that he himself had recently escaped an ambush by highwaymen, John suggested that the doctor might have fallen victim to the gang—a theory Colonel York found highly implausible. After questioning Kate—who offered to use her clairvoyant gifts to find the missing man—the colonel and his men took their leave. It was clear, however, that their suspicions had been deeply aroused.

Some weeks later, a neighbor of the Benders rode over to the inn and was surprised to discover that the place was deserted. From the mess strewn around inside—dirty dishes, an old clock, a German Bible, some hammers, a meat saw, a long-bladed knife, and the canvas partition, which lay bundled in a corner—it seemed clear that the Benders had abandoned their home in a hurry.

When word of this development reached Colonel York, he lost no time in assembling a group of men and making straight for the inn. According to some chroniclers, it was York who discovered the trapdoor in the floor of what had been the Benders' kitchen area. The moment it was lifted, a dreadful odor assaulted his nostrils. Closer inspection revealed the source of the terrible stench: a pool of dried blood, caked on the stone floor.

Prying up the entire cabin with stout poles, the men managed to move it clear of its foundation. With the cellar exposed, they used sledgehammers to shatter the stone floor but found nothing beneath. By the light of the late afternoon sun, however, one of the men spotted something suspicious in the soil of the nearby apple orchard: a strange, rectangular depression, like a slightly sunken grave. He called out to the others, who grabbed shovels and spades and began digging. In less than a minute, they had unearthed the remains of a partly clothed man lying facedown in the dirt. The base of his skull was completely bashed in. When the men turned the body over, they saw that the throat had been slashed from ear to ear. Despite its badly decomposed state, Colonel York had no trouble identifying the corpse as his missing brother, William.

By then darkness had fallen. Early the next morning, the men returned to the spot and, using metal rods to probe the soil, conducted a thorough search of the orchard. By the time they were done, they had unearthed eight more bodies, all but one of them adult males, subsequently identified as travelers along the Osage Trail who had never reached their destinations. They were all known to have been carrying substantial amounts of cash and had all died in the identical manner, the base of their skulls crushed, their throats slit. The single exception was an eight-year-old girl, Mary Ann Loncher, found beside her father's corpse with a silk scarf bound tightly around her neck. A postmortem exam determined that she had been strangled to the point of unconsciousness, then buried alive.

From the physical evidence—the size and shape of the men's head wounds, the matching dimensions of the hammers found in the cabin, certain telltale stains on the canvas curtain—as well as from the testimony of several people who had survived stays at the inn, a picture emerged of the Benders' diabolical MO. When a prosperous-looking traveler showed up, he would be ushered into the dining area and seated at the table with his back to the canvas divider. While Kate beguiled him with some dinnertime conversation, her father or brother would be lurking on the other side of the curtain, hammer at the ready. When the unsuspecting guest leaned his head back against the curtain, the hammer would come crashing down, shattering the back of his skull. The body would then be dragged to the rear of the cabin, where it would be robbed, stripped, and dumped through the trapdoor into the cellar. There, his throat would be slit for good measure. Later, the body would be taken out and buried in the orchard.

Three thousand dollars in reward money was offered for the apprehension of the fugitives. Despite a massive manhunt by lawmen, bounty hunters, and assorted vigilantes, however, the Benders eluded arrest. Rumors about their whereabouts would circulate for years: that John Jr. was working on a railroad gang in Texas, that Kate was running a brothel in San Francisco, that Pa Bender had committed suicide in Michigan, that the whole family had perished while attempting to cross into Mexico via hot-air balloon. But their fate remained a mystery.[7]

Following the ghastly discoveries on the Gunness farm, newspapers were quick to note the "remarkable parallelism" between Belle's atrocities and the "notorious doings of the Bender family." Indeed, so similar did the two cases appear in certain respects that wild rumors began to circulate about possible connections between Belle and the Benders. One widely printed article cited an anonymous correspondent who sent a letter to the editor of a Louisville, Kentucky, newspaper, claiming that Belle and Kate Bender were related by blood, "Kate's father [being] a brother to Mrs. Gunness' grandfather."[8]

Another writer ventured an even more remarkable theory: that "Mrs. Gunness was . . . Kate Bender." If such were the case, "she has outdone the ghastly achievements of her former life." However appalling the Bender crimes, the tally of their victims had already been surpassed by the findings in Belle's hog lot. Moreover, "the Benders had the support of one another—the terrible relief which comes to those who share a fatal secret." By contrast, while "Mrs. Gunness may have had an accomplice in Lamphere or another," it seemed equally likely "that many if not most of her crimes were committed by her alone."

However dubious the notion that the vanished Kate Bender had reappeared three decades later under a new identity in La Porte, there was no doubt in the mind of the writer that she and Belle Gunness would forever be linked "in the history of crime." Both had achieved "a terrible immortality, leaving names at which the world may well grow pale." And their enormities revealed a sobering truth: that "the possibilities of the human heart seem infinite in evil as in good."[9]

23.

DEAD OR ALIVE?

On Friday, May 8, E. R. Buell and A. J. Hunt, commercial travelers from Detroit, were seated beside each other in a Pullman car on the Atlantic Express, headed for Rochester, New York. At around seven o'clock in the evening, the train made a stop at Ashtabula, Ohio, where a woman boarded and took a seat across the aisle from the two men.

She was a large woman, perhaps five feet nine inches in height and weighing, from the looks of her, about two hundred pounds. She was dressed in widow's weeds and wore a heavy black veil.

Buell would later tell reporters that there was something peculiar about her behavior—that "she seemed eager to avoid attention on the car." Both men had recently been in Chicago and were keenly aware of the Gunness case and the conflicting opinions as to Belle's fate. In fact, Buell was carrying a copy of one of the Chicago papers with a large photograph of the "Female Bluebeard" on its front page.

At some point during the trip, the woman lifted her veil. At the sight of her face, the two salesmen exchanged a look.

When they arrived in Rochester, Buell and his companion proceeded straight to the Powers Hotel, where they informed the house detective of their suspicions. The detective immediately telephoned the police lieutenant Henry R. McAlester, who in turn put in a call to Captain Thomas R. Quigley in Syracuse, where the train would be making its next stop. Quigley promptly dispatched two of his detectives, Carl Neiss and John Donovan, to meet the train when it arrived.

It was a few minutes before 1:00 a.m. when it pulled into the Syracuse depot. Accompanied by the stationmaster, the two detectives boarded the train and spoke to the Pullman car conductor, O. S. Britton. They described the woman in black who had gotten on at Ashtabula and asked if she was still on board. When Britton inquired if they were friends of the woman, Neiss and Donovan displayed their credentials and explained the reason they were there. Britton immediately led them to the lower berth where the woman lay sleeping.

She would later describe the "terrible sensation" that had come over her when she was awakened by "two men's heads peering into [her] berth." Her first thought was that "the train was being held up by robbers." When they identified themselves and told her why they were there, she was "dumbfounded." They ordered her to dress immediately. She was still making herself ready, however, when the train—already fifteen minutes past its scheduled departure time— chugged out of the station.

The officers rode with her all the way to Utica, where they led her onto the platform, loaded her into a hack, and drove her to police headquarters. By then, word of the detectives' mission had spread throughout the train, generating intense excitement among the passengers, who felt that they had been present at a historical event: the capture of the country's most notorious fugitive, the "Indiana Ogress," Belle Gunness.[1]

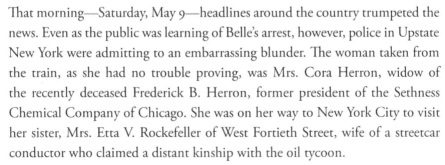

That morning—Saturday, May 9—headlines around the country trumpeted the news. Even as the public was learning of Belle's arrest, however, police in Upstate New York were admitting to an embarrassing blunder. The woman taken from the train, as she had no trouble proving, was Mrs. Cora Herron, widow of the recently deceased Frederick B. Herron, former president of the Sethness Chemical Company of Chicago. She was on her way to New York City to visit her sister, Mrs. Etta V. Rockefeller of West Fortieth Street, wife of a streetcar conductor who claimed a distant kinship with the oil tycoon.

Having established her identity to the satisfaction of the Utica authorities, Mrs. Herron was taken back to Syracuse, where—after sending a telegram to her sister—she spent the remainder of the night in the matron's quarters of police headquarters. Early the following morning, she was interviewed by Police Chief Condon, who offered his apologies and asked her to sign a release relieving his department of responsibility for the false arrest, a request she refused. She was then driven to the train station and given a ticket on the Empire Express to New York City.

Waiting to meet her at the Grand Central Station were her sister, Mrs. Rockefeller, and reporters from various papers, including the *New York Times*.

"This is a dreadful thing," Mrs. Rockefeller angrily declared after she and Mrs. Herron had exchanged an emotional greeting, "and I shall encourage my sister to seek legal redress for the stigma that the stupid Syracuse detectives have placed on her."

Asked how much she intended to sue for, an exhausted Mrs. Herron "named fifty thousand dollars as the sum she felt she was entitled to."

As Mrs. Herron climbed into a taxi for the short ride to her sister's apartment, the *Times* reporter called out: "Won't you say something about your experience?"

"Oh, what can I say?" she replied in a tremulous voice. "It is too awful."[2]

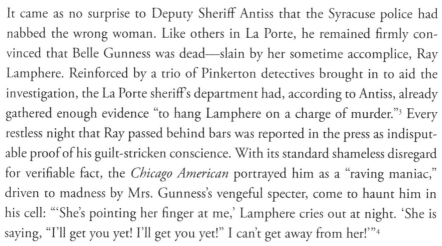

It came as no surprise to Deputy Sheriff Antiss that the Syracuse police had nabbed the wrong woman. Like others in La Porte, he remained firmly convinced that Belle Gunness was dead—slain by her sometime accomplice, Ray Lamphere. Reinforced by a trio of Pinkerton detectives brought in to aid the investigation, the La Porte sheriff's department had, according to Antiss, already gathered enough evidence "to hang Lamphere on a charge of murder."[3] Every restless night that Ray passed behind bars was reported in the press as indisputable proof of his guilt-stricken conscience. With its standard shameless disregard for verifiable fact, the *Chicago American* portrayed him as a "raving maniac," driven to madness by Mrs. Gunness's vengeful specter, come to haunt him in his cell: "'She's pointing her finger at me,' Lamphere cries out at night. 'She is saying, "I'll get you yet! I'll get you yet!" I can't get away from her!'"[4]

Rebutting Antiss's claim, Ray's attorney, Wirt Worden, issued a statement asserting his client's innocence. Having represented Ray in the various suits brought against him by Mrs. Gunness, Worden proclaimed that, though undeniably "a man of mediocre mentality," Lamphere was "without criminal proclivities.

"There are two reasonable theories as to the cause and origin of the fire," he continued:

> One is that Mrs. Gunness—thinking that Lamphere may have discovered things that would incriminate her, and knowing further that Asle Helgelien was coming to make an investigation—sought to cover up all evidence of her crimes and escape with her own life, if possible, and that she, in carrying this out, murdered the three children, placed them on the cellar floor with the adult corpse found, and fired the building and escaped. The other theory is that Mrs. Gunness, foreseeing the culminating of events upon the arrival of Helgelien, decided to end her own life and at the same time cover up all evidence of prior crimes and to do so, killed her own children, fired the house, and committed suicide.

"In either event," Worden concluded, "Lamphere, as I firmly believe, is innocent of any crime. He is simply a victim of circumstance."[5]

Proponents of Worden's first theory—that the headless woman found in the cellar was a decoy planted by Belle—were bolstered in their belief by the many reported sightings of the murderess. Police in Elkhart, Indiana, were on the lookout for a woman weighing about two hundred pounds "and of distinctly masculine appearance" who had aroused the suspicion of a bookstore clerk named Stillman when he noticed that she spoke in a Scandinavian accent and "had a number of gold teeth . . . that matched the description of the La Porte arch-fiend."[6] George G. Spurunewski, a druggist in East St. Louis, contacted the police to report "that a woman answering the description of Mrs. Belle Gunness" had recently taken up residence in his city.[7]

Sheriff R. S. Williams of Delta County, Colorado, convinced that Mrs. Gunness had settled nearby, telegraphed the authorities in La Porte, asking "if any reward was being offered for her capture, so that he might proceed with her arrest."[8] Another telegram to the La Porte police, this one from a resident in Willmar, Minnesota, claimed that Mrs. Gunness was currently working as a housekeeper for a local farmer and urged them to "come and get her."[9] Samuel Harvey of Kansas City, Missouri, wrote directly to Mayor Darrow, saying "he had met Mrs. Gunness in Ogden, Utah on May 4, six days after she was supposedly burned to death."[10] She was also seen in Grand Rapids, Michigan; Palouse, Washington; Hot Springs, Arkansas; Cincinnati, Ohio; Joliet, Illinois; Alberta, Canada; and "traveling through the wilds of the state of Chiapas, Mexico, dressed in man's attire."[11]

Closer to home, a self-declared "seer" named Jesse Dickenson appeared at Sheriff Smutzer's office on Saturday, May 9, announcing that Belle Gunness was still in La Porte County and that he had the power to locate her. "All I require," he said, "is something that has been in the possession of Ray Lamphere, and by the aid of this, I will be able to tell the exact location of her hiding place and the mystery will be solved."[12]

Another person claiming spiritualistic powers, Mrs. A. James of South Milwaukee, announced that, by studying the signs of the zodiac, she had discovered that Mrs. Gunness was presently living "either in Michigan City, Fort Wayne, Indianapolis, or Terre Haute . . . She will be found in a livery barn in one of these cities dressed as a man and doing man's work."[13]

Sightings of Belle became such a common occurrence that the press began treating them as a joke. One Indiana newspaper advised all "large-sized women [to] stay at home so that they are not mistaken for Mrs. Gunness and held by the authorities." Another wryly observed that Belle had "been seen in so many different places at almost the same time" that she seemed "to have solved the problem of rapid transit."[14]

Sheriff Smutzer, still convinced that Belle was dead, had come up with a novel way to prove it, "an original departure from the methods usually employed in the work of solving murder mysteries," as one Chicago paper wrote. Late

Saturday, May 9, he announced that he had retained the services of a veteran miner named Louis Schultz, who had spent nearly twenty years among the gulches of California and Colorado prospecting for gold. On Monday, Schultz would set up his sluice on the Gunness property and begin sifting the ashes in the cellar in a search for Belle's gold-capped teeth.

"I will take my time," said Schultz, "and go over every particle of the wreckage. If the teeth are there, I will find them. And if it was Mrs. Gunness who perished in the flames, the teeth are there."

Belle's dentist, Dr. Ira P. Norton, agreed with Schultz. "Mrs. Gunness had some dental work done by me a year ago. She made two visits and paid me $40 for my work," he told reporters. "The four incisors in her lower jaw were missing. I put gold crowns on the two lower bicuspids and bridged in four porcelain teeth between them. The four porcelain teeth were reinforced by a back of eighteen-karat gold. If it was Mrs. Gunness whose body was found in the ruins, her teeth are intact among the debris. The fire was not hot enough to melt the gold or incinerate the porcelain."[15]

Smutzer's announcement came at the end of a long and fruitless day of digging. For the first time since he and his helpers began their grim excavations, Belle's "garden of death" yielded no new bodies. When the search was abandoned at nightfall, the crowds that had gathered at the farm since early morning couldn't hide their surprise. By then, Belle had assumed such monstrous dimensions in the public imagination that it was generally assumed "she had sown every square yard of her 30-acre farm with the bodies of her victims."[16]

No digging was planned for the next day, partly in honor of the Sabbath but mostly because of the immense hordes that were expected to descend on the farm. Guards would be posted in the cellar and on the ruins of the farmhouse, but otherwise "spectators [would] be allowed to roam at will."

To cash in on the Gunness-related frenzy, the Lake Erie and Western Railroad had arranged for special excursion trains to bring visitors from Indianapolis and Chicago. Every hotel room in La Porte and nearby Michigan City had been booked and extra cots set up in the hallways. Restaurants were doing a booming business. "Generally speaking," one local newspaper observed, "the town presents the appearance of a fair or big convention."

Livery companies were hiring additional drivers to ferry sightseers to and from the Gunness place. They would have countless round-trips to make. According to one estimate, at least ten thousand people—"the equivalent of three-fourths of the population of La Porte"—were expected to flock to the "murder farm" on Sunday to gratify their morbid curiosity.[17]

24.

CARNIVAL

The predictions published in the Saturday papers were wrong. Ten thousand people did not descend on the Gunness farm on Sunday, May 10. According to the most reliable estimates, the number was closer to sixteen thousand, and possibly as high as twenty.

The first excursion train reached La Porte just after five o'clock in the morning. Others, packed to overflowing, arrived regularly throughout the day, disgorging passengers by the hundreds. Local hackmen were waiting at the station, ready to take the new arrivals out to the farm. The standard fare was ten cents for the one-mile ride. Once there, the passengers were informed that the return trip would cost them a quarter.[1]

By midmorning, the McClung macadam road was jammed with every variety of vehicle—carryalls, buggies, broughams, buckboards, wagonettes, and more—along with an army of pedestrians. An estimated fifty automobiles brought smartly dressed visitors from Chicago, Michigan City, South Bend, Elkhart, Goshen, Niles, Mishawaka, and other midwestern cities. Young men on bicycles, new mothers pushing baby carriages, and old-timers hobbling along on crutches "vied with each other for a place on the road, while motorcycles shot through the crowds at frequent intervals." Given the congestion, it seemed a miracle that only a single accident occurred, when an automobile spooked the horse pulling the buggy of Benjamin Zanelar and his wife, and Mrs. Zanelar was thrown from the rig and broke an arm.[2]

A festive atmosphere reigned at the farm. Newspaper commentators compared the scene to a "county fair," a "playground," and a "Sunday amusement park."[3] Vendors, calling their wares through megaphones, peddled peanuts, popcorn, and lemonade. Beside one of the graves, where the moldering remains of two of Belle's victims had been unearthed, a portly fellow manned a makeshift refreshment stand, dispensing "pink ice cream and cake."[4]

A crew of young men, hired for the occasion by a local printer, roamed the grounds, hawking picture postcards at ten cents apiece or three for a quarter. The photos of Andrew Helgelien's dismembered body sold out within minutes, though the ones showing the skulls of Belle's other victims were also popular. Other subjects included portraits of Belle and her children, panoramic views of the farmstead, and images of shovel-wielding diggers standing knee-deep in the graves. Many visitors brought Kodaks and took their own photos, posing their families before the ruins of Belle's farmhouse or at the edges of the pits in the excavated hog lot.[5]

Several enterprising youngsters went around offering human skeletal fragments allegedly dug from the "death garden," though the people who snapped up these supposed relics would eventually learn that they had purchased the bone shards of pigs. Other eager souvenir hunters came away with whatever treasures they could get their hands on: chunks of brick from the incinerated house, charred pieces of stovepipe, bent nails, burnt shoe buttons, even twigs from the orchard. Joe Zahner, member of the South Bend baseball club, "secured an old coffee pot and a disreputable looking shoe."[6]

Ignoring the guards posted at the site, scavengers climbed into the ruins of the cellar and emerged with whole bagfuls of debris. Other men hopped into the open graves and groveled in the dirt for ghoulish keepsakes. One handsome young woman was seen "with the skirt of her beautiful dress lifted up in which she carried about part of the carcass of a dead dog, supposed to have been killed by Mrs. Gunness while she was experimenting with poisons to use on her victims."[7]

The earliest arrivals to the farm made straight for the buggy shed, where the reeking remains of the exhumed corpses were lain out on wooden planks. Sheriff Smutzer, standing guard outside, lined the visitors up in single file and allowed them into the makeshift morgue a few at a time. By nine o'clock, however, the crowd pressing for admission became so large and unmanageable that

Smutzer was compelled to padlock the door. Sending up cries of frustration, several women "clawed at the little red carriage house . . . They stuck their fingers in the cracks and wrenched in an attempt to pry them apart far enough to see inside," while "men boosted each other to the window at the end of the structure and gazed until others pushed them from their places to make room for other gawkers."[8]

It was a perfect day for a picnic, and many of the families who arrived in the morning brought along lunch baskets. At noontime, they spread tablecloths on the lawn beneath the fir trees in the front yard or on the grass of the apple orchard and settled down for their meals. Laughing children darted among the crowds or trooped alongside a local character, "Uncle Ben," who roamed the property with a forked willow divining rod that could—so he claimed—detect the graves of undiscovered victims. "Thirty-seven in all," he solemnly announced to reporters at the conclusion of his search.[9]

The holiday scene at the Gunness farm was not only front-page news across the Midwest but the subject of widespread moralizing. For two weeks, papers had been gleefully exploiting the tragedy. Suddenly, their editorial pages rang with indignation at the unseemly behavior of the crowds who had defiled the Sabbath by turning the murder farm into a carnival ground. The normal Sunday atmosphere of "quietude and religious observance" had been supplanted by "noisy merry-making and wild frolic"—"ribald rioting and coarse and disgusting and almost insane frivolity." Such was the air of festivity that "one would have thought the Gunness farm contained a circus rather than a murder morgue." To one outraged commentator, the mad "scramble of 15,000 people" to the site of such "appalling and atrocious" crimes was a sad commentary on the moral state of supposedly civilized man—"galling, incontrovertible proof that the race is still but a little removed from a stage of actual savagery."[10]

Stung by these attacks, the editor of the *La Porte Weekly Herald* defended his community, arguing that the hordes of morbid sightseers at the Gunness farm deserved no special censure, "for the same would doubtless have been true of [people from] any other section of the state or the country." The ghoulish spectacle was merely "a magnified reflection of what transpires almost every day in every community. Our police courts are always crowded with people eager to brush against crime. The morgue is the center of attraction . . . Relics of a murder or of a terrible accident entailing the loss of life are eagerly collected and given a conspicuous place in many homes."

How to account for this "unhealthy appetite for the horrible"? Perhaps, the writer suggested, there was some strange comfort to be derived from the awareness of another's suffering. "One would think there was enough unavoidable tragedy in everyone's existence to keep him from seeking the hideous and unsightly," he mused. "And yet it may be the fact that each has his cross to bear that leads him to come in contact with the world's wretchedness as a sort of palliative to his own."[11]

Whatever the case, the public's fascination with every grisly detail of the Gunness case would continue unabated, as would the efforts of various hucksters to profit from it. The following Sunday would bring ten thousand sightseers to the farm. A few days later, an editorial in the *La Porte Weekly* noted with outrage that two theaters in South Bend were presenting a magic lantern show consisting of "twenty-two views of the Gunness farm. Next," the writer continued with bitter sarcasm, "they will probably be showing moving pictures of Mrs. Gunness murdering her victims."[12]

His comment proved prescient. Not long afterward, theaters throughout the Midwest began showing a moving picture produced by the Edison Company, titled *Mrs. Gunness, the Female Bluebeard.*[13]

25.

"THE MRS. GUNNESS MYSTERY"

The public couldn't get enough of the Gunness case. In La Porte, the printing presses worked overtime to meet the demand for the two local papers. The daily run of the *Herald* rose by as much as eight hundred copies, many readers "buying three and four extra copies" of every issue, one for themselves, the others "to send away to friends."[1]

In Chicago, the appetite for every juicy tidbit about the case was fed by the yellow papers, which—when no actual news was available—cheerfully dished out wild rumor, lurid gossip, and even rank fabrication. According to one Chicago daily, Mrs. Gunness was a grave robber who "stole a body from Pine Lake cemetery near her home and substituted it for her own in the burning house."[2] Another reported that she was a hypnotist who "was possessed of some remarkable power to compel unwilling victims to do what she commanded."[3] In a syndicated piece headlined "The Horrors of That Night," a writer named Robert Ash depicted the "multi-murderess" as a guilt-haunted wreck, tormented nightly by "the ghosts of her victims":

> For months following the death of her victims, the archfiend suffered the torments of the condemned . . . The woman's dreams were troubled. Specters of Helgelien, of Jennie Olson, of ten crumbling skeletons haunted her . . . Darkness was filled with horror for the woman. In nightly delirium the wraiths of the victims of the "death farm" passed in review before her.[4]

Citing sources in Norway, one widely circulated story claimed that Belle's father, "Peter Paulson," was "a traveling conjurer and magician" who performed at fairs throughout the country. Along with "her three sisters and brothers," Belle also "took part in the show," performing in front of the tent as "a rope dancer . . . in short skirts" to entice male customers inside.[5]

One of Belle's most diabolical letters to Andrew Helgelien was reprinted in newspapers across the country. "No woman in the world is happier than I am," it read in part. "I know that you are now to come to me and be my own . . . When I hear your name mentioned, it is beautiful music to my ears. My heart beats with wild rapture for you! My Andrew, I love you. Come prepared to stay forever." Only many years later would researchers determine that this sinister missive was a fake, concocted by one or more of the out-of-town newspapermen holed up at the Hotel Teegarden.[6]

Several Indiana communities seemed seized by a perverse envy. When rumors spread that "a new 'death farm' where Mrs. Belle Gunness buried many of her victims" had been discovered near Warsaw, "the citizens of that place were thrown into a fever excitement" and appeared crestfallen when the story proved false.[7] In Valparaiso, one newspaper reported that, before purchasing her farm in La Porte, "Mrs. Gunness wrote to one of our citizens inquiring about the price of a piece of land which he had for sale." Evidently, she "intended to start her private graveyard near this city." For unknown reasons, however, the "negotiations fell through. Thus," the article somewhat wistfully concluded, "our city missed a chance to gain world-wide notoriety."[8]

Jacob Rouch, a seventy-year-old resident of Warsaw, was said to have become so obsessed by the Gunness case that he "went temporarily insane . . . and while in that condition took his own life."[9] Even weirder was a story in the *New York Times*, headlined "Dog Gunness Hurt Her Lawn." According to the article, Mrs. Sarah D. Stubbert of Glen Ridge, New Jersey, had rented her "handsome home" to a Manhattanite named F. H. Sawyer. When she "returned to take possession of her home," Mrs. Stubbert—who had "always taken pride in her lawn"—was "shocked to find the beautiful plot marred by Mr. Sawyer's dog, Gyp, who had emulated Mrs. Gunness by burying bones in the lawn." Mrs. Stubbert promptly brought a suit against Mr. Sawyer for $500 in damages wrought by his "canine Gunness."[10]

The wildest tales of all appeared in a paperback "true crime" book hastily slapped together by some anonymous hack and published that summer by the Chicago firm of Thompson & Thomas. Priced at a quarter, this shameless cut-and-paste job—"a mess of undigested newspaper clippings spiced up with red-hot imaginary episodes," as one historian describes it[11]—was titled *The Mrs. Gunness Mystery! A Thrilling Tale of Love, Duplicity & Crime.* On its lurid cover, Belle—depicted as a statuesque beauty in a filmy nightgown—hovers over the bed of a slumbering farmhand, a candle held aloft in one of her hands, a bottle of poison clutched in the other. The prurient quality of the image prevails throughout the book, which opens with a chapter on Belle's ostensible childhood titled "The Sword Swallower's Daughter."

"It was a gala day in the gypsy camp near Trondheim, Norway," the chapter begins, "when Peter, the giant sword swallower, won the hand in marriage of the svelte little Arabella, whose tiny pointed toes dancing upon a swinging rope high in the air had set the nation on fire with enthusiasm." We learn how the "dashing and handsome" Peter swept the "pretty Arabella" off her feet by demonstrating his amazing skill at sword-swallowing, burying a long steel blade into the "human sheath" of his throat until only its "jeweled hilt" was visible between his teeth. "The brute horror of it fascinated the dancer. With the strange trait that characterizes her sex, Arabella found herself falling in love with this daring giant."

Soon, Arabella was serving as Peter's assistant in a new act he had invented called "The Decapitation," in which he created the shockingly realistic illusion that he was beheading his lovely young wife:

> The properties for the act were a great sword, a chopping block, a cheval mirror, and a head of wax fashioned to resemble the features of his pretty wife. Clad in the blood red tights and the black mask of the headsman, Peter would stand upon a platform beside the gruesome block, while the pretty Arabella laid her golden head upon its surface. Then, to the horror of the spectators, he would feel with his fingers for the white throat of the woman. A dazzling flash of the steel blade and down it

came with a sickening crunch. A spurt of "property" blood and
the head of the beauty dropped from the block into a basket
before it. Before the crowd could recover from their thrill of
horror, the woman would arise from behind the block, smile
at them with her dazzling teeth to prove that a dummy and
not her real head had been clipped off, and throw them a kiss.

One year after their marriage, a baby girl was born to the couple. "She
was christened Arabella after her mother, but everybody called her Baby Bella."
Accompanying her parents on "their yearly round of the towns in Norway and
Sweden," the blue-eyed moppet was soon emulating them in her own games of
make-believe. One day, "the big showman" and his wife came upon their little
daughter seated at the rear of their gypsy tent, "prattling merrily to her one
childish treasure," a rag doll named Dollie. As the parents looked on in horror,
Baby Bella reached for one of her father's swords and, "with a gurgle of delight,"
chopped off Dollie's head.

So shocked were Peter and Arabella by this behavior that they "temporarily
retired from show business" and opened a crockery shop in Christiana. Not long
afterward, during a visit from her grandfather, the child saw the old man "meet
a violent death when he tumbled from the top landing of the stairs, where she
stood, to the floor below, and broke his neck."

The worst, according to the book, was yet to come. Peter's crockery venture
having failed, he "was forced back into his old business of sword swallowing.
One day, as he stood before a great crowd and thrust a razor edged blade into his
vitals, he slipped and fell. The point of the knife was driven through his bowels.
Baby Bella saw her father die in terrible agony."

Though couched in characteristically overwrought language, the chapter
concludes with a question that continues to dominate debates over the relative
influence of nature and nurture in the creation of serial murderers. "Was it
hereditary or was it childish association with horror that led this child to grow
into an ogress, with the lust for letting human blood, the love of rending of
bodies limb from limb, and the greed for human heads that caused her to slay
and decapitate at least twenty-five children, women, and men whose names are
known?"[12]

The heart of the book is a wildly sensationalistic account of Belle's crimes, much of it plagiarized from the newspapers, the rest made up out of whole, highly colorful cloth. After dispatching her two husbands, Belle—variously referred to as "the sword swallower's daughter," "the sorceress," "the siren," "the ogress," and "the bloodthirsty monster, Mrs. Hyde"—"set about devising a cunning murder machine, baiting her trap to satisfy the wild blood lust that hungers in her heart." The first step was the construction of a "dungeon chamber" on her La Porte property. Soon after moving in, she hired a mason to build an ostensible "smoke house," with soundproof walls, no windows, and a heavy oaken door. She then equipped her intended "murder room" with meat hooks and a vat—"appurtenances that might be used in cutting up and making sausage—or dismembering a human body."

Next came the purchase of "the other accessories to this murder machine: some arsenic, a bottle of chloroform, a few keen edged scalpels and dissecting knives." The final step was creating a "death garden"—a "little private murder cemetery" where she could "plant the bones of her victims." At last, she was "prepared to enter the wholesale murder business."[13]

Putting her diabolical plan in motion, she "sent myriads of letters into the world"—"love letters, palpitating with passion, seductive in their hints at the fortune any man might have in marriage." It wasn't long before the "moths flocked to her flame."

In describing her atrocities, the nameless scribe pulls out all the salacious stops, rendering the scenes in the quasi-pornographic style of a Victorian penny dreadful. Typical is his depiction of the ostensible dual murder, on Christmas Eve, 1906, of Belle's foster daughter, Jennie Olson, and the Minnesota bachelor John Moe:

> Catlike, softly as a tigress stalking her prey, the sword swallower's daughter sought the chamber of the virgin girl. Lithe fingers felt the soft white throat. A half smothered scream in a childish treble and all was over.
>
> Now the tigress emerged and tiptoed to the room of Mr. Moe. From the belt beneath her nightgown she drew a tiny vial. No need for caution now. The man was drugged with wine.

Her eyes were small steel points. Her nostrils quivered with the scent for blood. Her hands were talons. Her face was a horrid gargoyle. By candlelight, Mrs. Hyde sat in the crimson-papered guest chamber and reveled in the final struggles of her prey . . .

Down to the dungeon chamber she lugged the heavy bodies. Down on the chopping block she laid the lifeless forms. With the sure, quick work of the adept, she stripped them of clothing. She raised above her shoulders the keen blade of a huge meat axe. Quick, sure, clean as the work of the surgeon was Belle's dismemberment. Conscienceless, trembling not, void of emotion, she separated limb from limb the slender form of the girl she had nursed from a babe.[14]

Once the bodies were planted in her "death garden," the fictional Belle would sprinkle them with chloride of lime to destroy all traces of her monstrous handiwork. "Every day, the acid was eating away the evidence, devouring bones, hair, flesh, carrying on the labors that the widow, with fiendish ingenuity, had begun."

Even as the acid did its work, "Belle's thirst for blood and her itch for gold grew on apace." Seating herself at her table, she composed one of her diabolical love letters, then—"smiling a vulture's grin as her tongue tip wet the stamp"—mailed it off to her next unwitting victim.

Soon "there was another blood orgy: A bit of powder on a silver spoon, a groan, a rattling in the throat, the swift deft surgery that clipped bone from bone as the chef carves a capon for the table, the midnight burial in the little garden—and the lime did the rest."[15]

Tallying Belle's victims, the writer asserted that she was responsible for twenty-five "known murders" and suspected of as many as fifty. The depredations of America's other notorious "multi-murderers" paled by comparison: "The Bender family, operating a murder ranch in Kansas, had but eight known victims. Dr. H. H. Holmes, of Murder Castle fame, killed not more than a score in all. Hoch, the arch bigamist, killed but ten."

The numbers spoke for themselves. Belle Gunness, "The Sorceress of Murder Farm," was, by a wide margin, "the most terrible criminal of the ages."[16]

26.

PAY DIRT

The white-haired prospector Louis Schultz, known to his friends as "Old Klondike," spent Monday, May 11, constructing his sluice box—a narrow wooden trough, about twelve feet in length and arranged at a downward angle on the ground. While he worked, Joe Maxson and a few other men began hauling shovelfuls of ashes from the cellar of the incinerated farmhouse and dumping them in a big pile beside the contraption. The next day, with a water wagon supplying the necessary stream, Schultz began the process of washing the debris in search of Belle's gold teeth.[1]

In the weeks since the fire, diggers in the cellar had turned up three men's watches. From its serial number, one had been traced to a store in Iola, Kansas, where, so the ledger showed, it had been purchased by Ole Budsberg. The other two timepieces were likewise presumed to be those of Belle's victims. Now, as Schultz worked his sluice, other watches came to light—five more over the course of the next two weeks, making a total of eight.[2]

As far as State's Attorney Smith was concerned, these finds settled one of the biggest questions about Belle's crimes. Contradicting theories that at least a dozen additional corpses would be discovered in her hog lot, Smith asserted his "confident belief" that "the graveyard of Mrs. Belle Gunness has surrendered its last victim. I base this belief," he explained,

> on the number of watches found in the debris. Eight watches have been recovered. It is the evidence of people who were

employed by Mrs. Gunness and who, by the working of a seeming miracle, escaped her execution room, that this queen of crime possessed a mania for collecting watches. It is reasonable to believe that each one of her victims possessed a watch, and that she came into possession of a watch with the taking of the life of each new applicant for her matrimonial favors.[3]

Over the next few weeks, Sheriff Smutzer would do some desultory digging around the property. He would find a man's skull in an abandoned privy vault, apparently the discarded head of one of the decapitated victims previously unearthed. Some hogs, rooting in the yard, turned up a couple of human bones. But as Smith had predicted, no more bodies would be found.[4]

➤ «◉» ⊂

On Saturday, May 16, the body of the first victim exhumed from the Gunness graveyard was returned to the earth.

Andrew Helgelien's remains had been transferred to the Cutler mortuary, where they awaited official identification. On Friday night, May 15, Edward A. Evans, the Chicago police department's specialist in Bertillon measurements—the standard system of forensic identification at the time, soon to be superseded by fingerprinting—examined the dismembered parts. Using Bertillon records obtained from Minnesota's Stillwater Penitentiary—where Helgelien had done ten years for burglary and arson—Evans confirmed that the remains were those of the South Dakota farmer.

Placed in a casket that had been paid for by Asle Helgelien—who, before returning home, had left two hundred dollars for his brother's funeral—the body was loaded into Cutler's "dead wagon" and driven out to Patton Cemetery, where it was stored overnight in a vault. The following morning, at around ten o'clock, a brief service was conducted at the grave site by Reverend August Johnson, pastor of the Swedish Lutheran Church. As he reached the passage "For dust thou art, and unto dust shall thou return," one of the participants—Charles H. Michael, proprietor of a local hotel—laid a bunch of lilacs on the casket. Then Andrew Helgelien—the first of Belle's victims to be exhumed from her secret graveyard—was lowered to his final resting place.[5]

———— ((●)) ————

Apart from one rainy day when work was suspended, Louis Schultz would conduct his macabre prospecting for a week. Besides the watches, he would turn
up several corroded knives, parts of a gilded picture frame, a plain gold ring,
some keys, a belt buckle, a few bone fragments, and the remnants of a book on
anatomy. The ashes, however, yielded no trace of the teeth.

Large crowds of spectators gathered at the farm each day to watch Schultz
work. Among them was a trio of Pinkerton detectives, brought in at the suggestion of Sheriff Smutzer to help gather evidence against Ray Lamphere. Their
presence did not sit well with Ray's lawyer, Wirt Worden, who issued a caustic
statement to the press. Alluding to the questionable tactics of which Pinkerton
operatives were often accused, Worden flatly declared that "evidence is now
being deliberately manufactured to make it fit the theory of the detectives."
There was no doubt in his mind, said Worden, "that the gold teeth of Mrs.
Gunness, with special identification marks of the dentist, will be found."[6]

———— ((●)) ————

Just before noon on Tuesday, May 19, Worden's prediction was fulfilled when,
moments after shoveling a large load of ashes into his sluice box, Schultz came
up with a pair of dental bridges, an upper and lower.

"They're found!" shouted Sheriff Smutzer, tossing his leather cap high in
the air. Taking the bridges from the grinning miner, Smutzer hopped in his car,
sped into town, and made directly for the office of Belle's dentist, Ira Norton.

Dr. Norton had no difficulty identifying the prostheses. The upper bridge
was the work of another dentist; Belle had been fitted with it in Chicago before
moving to La Porte and was wearing it when Norton first examined her. The
lower bridge was his own handiwork: four porcelain incisors backed with
eighteen-karat gold and anchored to molars on either side of her jaw. There was,
he told reporters, no mistaking the maker of the "dummy teeth," which "bear
my private style of workmanship. This lower bridge is positively the one I made
for Mrs. Gunness."[7]

"What's to have prevented Mrs. Gunness from having removed the teeth
and thrown them into the fire before she left?" asked one of the reporters.

Norton pointed to a charred fragment of molar still hooked to the lower bridge. "As you see," he explained, "a natural tooth still adheres to the bridgework. To do what you propose, Mrs. Gunness would have had to extract one of her own teeth."[8]

Not everyone was convinced. Wasn't Mrs. Gunness cunning enough to attach the bridgework to a tooth taken from one of her victims? And how was it possible that a conflagration hot enough to completely incinerate her skull would leave her false teeth so undamaged?

Norton's pronouncement, however, was sufficiently authoritative to persuade most officials that, as the *La Porte Argus-Bulletin* put it, "Again, and finally, Mrs. Gunness is dead."[9] Just a few days earlier, Coroner Charles Mack, who had still not issued his official report on the identity of the headless female corpse found in the ruins of the farmhouse, declared that he was likely to leave the verdict open. "Coroner Mack Not Yet Convinced That Body Is That of the Murderess," read the headline in the *Argus-Bulletin*.[10] The discovery of the two sets of bridgework changed his mind. At 4:00 p.m. on Wednesday, May 20, Mack filed his report with the clerk of the court. "It is my verdict," it concluded, "that the body . . . is that of Belle Gunness; that she came to death through felonious homicide and that the perpetrator thereof is to me unknown."[11]

Two days later, Friday, May 22, a grand jury returned indictments against Ray Lamphere, charging him with arson and the first-degree murders of Belle Gunness, her three children, and Andrew Helgelien.[12]

PART THREE

THE STATE OF INDIANA
V. RAY LAMPHERE

27.

GUNNESSVILLE

In mid-May, at the height of the Gunness mania, when stories about the Female Bluebeard dominated the front pages of dailies throughout the Midwest, prominent La Porte shoelace manufacturer F. W. MacDonald made a business trip to Cincinnati and St. Louis. Upon his return, he sent a concerned letter to the editor of the *La Porte Argus-Bulletin*.

Rather than their usual salutations—"Why hello, Mac, you're looking well. How's the missus?" and so on—the wholesalers he met had, to a man, greeted him with macabre jests: "Well, Mac, I see you haven't been killed yet," "Glad to see you, Mac, I thought all the men in La Porte were dead," and the like. It was clear to MacDonald that the Gunness tragedy had terribly besmirched the reputation of La Porte. He was writing, therefore, to urge "our officials, both city and county," to do whatever they could to dispel the dark shadow cast over their community by the Gunness case and "to make good the fair name of La Porte."[1]

MacDonald's wish that the world would cease associating La Porte with its most infamous inhabitant would never come true. Long after the Gunness property had passed into the hands of other owners, tourists from throughout the country would flock to the site, searching the yard for the spots where Belle's victims had once lain and tramping through the adjacent orchard, "ruining the apple trees . . . by breaking off branches" as souvenirs. Travelers to and from La Porte would elicit responses similar to the one experienced by a woman named Ford. On a train ride back to Memphis after a visit to La Porte in 1913, she handed her ticket to the porter, who took one look at her city of departure and gasped, "Gunnessville!"

"He knew all about the Gunness case," reported Mrs. Ford's daughter, "and he was very disturbed about it." And for the rest of the journey, he "kept his distance."[2]

—————————)((‡)) —————————

There were some in La Porte who swore that Belle continued to haunt the area. In early July, Daniel Hutson was driving a wagonload of hay past the Gunness farm when—so he claimed—he "saw through the trees Mrs. Gunness and a strange man walking in the orchard." His daughter, Eldora, reported a similar sighting. According to her story, she was out on McClung Road one day in July when she saw a buggy coming toward her, drawn by "a beautiful dappled gray horse I had seen tied up at Belle's gate once that winter. Then the buggy came closer, and it was Belle!" That same day, two boys walking by the Pine Lake Cemetery spotted a heavily veiled woman stop to take a drink from a water pump. When she lifted her veil, they, too, recognized Belle.

Another witness, identified in accounts only as "the town scavenger," had a similar, chilling encounter. Driving by Belle's farm one "rainy summer evening," he saw a woman dressed in black alight from a buggy and go "fumbling around on the ground near the southeast corner of the house," as though searching for something. As he stopped his team to "untangle the reins," she returned to her rig, muttering, "That money ain't here." All at once, "the lightning flashed." When he saw who it was, he went "cold and numb" and "drove on to town as fast as I could."[3]

In light of these and other accounts, one observer counseled that the best way to rid the community of Mrs. Gunness's baleful presence was to pile all her remaining goods in a great heap and purge them in a "purifying" bonfire.[4] Instead, the town held an auction.

Arranged by her executor, Wesley Fogle, the sale took place on Friday, May 29. Like the festive outings to the farm that had become known as "Gunness Sundays," the event drew an enormous crowd—as many as five thousand people, according to some estimates. By the time the auction ended, every item had been snapped up, bidders paying as much as ten times the original cost for the privilege of owning one of the Female Bluebeard's kitchen utensils or gardening tools. Belle's border collie, Prince, and her children's pony fetched the highest prices: $107 and $205, respectively. Both animals—along with two chickens, an old house cat and her kittens, and a few miscellaneous relics—were purchased by a huckster named W. W. Hans, who put them on display at Chicago's Luna Park.[5]

To the editor of one Indiana newspaper, the purchasers of Mrs. Gunness's personal effects—"the memorials of a she-devil whose like has not been known"—were making themselves vulnerable to insidious forces. Citing the paranormal theory of psychometry—the belief that physical objects retain the residual life-energy of their former owners—the writer warned that Belle's belongings possessed an "aura of evil" that might infect anyone who came into contact with them. Those foolish enough to have "spent the high dollar to obtain these blood-spattered goods" were behaving as recklessly as "a mother would be to buy rattlesnakes as playthings for her children."[6]

On the afternoon of Wednesday, June 17, under the supervision of undertaker Austin Cutler, the remains of the woman officially identified as Belle Gunness, along with the corpses of the three Gunness children, were loaded onto the Lake Shore train to Chicago. Arrived at Union Depot, the caskets were transferred into the mortuary wagon of a local undertaker, who proceeded directly to City Hall for the burial permits. At 10:00 a.m. the following morning, the four bodies were unceremoniously interred in the Forest Lake Cemetery. No service was conducted and no relatives were present, Belle's sister, Mrs. Nellie Larson, refusing to attend.

Readers of the *La Porte Weekly Herald* learned of the funeral in an article published on June 25. Its headline read: "Mrs. Gunness Dead At Last."[7]

Not everyone, however, shared that belief. Despite the coroner's verdict and the interment at Forest Lake Cemetery, "at least seventy-five percent of the people in and about La Porte are convinced that the arch-murderess . . . is still alive and in hiding," wrote journalist Arthur James Pegler.[8] Elsewhere in the country, sightings of the Female Bluebeard continued to be reported on a regular basis.

In the last week of June, less than two weeks after the funeral, the *New York Times* reported that the Detroit police were holding "two young women [who] are said to have met Mrs. Gunness since her supposed body was found in the ruins of her home." After receiving a telephone call from the sheriff of Hillsdale, Michigan, announcing that he had arrested Mrs. Gunness, Deputy Antiss and Police Chief Cochrane made an overnight trip to that city, only to find that the woman in custody was "a fortune teller of some nomadic tribe, weighing perhaps 150 pounds and without any resemblance to the murderess." Later that summer, Belle was spotted in Birmingham, Alabama; Minneapolis, Minnesota; Portland, Maine; Passaic, New Jersey; and Galveston, Texas, where she was seen boarding the Hamburg-American liner *Dania* prior to its departure for Hamburg, Germany.

Two men claimed to have seen Mrs. Gunness on trains passing through Texas. In late summer, a traveling salesman named George L. Robinson told police that, while riding the Katy Flyer to Denison, he was "standing at the water cooler, drawing a cup of water, when a woman in deep mourning approached and asked for a drink. In raising the cup to her mouth, she removed part of the veil, and I at once recognized her as Mrs. Gunness. When I spoke to her and called her by name, she suddenly turned and went back to her seat in a hurry, and after packing a few things that she carried, left the train at the next station." A few months later, Henrik Fritz, former resident of La Porte, reported a similar experience aboard a train from Fort Worth to Denver. Passing through a Pullman car, he saw Belle "emerge from the lavatory." Recognizing Fritz, she immediately "dropped a heavy veil over her face," hurried back into the lavatory, and locked herself inside.[9]

Fritz's reported sighting of the living Mrs. Gunness appeared in the press on October 9, 1908—one month to the day before Ray Lamphere was put on trial for her murder.

28.

THE MAYPOLE

Interviewed in his cell on the eve of his trial, Ray stoutly maintained his innocence, as he had from the start. "They can twist and turn the evidence all they like, but if they prove that I set fire to the house, they will have to do it by false testimony," he declared. "I have led a pretty loose life, maybe, and possibly I drank too much at times. But there are others who have done as bad as me who are walking the streets of La Porte today. I know nothing about the 'house of crime,' as they call it. Sure, I worked for Mrs. Gunness for a time, but I didn't see her kill anybody, and I didn't know she had killed anybody."[1]

Speaking to reporters, his aged mother, Hannah, proclaimed her unwavering faith in her boy. "With my own fingers I made all the clothes Ray wore until he was ten years of age," she said in a tremulous voice as she dabbed at her eyes with a handkerchief. "I sewed love into every stitch. He was my heart, my life, during his childhood. Every day that he has been in jail, my heart has ached for him. God knows—and *I* know—that he is not guilty! He has written this to me, and he has never told a lie to me in his life!"[2]

In a somber column published in the *La Porte Weekly Herald*, editor Edward Molloy reminded his readers that the sole "reason for the trial" of Ray Lamphere was to "determine whether it was his hands that applied the torch to the house on the hill, or whether he is innocent of the atrocity that has been charged to him." "It is not a show," he stressed. "Its purpose is not to furnish entertainment either for spectators in the courtroom or readers of the daily press."

As it happened, the same page of the *Herald* carried a prominent advertisement for an actual show that was about to open at Hall's Theater in La Porte: Father James Lawrence Vaughan's "Grand Moral Play," *A Woman of the West*, featuring, among other highlights, "the most reverential church scene ever written" and "a carload of scenic effects, including mountain stage coach and horses."[3] The show would earn plaudits from local reviewers and draw appreciative audiences willing to pay anywhere from twenty-five cents to one dollar per ticket. Still, it would not prove nearly as popular as Ray Lamphere's trial, which—despite editor Molloy's admonition—would be the biggest show in town.

The proceedings got under way on the morning of Monday, November 9, 1908. The onlookers crammed into the upper-floor courtroom were struck by the defendant's "air of jaunty confidence" as he was led in by Deputy Sheriff Antiss shortly before 10:00 a.m. Apart from the jailhouse pallor he had acquired during his six-month incarceration, Ray seemed healthy and alert, and—in a new store-bought suit and necktie, clean collar, and freshly polished shoes—far better groomed than his neighbors had ever seen him. During the noon recess, he seemed positively carefree as he posed for the "flash light cameras" of the newspapermen from the various Chicago dailies.[4]

His lawyer, Wirt Worden, was a figure of some renown in the community. Three years earlier he had been involved in a case that, while not nearly as sensational as the current one, generated a good deal of local attention. On that occasion, however, he was not the attorney but one of the defendants.

In December 1904, two sisters, Mrs. Stella Lula and Mrs. Mary Sobinsky, residents of Michigan City, Indiana, were arrested for shoplifting furs from the Herman Zeese Dry Goods Store. At their trial in early 1905, their defense attorneys—Worden and his law partner, La Porte mayor Lemuel Darrow—produced a witness, Mrs. Rose Duck, who identified herself as a salesclerk at a Chicago department store and testified that she had sold the furs to the two women the previous March. Both defendants were acquitted.

A subsequent investigation, however, revealed that Mrs. Duck, whose real name was Boyce, was a phony witness who had been paid twenty-five dollars by the defense team to lie on the stand. In March 1905, a committee appointed by Judge John C. Richter of La Porte submitted a two-page report concluding that Darrow and Worden—along with a third attorney involved in the case, John E. Talbot of South Bend—had "conspired, confederated, and connived in procuring [Mrs. Duck] to commit the crime of perjury."[5] At their trial in January 1906, Darrow and Talbot were found guilty of unprofessional conduct and permanently disbarred from the practice of law in Indiana. Worden, however, was acquitted.[6]

Presiding at Ray's trial was the same Judge Richter who had ordered the investigation into the conduct of Worden and his associates that led to the disbarment proceedings. Now, after overruling the defense's motion that the indictment be quashed, he directed that all witnesses be excluded from the courtroom during jury selection, as requested by the state.[7]

It would take four days to empanel the jury. One hundred and fifteen talesmen would be questioned: solid citizens, mostly farmers and merchants, ranging in age from thirty-one to seventy-two.[8] Each was asked the same set of questions: Had they read of the case? Did they know Mrs. Gunness? Had they formed any opinion as to whether she was dead or alive? Were they acquainted with Ray Lamphere? Had they arrived at any fixed belief about his guilt or innocence? Could they be impartial?

Unsurprisingly, the majority were rejected after admitting that, having followed the case closely in the local papers, they had reached firm conclusions both about Ray's involvement and Mrs. Gunness's ultimate fate.

With little of substance to report during this protracted and tedious process, Harry Burr Darling, editor of the *Argus-Bulletin*, found various colorful ways to keep his readers diverted. A writer much given to strained, often bizarrely incongruous metaphors, he outdid himself on November 10 with a front-page piece in which he compared the coming task of the Lamphere jury to "a May day celebration":

> In the spotlight is the May pole, and, stretching from its top
> are twelve long ribbons, each juror holding a ribbon. The
> entire case of the prosecution hangs on conclusive proof

that the Gunness woman is dead. Otherwise, the May pole falls in a crash and the state's argument is broken and shattered. If, on the taking of evidence, the jurors are persuaded as to the death of the woman, the May pole stands, but to convict Ray Lamphere, the state must play the right music. The jurors will refuse to budge from their positions and the ceremony will be over unless, on each of the ribbons, the state stamps in indelible letters the name of "Ray Lamphere." Circumstantial evidence must be so woven about this prisoner . . . as to dissipate the last shred of reasonable doubt. In that event, mystery unraveled, Belle Gunness dead and Ray Lamphere unseparably [sic] connected with her death and the deaths of her children, the jurymen might well turn in ribbons, blackened by human murder. Unless this spider web of circumstantial evidence is spun around the prisoner, the ribbons will be handed back as they were received, white and spotless.[9]

The seventh juror had just been selected on Tuesday the tenth when, shortly before the afternoon adjournment, "Lamphere's thin cheeks paled, he uttered a weak cry as if in pain, and his head fell on the table in front of him. He tried to rise, and blood gushed from his nose and his mouth."

Deputy Sheriff Leroy Marr immediately hurried to Lamphere's side, helped him to his feet, and half led, half carried him into the cooler air of the corridor. While the courtroom buzzed with consternation, Sheriff Smutzer rushed out into the hallway after Lamphere and the deputy. He returned a few minutes and announced that "Lamphere had suffered only a slight hemorrhage and would shortly be able to return."

Though Chicago papers speculated that Lamphere's collapse might jeopardize the entire trial, he returned to the courtroom the following morning, seemingly no worse for wear. Interviewed by reporters, however, the physician who attended the inmates at the La Porte jail struck an ominous note, expressing his "fear that [Lamphere] is afflicted with incipient tuberculosis."[10]

It was not a report on Ray's physical condition but a piece on his supposed psychological makeup that dominated Wednesday's coverage by the *Chicago Daily Journal*. Headlined "Hate-Cowardice: Predominating Elements in Ray Lamphere Told by Character Expert," the article featured a full-face portrait of Ray with a dozen arrows pointing to various facial and cranial features. According to the author, J. M. Fitzgerald, M.D.—identified as "Phrenologist and Expert in Character Study"—Ray was "exactly the sort that [Mrs. Gunness] would pick from all her acquaintances for her assistant, her Man Friday—weak mentally and morally and yet as stealthy as a cat, with less sense of gratitude than many members of the feline species":

> The first impression that one gets from his picture is that here is a mixture of the human and the tiger cat. The head is low in the frontal brain and especially pinched in the upper temples and forehead at the seat of ideality, or refinement of mind, benevolence or sympathy, veneration or respect for law, human divine, causality or logical reason, and power to comprehend consequences innately . . .
>
> He has none of the initiative [Mrs. Gunness] possessed in abundance for wholesale murder, but a person of his type would readily consent in carrying out the after work and doing away with the individual if he were crippled or maimed into helplessness.
>
> He is naturally a coward but would be revengeful and full of deadly hate for anyone who he believed had sufficient influence to jeopardize his liberty and who failed to give him money for the purpose of gratifying his animal nature, which possesses him body and soul. His whole head and face indicate the dissolute man of perverted appetites. The eyes are catlike, watchful, cunning, and cruel . . . The nose is well suited to the feral, catlike eyes; it further bears out the impression of stealth and low ideals.

Summing up his highly scientific and unbiased study, Fitzgerald concluded that Lamphere's "phrenology and physiognomy indicate a low-grade animal type of man of weak mental and moral faculties, whose animal propensities early in life instinctively crowded out of his mind any good training or fine example his mother might have tried to inculcate . . . He has, these many years, been anti-social in the higher sense, and the more human parts of his brain have become atrophied from lack of normal function."[11]

━━━━►((◗))◄━━━━

That same day, Wednesday, November 11—twenty-four hours after publishing his hopelessly muddled "May day" piece—Harry Burr Darling ran an eye-catching story headlined "Sensational Find of Bones," resurrecting a controversy that had been seemingly laid to rest several months before.

In the last week of May, State's Attorney Smith had received a letter from one Julius Truelson, an inmate in the Vernon, Texas, city jail. A small-time swindler who had been going under the name Jonathan G. Thaw—supposedly a cousin of the notorious Pittsburgh millionaire Harry K. Thaw, slayer of celebrity architect Stanford White—the twenty-two-year-old Truelson claimed that he had been an accomplice of Belle Gunness in several of her murders.

According to his literate and compellingly detailed letter, he and Belle had become acquainted in January 1903, when, after answering one of her ads, he "met her in Chicago and was offered employment by her." She told him that "she practiced an illegal form of surgery"—by which she meant abortions—"and occasionally had bodies to dispose of, and that she would pay him well for helping her."

Four and a half years later, in June 1907, now married to a young woman named Mae Frances O'Reilly of Rochester, New York, Truelson, having tired of his wife, took her to the Gunness farm "to have her put out of the way." He and Ray Lamphere then buried her body, along with that of another victim, "near the railroad tracks in the rear of the farm." In the following months, he "assisted [Lamphere] in disposing of six other bodies at the Gunness farm."

One evening in March 1908, fearing that Asle Helgelien's inquiries into his brother's fate were about to expose her crimes, Belle asked Truelson "to burn down the place and flee with her to Frisco." Truelson "cautioned her not to panic and thereby draw suspicion on herself." In town that night, he and Ray discussed the matter and "decided that we had to put her out of the way before she did away with both of us, so we tossed a coin to see which of us was to do the job. Lamphere lost and it was decided that he was to enter at night and knock Belle and her kids in the head and then set fire to the place to cover her crimes and ours. I left that night and went to Chicago." Eventually, he made his way to Texas, where he was arrested for passing forged checks. He was writing now because his "guilty conscience . . . haunted him most every night."[12]

In contrast to the countless crank letters sent to La Porte officials since the start of the Gunness affair, Truelson's missive sounded so persuasive that Sheriff Smutzer was immediately dispatched to Texas. Arriving in Vernon on May 21, Smutzer conducted a lengthy interview with the prisoner, who ultimately swore to and signed a nineteen-page confession.

No sooner had he been led back to his cell, however, than Truelson recanted everything he had said, explaining that the whole thing was a lie designed "to get him out of the hands of the Texas authorities." A subsequent investigation into his background revealed that he was locked up in the Elmira Reformatory during the entire time Belle was engaged in her crimes; that his ex-wife, Mae Frances O'Reilly, was very much alive; and that he was "addicted to drugs which sometimes aid the imaginative faculties." Interviewed at the family home, a three-story private residence at 34 West Forty-Seventh Street in Manhattan, Truelson's brother, Harry, flatly declared that his brother was "insane. He was struck by a trolley car at Twenty-Third Street and Broadway five years ago, and he has not been right since."[13]

Despite Truelson's retraction and the other hard evidence that he had concocted the confession, some people continued to believe that there must be some truth to it. It was "so minute in detail," they insisted, so full of "things that could only be known by a person actually familiar with them," that it could not have been a complete fabrication.[14]

Among these individuals were Belle's neighbor Daniel Hutson and Deputy Sheriff Marr. In the days before the start of Ray's trial, the two men went out to the Gunness farm and, as Harry Darling reported, "made excavations in the place described in Truelson's confession, where he said bodies of victims had been buried." Though they found no bodies, they did dig up some bones, which Marr "believe[d] were human."

The discovery occasioned Darling's sensational headline of November 11. The accompanying story, however, ended on a distinctly anticlimactic note: "This development is likely to have little bearing on the case on trial, except as giving some slight degree of credence to the confession of Truelson."[15]

Finally, on the afternoon of Thursday the twelfth, after the rejection of one hundred and three candidates, a jury was seated: twelve men, the youngest thirty-four, the oldest sixty-five, nine of them farmers, the others a carpenter, dry goods clerk, and a salesman. They would be sequestered for the course of the trial—not, however, in a local hotel, as was usually the case, but in the courthouse itself, where twelve cots had been set up in the jury room. They would be allowed a brief daily walk outside for some fresh air and exercise, but, to ensure that they engaged in no inappropriate interactions with the public, they would be "given close surveillance . . . by Sheriff Smutzer and his deputies."[16]

29.

SMITH

At 4:30 p.m., with time still remaining before court adjourned for the day, State's Attorney Ralph N. Smith rose to make his opening statement. He would hold the jury spellbound for the forty-minute duration of his speech. One listener, Harry Burr Darling, extolled the lawyer for his unpretentious style. "Prosecutor Smith does not indulge in flowery metaphors," he wrote admiringly. "He spoke in the plainest English and straight from the shoulder. During the entire time the dropping of a pin would have attracted attention."

Darling's own preferred style, of course, was the diametrical opposite of the unembellished English he commended in Smith. His fondness for florid and overblown language was evinced yet again in his description of the defendant's reactions to the prosecutor's statement. "A remarkable change came over the prisoner during the address of Smith," wrote Darling. "He was not the same Lamphere of the jury examination, listless and apparently unconcerned. The color of his face resembled a fresh tombstone, and his eyes shone out from sunken sockets like two pieces of burning charcoal would blaze from a sheet of snow."[1]

Thanking the jurymen for their "patience in the long and somewhat tedious examination" process, Smith explained that, owing to the "widespread notoriety" of the case, selecting the twelve most qualified men for the task was "a matter . . . of great importance." He stressed that—however aggressive he and his cocounsel, Martin Sutherland, might appear in their prosecution of the defendant—they were not out for anyone's blood. They were not agents of vengeance but servants of the law. "We have no animosity to satisfy," he asserted. "We have no axes to grind, no spleen to vent. We are not persecuting anybody. If we sometimes get zealous, it is because of our anxiety to fulfill our duty . . . A dark cloud has fallen upon our county. A dastardly series of crimes have been committed in La Porte County and we are here to do our duty."

He acknowledged that there would be very "little direct evidence" in the case. The guilt or innocence of the defendant would be determined almost entirely on circumstantial evidence. Of course, there was nothing unusual about that. Dark, premeditated deeds like arson were typically carried out in secrecy. As Smith put it, "People, when they set out to commit a crime, such as the burning of a dwelling, do not set out to do it with a brass band."

Having dispensed with these preliminaries, Smith got to the heart of the matter. "We charge Ray Lamphere with setting fire to the home of Belle Gunness on April 28 while she was in it," he declared, "and we expect to prove that she was burned to death there with her three children—Myrtle Sorenson, Lucy Sorenson, and Phillip Gunness. We expect to prove that when the ruins were cleared away, the charred bodies found in the ashes were those of Belle Gunness and the children.

"Our position is that it does not matter whether Lamphere intended to set fire to Belle Gunness when he set fire to her house. When we prove he did set the fire, remember the statute which says he is guilty of murder in the perpetration of arson where lives were lost, whether he intended to take a life or not. The state is not required to show that he went out there with the intention to kill Belle Gunness in the fire."

Before continuing to lay out the case against Ray, Smith paused to say a word about the woman who had brought such unwanted notoriety to La Porte. It was not his purpose, said Smith, either "to defend the character of Belle Gunness" or "to drag it down." From the "dismembered bodies of nine persons [that] were found on her premises," however, it appeared that she "engaged in the wholesale slaughter of humanity."

Returning to the issue at hand, Smith turned to the question of motive. "By his own admission," he charged, "the prisoner was a witness to the murder of Andrew K. Helgelien, a profit-sharer in the blood money, and because he did not receive what he considered a fair share of this blood money, he applied the torch to Mrs. Gunness's home."

At this dramatic accusation, Ray "half started from his chair, as if to shout a denial," only to be pulled back down by the restraining hand of his attorney.[2]

"We shall show by evidence," Smith went on, "that in January of this year a man by the name of Helgelien was induced by means of matrimonial advertisements and letters to come from South Dakota to the Gunness farm, bringing his worldly wealth with him. We shall prove that on the night of January 14, Belle Gunness sent Ray Lamphere to Michigan City on a wild goose chase on the pretext of leaving some horses there for someone who was to call for them. Lamphere was to stay in Michigan City. This was the night Helgelien disappeared.

"Instead of staying at Michigan City as he was instructed to do," continued Smith, "Lamphere came back on the streetcar and got off near the powerhouse, and the evidence will show that he made the remark to a man on the car that he was 'going over there to see what the old woman was doing.' We will prove that Lamphere bobbed up like Johnny on the spot and assisted Mrs. Gunness in the dastardly work of disposing of Helgelien's body.

"Helgelien had three thousand dollars on his person, and evidence will be introduced to show that Lamphere got part of the money. It was over money matters that Lamphere and Mrs. Gunness fell out."

Smith briefly sketched the growing animosity between the pair. "Mrs. Gunness had Lamphere arrested for trespass. Altogether she had him arrested three times. She served notice on him to keep away from her place." For his part, Lamphere had been overheard to make insinuating threats against his former employer. "We can prove," asserted Smith, "that Lamphere said, 'I can get the old woman down on her knees anytime I want to. I know something about her that would send her to the penitentiary.'"

Matters came to a head, recounted Smith, on April 27. After coming into town that afternoon with his current employer, John Wheatbrook, Lamphere had gone to spend the night at the home of Lizzie Smith—"Nigger Liz," as Smith, like everyone else in town, had no qualms about calling her. Lamphere had set his alarm clock for three in the morning and started out from Smith's home about twenty minutes after three.

"The fire occurred about four o'clock," Smith continued. "Instead of going by a direct route through the city park to the farm of his cousin to get a broad ax, we will show he took the Gunness road. By his own statement we will show he was on the spot at the time of the fire. When asked why he did not wake up the people when he saw the house burning he replied, 'I didn't think it was any of my business.'

"We will prove he ran along the foot of the hills afterwards, past the cemetery to get on another road and wound up at his cousin's farm at five thirty."

Lamphere's movements that morning clearly pointed to his guilt. So did his reaction when taken into custody. "At seven o'clock that evening when the deputy sheriff went to the Wheatbrook farm to arrest Lamphere, he said, 'Ray, get on your coat and come along to town.' Ray's answer showed he had the fire in mind. He said, 'Did those folks burn up in that fire?' 'What fire?' asked the sheriff. 'Why, that house,' answered Ray. The foremost thing on Lamphere's mind was the burning of that house."

Of course, Smith conceded, to convict Lamphere of murder, the state was obligated "to prove the *corpus delicti*, or that Mrs. Gunness is dead." Undoubtedly, the defense would seek to convince the jury of the opposite. Indeed, Worden had already let it be known that he planned to issue a subpoena for Belle, summoning her to appear as a witness for the defense.[3]

Declaring that he certainly did "not want to convict a man for the murder of anybody who isn't dead," Smith proceeded to outline the evidence he would offer to prove that Mrs. Gunness "died and was burned in the fire.

"On the day before the fire," he related, "Mrs. Gunness went to attorney Leliter in La Porte and drew up her will and at Mr. Leliter's suggestion rented a safety deposit box in the bank and into that box she put the will and her private papers and some $700 in money. After that she went to Minich's grocery store for her week's supply of groceries and she also got toys and games for her children, spending some eight or ten dollars.

"That night," he continued, "Joe Maxson ate supper with them. About nine thirty he went up to bed and at that time the mother and children were at the table in the home playing games and nothing unusual had happened. The children played with the toys and games around the fireside.

"About four in the morning Maxson was awakened. He was occupying the upper story of the frame part of the house. Mrs. Gunness occupied the southeast corner room with the little boy. It was the custom of the children to occupy the northwest corner room. Maxson heard them retire. He was awakened by smoke in his room. There was a gale blowing that night from the northwest. He rushed to the window and the whole interior of the brick house was on fire. Maxson beat on the door of the family apartments without success and escaped from the house.

"The fire had evidently been started in the outside cellarway. Others came on the scene. They climbed to the room occupied by the children, but there was no one in the room. Our contention will be that Mrs. Gunness became suffocated and died, that the children were awakened by the smoke and ran over to their mother's room, into the thickest of the fire, and were suffocated.

"The house was completely burned. Not a bit of wood was left. The bodies were burned in the hot debris for twelve hours. Two hundred pails of water were necessary to cool the hot bricks so the bodies could be got at. All four were found together. That of Mrs. Gunness was lying on the back with the body of the boy clasped in her left arm."

That the charred female corpse was that of Mrs. Gunness would be shown by hard evidence. "We shall prove by the coroner's inquest," said Smith, "that the coroner found on the hand a ring or rings belonging to Mrs. Gunness. We shall prove by a reputable dentist here in La Porte that he did crown and bridgework for Mrs. Gunness. We will produce those teeth, and also her upper teeth. I think you will agree when the evidence is all in that the old woman is dead."

Of course, it was natural to feel that Mrs. Gunness "got what was coming to her." That sentiment, however, must have no bearing on the jury's decision. "I want to impress upon your mind," Smith stressed, "that the principal—the salient—points in the case are these: Did Ray Lamphere burn this house? Did he feloniously and willfully do this? Did Belle Gunness and her three children meet death because of this act?

"If we prove beyond a reasonable doubt an affirmative answer to these questions, and I believe we can," concluded Smith, "we shall expect a verdict accordingly."[4]

30.

CORPUS DELICTI

After their first night in what the *La Porte Weekly Herald* described as their "comfortable quarters"—a small deliberation room crammed with a dozen cots—the jurors were taken for a walk by Bailiff Carl Matz, then escorted to breakfast at the Hotel Teegarden, where they were "permitted to peruse the morning papers, from which all references to the trial had been removed." Having caught up on the other news of the day—the self-inflicted wound of an amateur magician named Don V. Smythe, who "accidentally shot himself in the hand with a blank cartridge while giving a sleight-of-hand performance in Noblesville"; the deplorable "lack of appreciation" shown by Miss Cora Harness, who failed to reward ticket agent Henry Benford after he found the "much-prized" gold watch she had lost during a shopping expedition; and the plans of the International Egg Carrier & Paper Co. to open a factory in La Porte—the jurors were led back to the courthouse for the first day of testimony.[1]

In the weeks leading up to the trial, the state had issued subpoenas for forty witnesses. All had been found except one: the gold miner Louis Schultz, who had produced the dental bridge declared to be that of Belle Gunness. Evidently, the old prospector, possessed of the perennial optimism of his breed, had decamped for the west in pursuit of the big strike that had so far eluded him.[2]

To establish the *corpus delicti*—proof that Mrs. Gunness had in fact been murdered—the prosecution began by calling the coroner, Dr. Charles S. Mack. A graduate of Harvard and the Columbia College of Physicians and Surgeons, where he received his M.D. in 1882, Mack had gone on to teach at the medical school of the University of Michigan before entering into private practice, first in Chicago and then in La Porte. He had held the office of coroner for the past two years.[3] "Snowy-haired [and] snowy-bearded," the fifty-one-year-old physician was described by one chronicler as resembling an Old Testament "prophet"[4]—an apt analogy since he had recently been ordained as a Swedenborgian minister and announced his intention to resign from his medical practice and take up a new life as a pastor in Toledo, Ohio. Indeed, just a few days before, a farewell banquet had been held for him at the Methodist church, where his fellow members of the La Porte Physicians Club "presented him with a beautiful gold-headed cane," symbolic of the upright manner in which Mack had "ever walked . . . as a physician, as a citizen, and as a man."[5]

From the point of view of any audience members anticipating high drama, Mack's testimony got the proceedings off to a disappointing start. Questioned by Smith's associate, Martin Sutherland, the coroner stated that he had first seen the "body of a woman and three children" on the afternoon of the fire. They "were badly burned. One of the children had a hole in the forehead. The head of the adult body was missing, and also the right leg was burned below the knee. The left foot was missing and one arm was off. I disremember as to whether or not the hand was attached to the arm."

Asked what "disposition" he had made of the bodies, Mack replied that they had been "taken to Cutler's morgue," where he had called in four "autopsists"—Drs. Gray, Wilcox, Long, and Meyer—to conduct the postmortem. As for himself, he "did not make a minute examination of the bodies. I did not pay any more attention to the bodies than in any ordinary case."

It quickly became clear to Sutherland that Mack would be unable to provide much useful testimony concerning the *corpus delicti* without consulting the notes he had made on the day of the fire. Mack, however, had failed to bring the notes with him. "Realizing the futility of obtaining an accurate description of the bodies unless the mind of the witness were refreshed by [the] notes," wrote Harry Darling, a somewhat exasperated Sutherland abandoned that line of questioning.[6]

A pair of sealed jars sat on the prosecution table. Retrieving the larger of the two, Sutherland undid the lid and removed the contents—a few badly charred bones recovered from the cellar along with the bodies. He then showed them, one at a time, to the witness, who identified them as a heel bone, a left jawbone, and—insofar as he was able to judge—a "seventh vertebrae." The second jar contained something that Mack was able to identify only as "animal tissue." It was difficult to see what advantage the prosecution had achieved by exhibiting these "ghastly relics," though—to judge from the excited stir among the spectators—it was a high point for courtroom sensation seekers.

Worden's cross-examination, which began a few moments later, proved such an "utter rout" that an audible "sigh of relief rippled through the crowd" when Dr. Mack—a beloved figure in the community—was finally permitted to step from the witness chair.[7] Under the defense attorney's relentless grilling, the coroner was compelled to admit that he was "not present when the bodies were discovered"; that he did "not know the condition of the bodies when found"; that he could not "state whether the arms [of the adult] were disjointed or not"; that he did not "weigh the body of the adult person"; that he did not "know there was a question as to the identity of that body"; that he "could not say whether any of the vertebrae were missing"; that he had no idea "how many cervical vertebrae there are in a human person"; that he did not examine "the upper terminus of the spine" with "any care"; that he could not "tell from its appearance whether the leg had been cut off or burned off," or "whether the head had been burned off or charred after it had been severed"; that he had not "examine[d] the hole in the skull of the child," could "not undertake to say" what "caused the hole," and had not checked to see if "there were holes in any heads of the other children."

By the time Worden got around to questioning Mack about the three charred bones, the coroner was so worn down that his testimony lapsed into self-contradiction.

"Are you positive," asked Worden, holding up one of the fragments, "that this bone I show you is a cervical vertebra?"

"I am not," said Mack.

"Well, Doctor, are you positive that this bone I present is a jawbone?"

"It is."

"Is it the bone of a human being?" Worden pressed.

Mack let out a sigh. "I do not know."

"Would you state, Dr. Mack, from present observation, that this bone is from the upper or lower maxillary?"

Just a moment before, Mack asserted that he was "positive" the bone was a jawbone. Now, "bedeviled to the end of his patience," he snapped, "I could not positively state that it is a bone at all."

With that, the coroner's ordeal came to an end. "The first medical testimony for the prosecution," as one historian put it, "had been turned into a triumph for the defense."[8]

⟩ ((◉)) ⟨

The state fared somewhat better in the afternoon session. The first witnesses called to the stand were Drs. Harry H. Long, Franklin T. Wilcox, and J. Lucian Gray—three of the "autopsists" called in by Mack. While the examination of Long and Wilcox, who had conducted the postmortems on the two Gunness girls, was somewhat perfunctory, Dr. Gray's testimony, as one reporter noted, proved to be "of material value to the state."[9] The former coroner of La Porte County and onetime coroner's physician in Cook County, Gray, under questioning by Sutherland, estimated that, before shrinking in the fire, the body of the adult woman would have stood "five feet, 4.44 inches" and weighed "about two hundred pounds." The "tissue of the abdomen [was] fatty, about two inches thick" and the breasts were "fat and large"—traits that corresponded to Belle's physique. Moreover, while acknowledging that he could not definitively state the cause of death, it was his opinion that "death was due to asphyxia"—a crucial point for the state, which was seeking to prove that Belle had been killed in the fire set by the defendant. In part, said Gray, his opinion was based on the condition of the "tightly clutched" fingers of the corpse's right hand. "Muscles are contracted that way in all cases of suffocation," he explained.[10]

Under Worden's aggressive cross-examination, however, Gray conceded that the clenching of the corpse's right hand could have been "a postmortem spasmodic contraction" caused by strychnine poisoning. He also admitted that he could not tell whether the body's left arm and right leg "had been cut off or burned off." His explanation of how he had computed the probable weight of the woman also raised eyebrows, particularly among the housewives in the audience. Including the arm, the charred remains weighed seventy-three pounds, explained Gray. "By comparing [it] with other meats which had been cooked, I estimated that it had shrunk about two-thirds." By this logic—as one crime historian points out—a nine-pound standing rib roast, when cooked, would end up as "a stingy three pounds on the dinner table."[11]

Observers agreed that, by the time he was done, Worden had "scored an impressive list of reasonable doubts" by suggesting that the dead woman had not died of suffocation but "been killed with strychnine and partially dismembered, and that Dr. Gray's identification of the seventy-three-pound remains as Mrs. Gunness was close to wishful thinking."[12] As for the other witnesses, wrote Harry Burr Darling, "it is the general opinion that [they] failed utterly to establish the state's contention as to Mrs. Gunness' death . . . Dr. Mack's testimony in particular is considered practically worthless in the way of identification of the adult body.

"Today," proclaimed Darling, "was decidedly Lamphere's day."[13]

31.

THE DENTIST

For the sake of the jurors—who would otherwise be forced to spend two idle days largely confined to their makeshift quarters—all the principals involved in the trial "deemed [it] advisable to hold court on Saturday."[1] The morning began with an unforeseen setback by the state. Following the completion of Dr. Gray's cross-examination and a brief reappearance by Coroner Mack—who testified that, besides the four bodies retrieved from the rubble, ten decomposed corpses were "removed from the place"—the prosecution called its next witness, Dr. Johann H. William Meyer.

A native of Buer, Germany, who emigrated to the United States at seventeen and still spoke with a pronounced accent, Meyer had begun his working life as a salesman for the Wile & Fox dry goods firm in La Porte before entering Rush Medical College in Chicago. Following his graduation in 1876, he interned at the Cook County Hospital, then returned to La Porte, where—apart from a year's study in Heidelberg and Vienna—he had practiced ever since, specializing in diseases of the ear and eye. In addition to his large private practice, he served on the faculty of the Practical School of Watchmaking in La Porte, where he lectured on the anatomy and diseases of the eye to aspiring opticians, and held the post of local physician for the Lake Shore & Michigan Southern Railroad.[2]

Despite his high standing in the community, Meyer would find himself in serious legal trouble just a few years after Lamphere's trial, when he was charged with murder for performing an abortion on a local farmer's wife, Florence Greening, that resulted in her death. Mrs. Greening's husband, William, who turned state's evidence in return for immunity, was the primary witness against him at his ten-day trial in February 1913. After fifteen hours of deliberation, however, the jury would acquit him.[3]

At the autopsies of the four corpses recovered from the fire, Meyer had performed the postmortem on four-year-old Phillip Gunness. Asked now about the condition of the little boy's body, he provided a description that—though delivered in a dry, clinical tone—was ghastly enough to induce shudders in the listeners.

"The body was severely burned," said Meyer. "The legs were burned off at the knees entirely. The forehead was burned away, exposing the brain. The back was badly burned, the spinal cord was exposed."

"How much of the limbs was burned off?" asked Sutherland.

"Nearly to the knees."

"Were the arms burned off?"

"One of the arms was missing," said Meyer. "The lungs were partially preserved by cooking. The heart was contracted, containing no particle of blood. All the organs were well cooked."

Sutherland paused for a moment, as though to let the jurors fully take in the hideous picture. Clearly, the person responsible for inflicting such horrors on a four-year-old child deserved no mercy. Unfortunately for the prosecution, its own witness was about to raise serious doubts as to the identity of that person.

"Could you form any fixed idea as to the cause of death?" asked Sutherland.

Meyer replied that he could not.

"What is your professional opinion, Doctor?" asked Sutherland.

"Contraction of the heart, like some case of poisoning," said Meyer. "From the examination of the stomach, I would say that the contraction was probably due to strychnine."

Any suggestion, of course, that Belle and her children had not been killed by arson undermined the state's argument against Lamphere. "Here," as one writer says, "was a prosecution witness in effect testifying for the defense."[4] Sutherland, clearly caught off guard by Meyer's response, quickly brought his examination to an end.

Meyer helped the defense again when Worden took over a moment later. Asked if there had been any ecchymotic spots on the little boy's body— small discolorations caused by ruptured blood vessels, a common sign of suffocation—Meyer replied with an emphatic "No, sir, none." He also confirmed that "there was a hole in the boy's forehead," reinforcing the notion that the children had died at Belle's hands before the conflagration.[5]

Worden faced a much tougher challenge when Belle's dentist, Dr. Ira P. Norton, took the stand. Like Dr. Meyer, the forty-year-old Norton had gotten his degree from Rush Medical College, financing his education with a job as an engineer on the Chicago elevated railroad.[6] A few years before the trial, he had won wide recognition in professional circles for his invention of a patented dental forceps equipped with a detachable lancet.[7]

Though the previous direct examinations had been handled by the assistant prosecutor, it was Frank N. Smith who now approached the witness chair—a sign of Norton's importance to the state. The dentist began by offering a detailed description of the work he'd done for Belle.

"I extracted three lower teeth," he explained. "Upon two cuspids I put two gold crowns and swung between these certain dummies in bridgework. It was an unusual construction. There was 18k-gold solder used to reinforce this. Afterwards, I drilled through one of the dummy teeth and placed two platinum pins, riveted in the end. I hung this bridge upon the two natural teeth remaining in Mrs. Gunness's jaw."

"Now, Doctor," said Smith, "did the sheriff bring to your office some teeth?"

"Yes, sir."

"When was that?"

"May 19, 1908."

"I now hand you some teeth. Are these the teeth the sheriff gave you?"

"Yes, sir."

"Did you ever see these teeth before?"

"Yes."

"Where?"

"I constructed them."

"For whom?"

"Mrs. Belle Gunness."

It was a dramatic moment—the positive identification of the bridgework found in the ruins—and Smith underscored it with a pregnant pause. After offering the teeth in evidence as State's Exhibit Number 16, he then set about to demolish the theory that Belle had deliberately planted the bridgework in the ruins as a decoy.

He began by eliciting a key bit of testimony from Norton: that "portions of the roots" of two of Belle's "natural teeth" were still "contained in the crowns of the bridgework."

"Now, Doctor," Smith asked, "how could these teeth be removed?"

"Only by splitting the gold crowns."

"Could they have been pulled?"

"No, sir," declared Norton. "Not even a dentist could have pulled the natural teeth from Mrs. Gunness' jaw with the crowns still attached, as these are." There was no question in his mind that the teeth had been "severed from the mouth of Mrs. Gunness by burning."[8]

When Worden's turn came a few minutes later, he sought to instill doubt in the jurors' minds by suggesting that—since neither the gold crowns nor the remaining roots could have possibly survived the inferno—the bridgework was a fake.

Wouldn't a fire "intense enough to destroy a skull" also "destroy a tooth?" he asked.

"No, sir," said Norton.

"Why?"

"Because of being protected by the gold crown."

"Wouldn't the dental gold melt before a skull would burn?" Worden pressed.

"It would not," said Norton.

Far from helping his cause, it was clear to Worden that, as Harry Burr Darling observed, his "cross-examination was only serving to strengthen the direct testimony."[9] He brought his questioning to a hasty close.

The final witness of the day was a neighbor of Belle's, Mrs. Florence Flynn, who offered a particularly ghoulish bit of testimony. Confirming that she been present at the farm when the four bodies were found, she was asked if she had seen them.

"Yes, sir," she replied. "I could recognize them as they were taken out. There was a sort of bed and mattress under them. The little boy lay upon the woman's body as if he had been wrapped in her arms."

"Well, were the arms about him?" asked Prosecutor Smith.

"It did not seem to me," said Mrs. Flynn, "that there were any arms."

On that grim note, the first week of Ray Lamphere's trial came to an end.

32.

ASLE

If the *Weekly Herald* could be believed, Ray's initial optimism had been completely wiped away by Dr. Norton's testimony. According to the paper, he was "particularly gloomy and downcast" throughout Sunday and spent much of his time poring over his Bible, "a thing he has not done to any extent since last spring." He seemed so deeply troubled that his jailers "believed he might break down and confess" at any moment.[1]

Whether Ray was really as despondent as reported is impossible to say. If so, he made a rapid recovery. By the next morning, he "seemed greatly refreshed and entered the courtroom with a smile on his face and a nod of recognition to several friends whom he noticed among the spectators."[2]

One of the spectators that morning was a visiting celebrity, Thomas Jefferson—not, of course, the long-deceased president but the son of one of nineteenth-century America's most beloved actors, Joe Jefferson, who had starred in a wildly popular stage production of *Rip Van Winkle* for over forty years. Following his death, his son had taken over the role and was scheduled to perform it that night at Hall's Theater. In a gesture much welcomed by the jurors, W. J. Hall, business manager of the theater, had invited them, along with Judge Richter, to be his guests at the show, an offer they had gratefully accepted.[3]

The first to take the witness chair that morning was Florence Flynn, who had not finished her testimony when court was adjourned on Saturday afternoon. At one point during Worden's cross-examination, juror Jared Drollinger interrupted to ask Flynn if she knew how much Belle weighed. Two years earlier,

Flynn replied, Belle, following a visit to her doctor, had revealed that she was tip-
ping the scales at 280 pounds—sixty more than Dr. Gray's estimate. The answer
reinforced the doubts of those who believed that Belle hadn't died in the flames,
since the notion that a body that size could shrink to a mere seventy-three
pounds seemed flatly incredible to anyone who had ever roasted a hunk of beef.[4]

For the most part, the morning produced little in the way of compelling
interest. Mrs. Ray Turner, who had been retained by State's Attorney Smith
to translate Belle's letters to Andrew Helgelien, explained "that the grammati-
cal construction of the letters was extremely faulty and evidently the work of
an ignorant person. The letters were all one long sentence without capitaliza-
tion." Belle's attorney, Melvin Leliter, testified "that there was some contention
between Mrs. Gunness and Lamphere as to wages," though under cross-
examination, he admitted that "he knew of the controversy between the two
parties only by hearsay." Insurance agent D. H. McGill put the value of Mrs.
Gunness's house at between three and four thousand dollars, and surveyor Clyde
Martin displayed a map showing the shortest route between the Gunness property and John Wheatbrook's farm.[5]

The proceedings, largely perfunctory up to that point, took a dramatic turn
when the next witness was called: Asle Helgelien.

The "stringy and shabby" Norwegian began with an abbreviated account of
his brother's life in America, omitting Andrew's ten-year stretch in the Stillwater
penitentiary.[6] The rest of his testimony—which ran through the noon recess,
then picked up again after lunch and occupied the remainder of the day—concerned his efforts to locate his missing brother. He recounted his discovery of
Belle's correspondence with Andrew, which began in 1906 and continued until
Andrew "left his home to meet his fate in the 'House of Death.'" He then
described his own letters to Belle, inquiring about his brother's whereabouts.

Three of her replies were read aloud to the jury: those of March 27 and April
24, in which she claimed that Andrew had gone off in search of his gambler-
brother "in Chicago or New York, or possibly . . . Norway," and a third, dated
April 11, in which she cunningly cast suspicion on a man "who worked for me
for a while" named Lamphere, whom she characterized as a mentally unstable
drunkard who was "jealous of Andrew."[7]

Following the introduction of these letters as evidence, Asle was asked about
his visit to La Porte after receiving the newspaper clippings on the fire sent to

him by bank clerk Frank Pitner. He proceeded to relate the tale of his search of the farm—already the stuff of local legend—culminating in the awful discovery of his brother's body "in a three-foot grave" and the disclosure, to a dumbstruck world, of the Gunness horrors.[8]

In an interview with Harry Burr Darling conducted that evening, Asle insisted that the full extent of those horrors had yet to be uncovered. "I know there are more bodies on the place," he declared. "I have learned of another soft spot which has never been explored. If the people here would let me, I am convinced I could find further trace of the woman's crimes."[9]

In Asle's telling, his brother—the burly ex-con who had once robbed and torched a village post office and was reportedly involved in a horse-rustling case[10]—was a sensitive, poetic soul, who pined for the faraway beauties of Norway.

"Andrew Helgelien was something of a mystic," said Asle. "He lived too much in his imagination for a farmer in Dakota. He could not forget the fjords and mountains of his native land. Anything that brought a touch of home with it moved him to melancholy."

It was Andrew's homesick yearnings that made him susceptible to the wiles of Mrs. Gunness. "She was a clever woman," said Asle. "She wrote of the things he loved. She discussed Norwegian places and Norwegian ways. When she told him she loved him, he believed it, because the poor fellow was in that mood where he would have renounced richness in America for a crust at home. I did not know these things until long after, when her letters to him came into my possession, and the ogress began writing to me.

"She held him spellbound," he went on, then let out a ragged breath. "So he went to his death."[11]

Asle did not remain in La Porte for the rest of the trial. Before returning home to South Dakota, he ordered a tombstone for his brother's grave in the Patton cemetery. The chiseled inscription read:

"Andrew Helgelien, 1859–1908, the last victim of the Gunness horror, remains found by his brother, Asle K. Helgelien, May 5, 1908. Rest in peace."[12]

33.

THE PROSECUTION STRIKES

In Washington Irving's classic story "Rip Van Winkle," the feckless title character stumbles upon the ghostly crew of Henry Hudson, who gather every twenty years in a hollow of the Catskill Mountains to drink beer and play at ninepins, "the sound of their balls" reverberating "like distant peals of thunder."[1] Perhaps it was Harry Burr Darling's attendance at Monday evening's theatrical performance that inspired his typically muddled metaphor in the next day's edition of the *Argus-Bulletin*:

> The progress of the Lamphere trial suggests a thunderstorm. The elements got to work a week ago, and a steady downpour of rain, punctuated by a few peals of thunder, some loud, some almost inaudible, together with a correspondingly small number of flashes of lightning, has been in order ever since.
>
> Prosecutor Smith is now playing the part of the great Jupiter who rolls the balls down the bowling alleys of the heavens. He started off with a rush Thursday afternoon, and in his opening statement scored a clean "strike." Since then, several "spares" have been recorded to his credit, but withal it will be necessary to land several more "strikes" to anywhere near approach a 300 score.
>
> There'll be another sharp peal of thunder at any moment.[2]

Darling was right about one thing. Tuesday's proceedings did produce another peal—not of thunder, however, but of laughter. The day got off to a delayed start. As soon as the doors opened that morning, a jostling crowd surged inside, filling the seats, jamming the aisles, arraying themselves along the walls. It was a frigid day, however, and, even packed with scores of people, the courtroom was so teeth-chatteringly cold that Judge Richter ordered a postponement until the building's custodian could shovel enough coal into the furnace to generate "a proper degree of heat."

When the trial finally resumed at 10:00 a.m., Smith, seeking to elicit incriminating testimony against the defendant, began summoning a string of Ray's acquaintances. John Rye, Ray's companion on his aborted trip to Michigan City the night Andrew Helgelien vanished, testified that "Lamphere had said he 'would get even with the old woman sometime.'" He was followed to the stand by Bessie Wallace—variously described as "Lamphere's sweetheart," "a woman of the underworld," and "a whore"[3]—who likewise testified that, during a conversation with Ray, he had said something "about Mrs. Gunness owing him money and how he would get the money or make it unpleasant for her and get even with her."[4]

It was another friend of Ray's, William Slater, who set the courtroom roaring with laughter. Under questioning by Smith, Slater detailed Ray's increasingly bitter conflict with Belle after Andrew Helgelien appeared on the scene. Soon after leaving her employ, Ray had told Slater that he had overheard "Mrs. Gunness and Helgelien talking about giving him poison" and that "Helgelien had suggested that they try it on Lamphere's dog." What made this perfidy particularly galling to Ray was the fact "that the woman had promised to marry him."

"What do you know about Lamphere's relations with Mrs. Gunness?" asked Smith.

Slater shifted uncomfortably in his chair. "He said she used to come to his room at night."

"Did Lamphere tell you that he slept with Mrs. Gunness?" Smith asked.

"No," said Slater. "He said she slept with him."

The remark produced such an explosion of hilarity that Judge Richter, after banging his gavel repeatedly, threatened to clear the courtroom if any such outburst happened again.[5]

The titillating testimony about Belle's sexual habits continued with state witness Peter Colson, Ray's predecessor in the role of handyman-lover. Under cross-examination by Wirt Worden, Colson described "how he fell under Mrs. Gunness' spell and how she made love to him with sweet words and caresses." Even while "obsessed with love of the woman," however, he was "possessed with fear of her.

"She made me love her," said Colson, "and she scared me at the same time. I was suspicious of her on account of the way her husband, Peter Gunness, died."

As the spectators listened in riveted silence, Colson explained that, eventually, her sexual demands became so insistent that he had to flee. "She made such love to me that I finally had to run away from the place. For six months I slept in a haymow on a farm a half mile away.

"I loved Mrs. Gunness in spite of myself," Colson concluded. "I didn't want to, but I couldn't help it. She attracted me and repelled me at the same time."[6]

Belle's final handyman, Joe Maxson—who began his testimony at the tail end of Tuesday and resumed it Wednesday morning—had no salacious tidbits to offer, though he did provide a dramatic account of his actions on the night of the fire. Under direct examination, he described his final meal with Belle and the children, their after-dinner game of Red Riding Hood and the Fox, his going off to bed and being "awakened about four o'clock by a room-full of smoke." He told of his efforts to "kick and beat down the door" separating his room from the main part of the house, until—"almost overcome by the dense smoke"—he grabbed a few belongings and "dashed madly downstairs."

After depositing his stuff in the carriage shed, he grabbed an ax and tried, unsuccessfully, to chop through the front door. At this point in Maxson's recital, State's Attorney Smith introduced the ax as evidence. It was, observed one reporter, "big enough and strong enough for an Oregon lumberman," and the possibility that it might be the very weapon with which the ogress had dismembered her victims sent a ripple of excitement through the courtroom.[7]

For the most part, Maxson's testimony was unrelievedly grim, but he did provide one inadvertent moment of levity. It happened during his cross-examination, when Wirt Worden's cocounsel, Ellsworth Weir, asked about the items Maxson had rescued from his room and deposited in the carriage shed.

"Didn't you take a few novels, pick them up and put them in your pocket?" said Weir.

"No, sir!" cried Maxson, clearly incensed at the suggestion that he might engage in an activity as effete as reading fiction. "I want you to understand here and now that I do not read novels, no kind of novels!" The sheer depth of his indignation produced scattered chuckles among the spectators.

Though Maxson's eyewitness account of the fire had been exhaustively covered in the press and was familiar to anyone who read the newspapers, he now added one previously undisclosed detail. At the end of his dinner with the Gunness family on that fateful night, Belle had handed Joe an orange that he had promptly "made away with." Though it "tasted sort of queer," he kept on eating it.

"I never thought much about it until after the fire," he continued, "and then I told my sister that I thought something might have been placed in the orange. I remember that I struck the bed like a log that night and went to sleep barely a moment after my head touched the pillow. If there were any noises the next morning when the fire broke out, I didn't hear them because I was in such a sound sleep. I don't usually sleep so soundly. I did not awake, as I said before, until the room was full of smoke, and then I was so dazed that it took me a while to realize that the place was on fire."[8]

Maxson's revelation about the ostensibly drugged orange inspired yet another of Harry Burr Darling's dizzying rhetorical flights, published that evening under the heading "A Gunness Lemon":

> Beware of this kind of fruit. It is dangerous, and the man or woman who offers it to you has evil intentions. Just because the lemon has the exterior appearance of an orange, don't be deceived. You may think it is a nice, sweet juicy Florida orange. Perhaps at one time it was. But the "Gunness" system has converted it into a "lemon" of the worst variety. It contains some kind of dope, which, as soon as you have

eaten it, will put you to sleep.

This is the warning sounded today in the testimony of Joe Maxson. This witness, it is believed, revealed Mrs. Gunness' favorite method of murder. She first secured control of her victims by throwing them into a sound sleep via the doped orange route. Then she could do the dirty work in any manner she chose, whichever was the most convenient, a sausage cutter or a sharp knife. If "she" had been a "he," it is probable that a poisoned cigar, rather than a doped orange, would have been used.[9]

On Wednesday afternoon, the state called one of its most important witnesses, a man who had never wavered in his belief that Belle Gunness was dead and that Ray Lamphere set the fire that killed her: Sheriff Albert Smutzer. "Dapper in polka-dotted bow tie, his curly brown hair parted with a double flourish," he took the witness stand "with affable self-confidence, a smile on his pleasant, rosy face."[10] As the prosecution hoped, his testimony—which closed out the day and resumed on Thursday morning—made for damning evidence against the defendant.

Smith began by asking Smutzer what he knew about the bad blood between Ray and Belle.

"About the middle of February," said Smutzer, "Mrs. Gunness wrote a letter to me and complained that Lamphere was annoying her in all sorts of ways, sticking his face in the windows at night, prowling around the house, and so on."

"What reply did you make to Mrs. Gunness?" Smith asked.

"I wrote her that if he kept it up to have him arrested."

"What did Mrs. Gunness reply?"

"She wrote me another letter saying that she was afraid Lamphere would do her some harm and that he was still bothering her."

"What steps did you take, Mr. Smutzer, in consequence of this second letter?"

Smutzer explained that he had immediately telephoned Ray's favorite watering hole, Smith's saloon, and told the proprietor "to send Lamphere around to me." When Lamphere showed up at the jail about an hour later, Smutzer "told him to keep away from Mrs. Gunness' house or I'd have to arrest him." When Ray protested that he had only gone there to fetch the tools he'd left behind when he was fired, Smutzer advised him to "send the constable for them."

And how, asked Smith, did Ray react to that advice?

"He shuffled away a few steps," Smutzer recalled, "and then turned to me with a queer look in his eyes and said, 'If I tell what I know of that woman, I can make it mighty hot for her.'"

According to Smutzer, Ray had informed him that Belle was presently consorting with "a man named Helgelien who owned a gambling house in Aberdeen, South Dakota. A man was killed there and ten thousand dollars was stolen. This man Helgelien fled with the money, and she has him there in that house." Smutzer had investigated this charge by writing to Aberdeen but dropped the matter after receiving a reply assuring him that "Helgelien was a well-to-do farmer living near Mansfield, that he was of good repute, and not wanted for any crime whatever."

Returning to the subject of Ray's conflict with Belle, Smith asked the sheriff what he knew "of Lamphere being arrested at the insistence of Mrs. Gunness." Smutzer's answer provoked an angry reaction from Wirt Worden.

"When Mrs. Gunness and her hired man, Joseph Maxson, came to me to have Lamphere arrested," Smutzer said, "Maxson brought with him a bar of iron a foot and a half long which he said Lamphere had left on the place while prowling around the night before. I thought then, and I still think, that Lamphere intended to kill Mrs. Gunness with that bar of—"

Worden, face flushed, was on his feet at once. "Objection!" he cried. "This witness must be warned! He is trying to get matter into the record that he knows will be ruled out. He knows he must not offer his conclusions but only the facts! He knows that conclusions are for the jury!"

The objection was sustained but, as in all such cases, the witness's words could not be unheard. When, after a largely fruitless cross-examination, a smiling Smutzer left the stand, observers agreed that his testimony had delivered exactly what the prosecution was aiming for, that it had been—as Harry Burr Darling would say—a "clean strike" for the state.

Smutzer was followed to the stand by Leroy Marr, the deputy who had driven out to John Wheatbrook's farm to take Ray into custody. Even before he announced why he was there, said Marr, Ray had asked if Belle and her three children had made it out of the burning house. When Marr asked how he knew about the fire, Ray replied that he had been walking "along by the house" and saw "smoke coming out of the windows and around the roof." Asked why he "didn't yell," he could only offer the lame excuse that he "didn't think it was any of my business."

Marr then added a detail that, in a courtroom full of white-only faces, cast Ray's already dubious character in an even more unsavory light. After being taken to jail, Ray had been interviewed by State's Attorney Smith. In the course of their conversation, said Marr, Ray admitted that "he had slept with Nigger Liz" but begged Smith not "to put that in any statement."[11]

The testimony of Marr's colleague Deputy William Antiss—the next witness to take the stand—was particularly damaging to the defense. According to Antiss, Ray not only admitted that "he saw [Mrs. Gunness] killing Helgelien" but stated that, were it not for his concern over hurting his mother, he "would plead guilty to arson." As the correspondent for the *Chicago Examiner* put it, Antiss's "version of what Lamphere said amounted almost to a confession on the part of the prisoner."

Following a brief cross by Wirt Worden, the witness was dismissed. The town clock was just striking 10:00 a.m. as he stepped from the stand. At that point, having "fired its biggest guns" with the testimony of the lawmen, the state abruptly rested its case.[12]

34.

SCATTERSHOT

Believing that the prosecution's case wouldn't conclude until the end of the day, Wirt Worden was caught off guard by Smith's announcement and requested a recess until Monday morning. When Judge Richter denied the request, Worden had no choice but to proceed with his opening statement.

Though delivered extemporaneously, his address, according to the rapturous account of Harry Burr Darling, was a model of lawyerly eloquence. "He spoke slowly and with the utmost deliberation," Darling reported, "and each word fell clearly on the ears of the entire courtroom. Several of the jurymen edged over to the front of their seats as if drawn toward the speaker like a needle attracted to a magnet. When he was finished, there was a profound quiet. Women sunk back in their chairs, and a peculiar light played over their faces. The spectators realized that Worden had made assertions in such a masterly manner that, if he proved able to back them up with witnesses, Ray Lamphere's neck was saved from the noose."[1]

Step by step, in his strong, sonorous voice, Worden set out the main points of his argument, all leading to a conclusion that would exonerate his client: that Mrs. Gunness had plotted the fire, substituted a female body for her own, and was still alive.

"Mrs. Gunness was not burned in the fire of April 28," Worden began. "We will show by evidence that the body of the adult female found in the ruins could not have been that of Mrs. Gunness. We will produce as a witness, John Ball, a local undertaker, who knew Mrs. Gunness very well. He will testify that the adult female body could not have been that of Mrs. Gunness.

"We will produce a witness who saw her with a middle-aged man, driving past her old home in a top buggy on the afternoon of July 9," Worden continued. "The two daughters of this witness also saw Mrs. Gunness that day.

"We will show that Mrs. Gunness had a motive for setting fire to her house. We will show that the crisis in her life came on April 27, that she was in constant dread that Asle Helgelien, brother of one of her victims, Andrew Helgelien, might arrive in La Porte any minute and begin an inquiry which would reveal the fate of his brother, buried in the Gunness cemetery.

"Our evidence will show that on the afternoon before the fire, Mrs. Gunness went to Minch's grocery store and bought an unusual quantity of kerosene, more than she was in the habit of buying.

"We will prove by testimony that on the afternoon of April 27, Mrs. Gunness had a conversation in front of the First National Bank building with a certain man in which she said, 'It must be done tonight, and you must do it.' That night, the house burned to the ground and the bodies of the three Gunness children were found in the ruins.

"Our evidence will further show that on the Saturday preceding the fire, she was seen driving out to her house with another woman, slightly smaller than herself, who has never been seen since, unless it was her body that was found in the ruins of the fire.

"We will show that the teeth found in the ruins could not have withstood the terrific heat of the fire without crumbling to pieces. Consequently, the teeth found in the ruins must either have been thrown there, or else the fire could not have been as hot as it is generally supposed to have been. This being the case, the skull of the female could not have been burned away. We will further show that the bridgework made by Dr. Norton for Belle Gunness could have been removed from the mouth in various ways.

"We will show by the testimony of local physicians that the three children came to their end by strychnia poisoning rather than burning. We will show that the bodies showed all the symptoms of strychnia poisoning rather than those of suffocation. We shall show from testimony already introduced that it would have been impossible for Ray Lamphere to have gone there and administered poison.

"Did Mrs. Gunness poison the children, place the adult body with them, remove her bridgework and leave it behind, and escape? If this be true, Lamphere cannot be guilty.

"On the strength of all this evidence," Worden concluded, "we will show that Ray Lamphere is an innocent man and the object of untrue accusations."[2]

⟫ «(◉)» ⟪

"The defense pressed the trigger of its revolver this morning," enthused Darling, "and the report will echo through Judge Richter's courtroom long after the Lamphere trial has passed into history." If Worden opened with a bang, however, he followed with a misfire. His first witness was John H. Ball, a pioneering figure in La Porte, renowned as the "first white boy born in the county."[3] After years spent as a bricklayer, cattle drover, miner, and US cavalryman, Ball had opened La Porte's first funeral home, selling the business to Austin Cutler upon retirement. Following the fire at the Gunness farm, the seventy-four-year-old Ball had been called in by Cutler to assist in the removal of the four bodies from the ruins.

In his opening statement, Worden had promised the jury that he would summon Ball as a leading witness to testify "that the adult female body could not have been that of Mrs. Gunness." When, however, Worden posed the key question to Ball—"From your knowledge of dead bodies and your acquaintance with Mrs. Gunness, was that the body of Mrs. Gunness?"—Smith objected on the grounds that it "called for a conclusion": that the question improperly asked Ball, a lay witness, to offer a legal opinion. The objection was sustained and Ball excused.[4]

Worden fared somewhat better after the lunch break. Calling the first of several dental experts—Dr. George Wasser, a prominent Cleveland dentist and graduate of Western Reserve University—Worden asked if, in his professional opinion, "the crownwork found in the ruins of the fire could have passed through the heat which destroyed the skull bones."

"I do not think so," said Wasser.

"In your opinion," Worden continued, displaying a fragment of tooth, "was this piece of tooth ever covered by the crown in the other set of teeth?"

"If it did cover this tooth," Wasser replied, "it was an awful misfit."[5]

Another dental witness, W. S. Fischer, agreed "that the teeth could not possibly have gone through the fire that destroyed the skull," as "the porcelain was free of cracks such an intense heat would have caused." Shown a pair of excising forceps, Fischer also explained "how they could be used in snipping live teeth from a person's head."[6]

Worden closed out the day with a hodgepodge of witnesses. Mrs. George Wright, a neighbor of Belle's, testified that she had seen the blaze through her bathroom window just as her mantel clock was "striking the hour of three"—twenty-five minutes before Ray Lamphere, according to his claim, left Liz Smith's house.[7] Undertaker William C. Weir told of visiting the farm on the day of the fire and "seeing a five-gallon can in the cellar. The can was empty and the solder melted away." Joe Maxson, recalled to the stand, verified Weir's statement, testifying "that on the evening before the fire, he placed the oil can in the hallway at the end of the stairway in the frame part of the house. After the fire it was in the cellar."[8]

In a move that seemed to promise a dramatic revelation but ended up amounting to nothing, Worden called his opponent, State's Attorney Smith, to the stand, to question him about a mysterious trunk he had surreptitiously hauled away from the Gunness carriage shed the previous spring. When the trunk was brought into the courtroom and opened, however, it "revealed neckties, books, and letters, none of which had any relation to the case."[9]

Reporting on Friday's developments, most newspapermen agreed that, following Worden's strong opening statement, the defense had gotten off to a scattershot start—that "no groundwork was laid for its theory that Mrs. Gunness is alive, or, if dead, that she was poisoned and not burned to death in the fire."[10] Locally, however, the biggest story of the day had nothing to do with the lawyers, the witnesses, or the defendant.

It had to do with the spectators.

35.

CESSPOOL

Throughout the nineteenth and early-twentieth centuries, newspapermen covering highly publicized murder trials rarely failed to comment, generally in tongue-clucking tones, on the large number of women who flocked to these proceedings and often made up the majority of spectators. That ordinary housewives and mothers should evince such eager interest in gruesome and salacious crimes seemed a shocking violation of every prevailing belief about the so-called gentler sex.

The situation was no different at the Lamphere trial. Owing to the scandalous nature of the anticipated testimony, efforts had been made to limit attendance to men. Apart from the opening day, however, when no ladies were permitted inside, the womenfolk of La Porte showed up at the trial in droves. "Women elbowed into the courtroom by the hundreds and occupied all the seats inside the rail that were not used by members of the bar," noted one Chicago reporter on the trial's third day; while the correspondent for the *Indianapolis News*, writing a few days later, estimated that "the number of women present has run as high as 400, many of them handsomely gowned and occupying front seats."[1]

This flagrant display of prurient fascination among the community's female population provoked the predictable outcry. Its source was the Reverend M. H. Garrard, who had recently assumed the pulpit of the First Christian Church. On Thursday evening, November 19, Garrard veered off the subject of his midweek sermon—"Beginning of Family and Business Life"—to deliver a fiery harangue against the eager horde of women trial-goers.

"I have been thoroughly disgusted with the way women have flocked into the courtroom in large numbers and at all hours both morning and afternoon, to have poured into their ears all the filth connected with the trial now in progress in our city," he began, deliberately avoiding so much as a mention of the foul name that had brought such infamy to La Porte. "It seems these women have camped out near the cesspool and mean to stay there until it is drained of its rot. It is bad enough to see many men there, but when I see the women sitting right up in front, as near to the filth as it is possible for them to get, I presume they are there out of fear that one of the rotten words or scenes might be missed if they were further back.

"When I see this thing, I am at a loss as to how to adequately describe it," continued Garrard, his voice ringing with indignation. "It is a strange thing that women, under no compulsion whatever, are found in large numbers in every notorious trial everywhere, and the more dirty the trial, the more women will usually be found in attendance. What are we to say of such women? Of their modesty? Of their refinement? It is mild to say they are not of the genteel type."

Curious about the type of people who would be drawn to such "dirty, rotten stuff," Garrard, as he explained, had visited the courtroom "one afternoon and also one morning" and was appalled at what he saw. "One young woman was comfortably located near where all could be heard and seen, and gave evidence of her very great pleasure in being so fortunately situated. She was artistically squishing a big piece of gum," he said with full-throated contempt, "her cheeks bulging out on both sides with the fat cud, and her head bobbing like a cow's.

"Well," he concluded, "many other things could be said, but I have more pleasant things to say. I hope that all decent women will keep away and frown on those who do go. Let modest, refined, well-bred ladies keep away from the very appearance of evil."[2]

Printed in its entirety in Friday's local newspapers, Garrard's diatribe set off an uproar. Both Harry Burr Darling and Edward Molloy, editor of the *Herald*, were inundated with letters defending the targets of the pastor's attack. Typical was the letter from a writer identified in headlines only as a "Well-known La Porte Lady," who charged Garrard with "desecrat[ing] his pulpit and his own profession by casting slurs" upon the women of La Porte.

Having "attended the Lamphere trial several times" herself, the writer affirmed that she had "seen the very nicest and most refined ladies of town there." Moreover, she had "heard nothing said by anyone in the court proceedings which contained one-tenth part as many obscene words and low phrases as" Garrard had claimed.

Striking a self-assertive note, very much in keeping with feminist sentiments of the time, the writer insisted on a woman's right to be educated in the workings of the legal system. "This is not an age when women are kept underfoot and in ignorance. A mere desire to see justice done and to learn the ways of justice should not be construed as a gratification of evil tastes." Stating that Garrard had done nothing but "bring ridicule upon his own head" with his intemperate remarks, she reminded him that "from a minister of the gospel, we naturally expect 'Charity for all and malice toward none.'" She ended with a swipe at Garrard's newcomer status, declaring that, as a newcomer to town—"a distinct outsider"—it was not his place to denounce the "genteel" trial-going women, whose "characters are far above reproach."[3]

Women weren't the only ones offended by Garrard's sermon. "Husband Takes Exception Also," declared a headline in the *Weekly Herald*. Reprinted below is an outraged letter sent to the paper by an unidentified gentleman of the city. Echoing the author of the earlier letter, the writer maintained that, as a recent arrival in La Porte, Reverend Garrard had little right to make such a sweeping condemnation. "The brother has not been a resident of this beautiful city long enough to be qualified . . . to dictate the tastes and desires of the ladies of this community." He then launched into a lengthy lecture of his own, part blistering attack on the minister, part gallant defense of his wife, part ringing tribute to American womanhood:

> My wife attended the Gunness trial, as did large numbers
> of other women, and now up bobs the Rev. M. H. Garrard
> and says that she and all the others are virtually not mod-
> est, refined, or genteel; in short, not respectable ladies.
> He would lead people to believe that the gentler sex of La

Porte are a carnal-minded lot who like to revel in what he calls filth and rot . . . Talk about arrogance, presumption, and the old criticaster's trick of "curving a contumelious lip"—all that is a mild sort of stupidity compared with this. Since when was this man commissioned to sit in judgment on the question of our women's modesty, refinement, and gentility? . . .

I glory in the American girl's stability and spunk. We all should be proud that her noble attributes of mind and soul do not break like blown glass before the various little naughtinesses of everyday life. If so sensitive and fragile as that, they would have shattered long ago. And I submit to any knowing man or woman whether the "racy" and unseemly words unavoidably spoken at the Gunness trial were really more vulgar, rotten, and suggestive than those that oft come from preachers' lips when discussing dancing, the white slave traffic, and kindred delicate topics . . .

I consider that woman's curiosity, her desire to see and hear and learn, is as legitimate a part of her life as of a man's, and that if her refinement and modesty are of a genuine and sensible quality, they will withstand all necessary indelicacies of the rough world all about her . . . Mr. Garrard will come in contact with just as good a moral element attending the trial as he will meet anywhere, church not excepted. My wife went to that trial a good woman, and she came from there a good woman still. True virtue can be trusted anywhere. I am not afraid to trust my wife . . . Mr. Garrard is not qualified or commissioned to sit in judgment over her.

Decrying the minister's lecture as "scurrilous," "ungentlemanly," and "unspeakably offensive," the writer concluded by referring to Garrard's sneering description of the young, gum-chewing woman seated up front. "I think," he wrote, giving full vent to his anger, "that the young lady . . . was engaged in a much better business than the immoderate Mr. Garrard spitting out unholy and gratuitous insults on the character of our women, thereby dragging the pulpit down to a level with the scandalmongering street."[4]

Not everyone offended by Garrard's finger-wagging sermon responded with an angry letter. One local writer, Mollie Long, was moved to compose a humorous poem. This bit of light verse, published in the *Weekly Herald*, took the form of a letter from the author to her friend Bessie Short of Chicago:

> We're having lively times, just now,
> Dear Bess, in old La Porte,
> For that mysterious "Gunness case"
> Is going through the court.
>
> They found a jury for the case,
> Most fit in every way:
> For what they thought about it all
> They really could not say.
>
> We don't know whether she's alive,
> Or whether she is dead,
> Or whether, when she went away,
> She took along her head.
>
> But this we know—she left her teeth:
> They're mostly made of gold,
> And every time we go to court
> We hear the story told.
>
> One preacher scolds us dreadfully
> Who go. Perhaps he's right.
> But where a preacher goes 'twould seem
> That women surely might.

And so I'll go again and see
What curious things they do,
To find out whether teeth will burn
And come out good as new.
And then, when I get home, Dear Bess,
I'll write it all to you.[5]

Despite the mockery and disdain he incurred, Reverend Garrard refused to back down. In a follow-up talk at his church, he insisted that he had "the greatest respect" for the "real women of the city," who were of the "highest caliber." His previous remarks had been addressed strictly to "a certain class of women" who were drawn to the trial "by morbid curiosity"—the type who "delight in the weird and sensational" and were "flocking like sheep" to the courtroom purely "out of a desire for entertainment."

Replying directly to the writer who had claimed her prerogative "to learn the ways of justice" by attending the trial, Garrard presented himself as a defender of female rights, even while asserting a thoroughly hidebound view of the proper role of women. "I certainly would not keep down the liberty of women," he declared, "but liberty does not mean license. I repeat my belief and say God made man and woman. He made man the stronger and set him over a particular field. He gave woman a peculiar nature and set her in the home to be the presiding spirit there. Her powers are represented by gentleness, sympathy, purity, devotion to principle, and love." The same unnatural impulses that drove certain women to sensational trials like those of Mrs. Gunness and Harry Thaw—killer of famed architect Stanford White—were responsible, he claimed, for the "multitudinous divorce proceedings" that were destroying the moral fabric of the nation.[6]

Garrard's hectoring appeared to have a discernible effect. On the afternoon of Saturday, November 22—one day after his original harangue was reprinted in the papers—more women than ever showed up at the trial. As the special correspondent for the *Chicago Daily Journal* noted, "This was attributed in large part to Rev. M. H. Garrard's attack on those who previously were spectators in the courtroom."[7]

36.

PARADE

To bolster its central arguments—that Mrs. Gunness was alive, that she had faked her own death, and that Lamphere was not her accomplice—the defense brought on a parade of witnesses over the next two days of the trial.

Belle's neighbor, Daniel Hutson, repeated his widely publicized story of having seen her and a "strange man" walking in her orchard on July 9, an account corroborated by his two young daughters, Evalina and Eldora.

"I was on the road, returning from town with a hayrick, and I saw two people at the Gunness place," said Hutson. "Even from that distance I could recognize her plainly. I knew her shape and I knew her lumbering walk. I never saw a woman walk like that. I started up my horses to try to get up the hill to the orchard before she could get away, but she saw me first and she and the man ran to their buggy, clambered in, and raced straight to the main road. I was within twenty feet of her and could plainly see her face."

Under cross-examination, Hutson was compelled to admit that the woman had been wearing a "wide-rimmed hat" with a double veil, one white, one black, "that came down to her chin." How he could "plainly see her face" under those circumstances was an interesting question. Hutson stubbornly insisted, however, that he "knew Mrs. Gunness well enough that he could not be mistaken."[1]

The testimony of another of Belle's neighbors, John Anderson, was offered to advance the theory that the headless body found in the ruins was that of a different heavyset woman, lured to the farm to be slain by and substituted for the murderess.

On the Saturday evening before the fire, Anderson recalled, he was tending to his flower garden, when Mrs. Gunness drove by in her buggy and stopped to chat with him. Seated beside her was "a strange woman." She was "a large woman," said Anderson, if "not quite so large as Mrs. Gunness."

"Did you ever see her again?" asked Worden.

Anderson gave an emphatic shake of his head. "Never," he said.

To support his contention that Belle had a partner in her murder business— someone other than Lamphere—Worden summoned Fred Rittman, described in the papers as a "surprise witness." A former farmhand of Belle's, previously unheard of in all the months since the fire, Rittman told of a strange afternoon, when—so Worden wanted the jury to believe—Belle's coconspirator had driven a victim to the "death homestead," where he would be drugged, killed, and planted in a freshly dug grave.

Two years earlier, said Rittman, he was plowing in the cornfield, when "Mrs. Gunness hitched up her favorite horse and said she was going to drive to town. Before departing, she told me to inform any visitors that she would return shortly and to make themselves right at home.

"Shortly after," Rittman continued, "a big, green automobile whizzed up the driveway and a couple of men, one elderly and the other medium but not so heavyset, got out. I exchanged greetings and asked what they wanted. They said they must see Belle Gunness at once. I explained that she was not at home but asked them to step inside and take things easy.

"I went back to my plowing and had been working about an hour when Mrs. Gunness came back. She put up her rig and came at once to me. 'I want you dig a hole for me,' she said.

"'What kind of a hole?' I asked.

"'Just a hole for a brick foundation,' she said. 'The masons will be here tomorrow.' She showed me where to dig, and put stakes to mark the corners. 'Dig it five-and-a-half feet deep,' she said.

"It did not occur to me at the time," said Rittman, "that it was about the size of a grave."

Rittman went on to relate that, before quitting for the day, he had gone up to the house to get paid and found Belle and the two men seated in the kitchen with several bottles of wine on the table. He himself had been offered half a glass, which left him feeling so "queerly" that he was certain the wine had been "doped."[2]

The testimony of Mrs. Louise Gackle—a young skirt factory worker who lived on Park Avenue, the direct road from La Porte to the Gunness farm—was meant to persuade the jury that Belle had escaped the burning house in the company of an accomplice after setting it ablaze.

In the early morning hours of April 28, said Mrs. Gackle, she awoke to drink a glass of medicine, having been unwell for the past few days. She saw by the clock on her bedside table that it was three in the morning. Just then, she noticed a "red glow, as of a fire and went to the window. I saw that it was coming from the Gunness farm." As she looked outside, a red automobile with a canvas top came speeding down the road from that direction. Later that morning, as other witnesses attested, "the same auto, or one of the same description, was seen going through the town of Hobart and also through Valparaiso."[3]

Joe Maxson was recalled to the stand to offer testimony that, if believed by the jury, would deal a serious blow to the prosecution. The handyman stated that, on the morning of May 19, he was standing beside Louis Schultz when the miner suddenly cried out, "I found the teeth!" According to Maxson, however—whose account was corroborated by his brother-in-law, Isaiah Alderfer—the miner did not remove the bridgework from the ashes he was sluicing but from his vest pocket. He "then stowed the teeth in his pocket again. It was near noon when Smutzer appeared. The sluice man pulled out the teeth and gave it to him."

The person best qualified to rebut this testimony was, of course, Schultz himself. But "Old Klondike" was nowhere to be found.[4]

A few other witnesses were called on Monday: Dr. Bo Bowell, who testified that, in his professional opinion, "the crown work exhibited could not have gone through the fire of April 28"; W. H. Ludwig, a former crematory attendant, who declared that "two or three hours were necessary to consume a human body in a heat of three thousand degrees intensity" and that the "skull was the last to burn"; County Commissioner William P. Miller, who told of finding "a flat stone in the Gunness basement." He "lifted it and saw a hole that looked as if a human skull had been concealed there. The skull was gone."[5]

The defense had one last, critically important witness to call: Dr. Walter S. Haines of Rush Medical College. When, just before lunch recess on Monday, Worden announced that Haines would not be able to travel to La Porte until the following day, Judge Richter declared a recess until Tuesday afternoon, when the jury would hear the final testimony of the trial.

37.

THE CHEMIST

Though he lived to be seventy-two—a ripe old age at a time when the life expectancy for an American male was forty-nine—Walter Stanley Haines was a semi-invalid for much of his adulthood, being afflicted with a debilitating respiratory condition. Despite this handicap, he managed to lead a remarkably active life. Born in 1850—the son of John C. Haines, twice elected mayor of Chicago during Walter's boyhood—he attended the Massachusetts Institute of Technology before training as a physician at the Chicago Medical College. In 1874, he joined the faculty of Rush Medical College as a professor of chemistry and remained there for fifty years, a revered figure to generations of graduates.[1]

By 1884, Haines was a figure of such renown that he became an early celebrity pitchman, touting the virtues of a popular brand of baking powder in newspaper ads. "I have recently examined a package of Royal Baking Powder and have found it entirely free from adulteration and injurious substances of all kinds," read one such testimonial (an endorsement that speaks volumes about the concerns of consumers in the days before the creation of the FDA).[2] Ten years later, Haines was still promoting the baking powder in a newspaper ad that read: "'I find the Royal Baking Powder superior to all others in every respect. It is the purest and strongest.'—Walter S. Haines, M.D. Consulting Chemist, Chicago Board of Health."[3]

Owing to his expertise as a toxicologist, Haines became a leading figure in the still-nascent field of forensic science. Along with a pair of eminent collaborators, he edited the two-volume *Text-Book of Legal Medicine and Toxicology*, a pioneering work covering such subjects as "Gunshot Wounds," "Mental Perversions of the Sexual Instincts," and—in one chapter singled out for particular praise by reviewers in professional journals—"The Destruction and Attempted Destruction of the Human Body by Fire and Chemicals."[4]

In the course of his long and distinguished career, he was involved in a string of sensational murder cases, testifying at the trials of Adolph Luetgert (the Chicago sausage maker charged with murdering his wife and dissolving her corpse in one of the vats used to make his product), Thomas Neill Cream (the serial poisoner whose last words on the gallows were "I am Jack the—!"), and Dr. Bennett Clark Hyde, accused of dispatching millionaire Thomas H. Swope with strychnine.[5]

There was no secret about the testimony Haines was expected to offer when he took the stand on Tuesday. Days before he arrived in La Porte from Washington, D.C.—where he had been engaged in official business related to his work on the revision committee of the *United States Pharmacopeia*—newspapers were reporting that he would "tell of finding poison in the bodies taken from the ruins."[6]

After listening to the distinguished toxicologist, the jury would naturally conclude that Belle, fearing imminent discovery, had killed her children and committed suicide, and Ray would be acquitted of murder. Or so Worden and his cocounsel hoped.

On the stand, which he occupied for just over thirty minutes, Haines explained that, on May 27, he had received several sealed jars from Coroner Mack, one containing the stomachs of Belle and two of her children. Cracking open the jar, he discovered that the organs were so badly decomposed that they "had run together, so that the material was like thick mud. A few fibers from the original wall were observable. The only possible analysis was by using the mass together." He blended the fetid sludge "to obtain uniformity and removed one-third of it for examination.[7]

"I found an abundance of arsenic and a quantity of strychnine," said Haines. "There was enough strychnine to have caused the death of three persons."

Apart from one qualifying observation—that "it was impossible to tell whether the poison was in one, two, or all of the stomachs"—Haines's testimony was everything that Worden could have hoped for.

Then came the cross-examination.

Asked if he could state with certainty "that the three persons whose stomachs he analyzed had died of strychnine poisoning," Haines replied that he could not. "The poison found in the stomach after death," he explained, "is not usually the poison which has caused death, for that has been absorbed and has gone to the remote arteries of the body." Indeed, Haines added, "owing to the condition of the viscera submitted to him," he "could not possibly determine the cause of death at all."[8]

Noting that, for ten days, "the bodies lay at the morgue and were viewed by several hundred persons," Smith wondered "if the strychnine may have been injected into the stomachs" during that time.

Yes, Haines conceded, "The poison might just as easily have been introduced after death."[9]

Haines was followed to the stand by La Porte undertaker Austin Cutler, called by the state as a rebuttal witness. In the view of the correspondent for the *Chicago Examiner*, Cutler's testimony added "a touch of farce comedy to the proceedings." To Ray Lamphere's defense team, however, there was nothing amusing about it.

No sooner had the mortician been sworn in than Prosecutor Smith asked if he had treated the remains with any poisonous substances.

"Why, yes, I put poison on those bodies. I thought it was strange you never asked me before," Cutler said. "I scattered about two gallons of formaldehyde embalming fluid and fifteen pounds of arsenic preserving powder over them while they were in my place."

Smith allowed himself a small smile. "Was this before the autopsy, when the stomachs were put in the jar for chemical exaggeration?"

"Why, of course it was," Cutler answered, as if astonished at being asked such a question.

"Tell me, Mr. Cutler," said Smith. "Why have you waited until now to make this fact known?"

"No one ever asked me," Cutler exclaimed. "That's why I didn't tell about the arsenic. When the bodies of the woman and the three children were brought to me the morning after the fire, nobody said anything to me about anything being wrong. All they told me was to get the bodies ready for shipment to Chicago, as they were to be buried there. Anyone knows that in my business we have to embalm bodies for shipment. The railroad will not receive them otherwise. I could not embalm in the ordinary way because the bodies were burned so badly, so I just scattered a lot of arsenic over them."

Though Cutler's testimony clearly helped the state in one regard—by offering an alternate explanation for the arsenic found in the corpses—it failed to account for the presence of the lethal dose of strychnine. Worden immediately put Dr. Haines back on the stand and asked if "strychnine [was] used in embalming fluids or preservatives."

"Strychnine has no antiseptic or preservative qualities," answered the chemist.

Haines's reply undid some of the damage done by Cutler. Overall, however, he turned out to be such a disappointing witness that, in its daily coverage of the trial, the *Detroit Free Press* reported his testimony under the headline "Defense Expert Aids Prosecution." Haines's failure to definitely state "that the four persons whose bodies were found in the ruins came to their end by poisoning rather than suffocation and burning" was more than a setback for the defense. It was, wrote the paper, "a death blow."[10]

38.

CLOSING ARGUMENTS

On Wednesday, November 25, in honor of the impending holiday, the *Argus-Bulletin* devoted the middle of its front page to a piece titled "Why We Are Thankful" by the Reverend John B. Donaldson, pastor of the First Presbyterian Church. After paying tribute to the New England Puritans, "those stern and stalwart souls" who "established Thanksgiving Day," and to Abraham Lincoln, who proclaimed it a national holiday, Donaldson offered thanks for America's "civic, commercial, and political" institutions, its upstanding elected officials, and its "just and sensible" citizenry. Looking closer to home, he gave thanks for the continuing "betterment of La Porte"—for "the influence of her schools and her public spirit," for "her growing factories and widening markets," for "the lanes that will be boulevarded and the macadam highways that will gridiron the county," for "the shrubs that will beautify her waste places" and for "a water plant that will furnish good drinking water before the wells shall produce a pestilence."

Most of all, he was thankful to the Lord for having lifted a terrible curse from his beloved community. "We praise God for the conflagration of the scarlet house whose visitors' feet took hold on the earthly hell." With heartfelt gratitude, he foresaw "the approaching day when our scandals shall cease to heat the wires of two continents"—when the Gunness case was a thing of the past, and La Porte was restored to its former blessed obscurity.[1]

Occupying the front page along with the Reverend Donaldson's essay was Harry Burr Darling's daily report on the trial. With the testimony finished and final arguments about to begin, he summed up the situation with one of his usual overwrought metaphors:

> On this day, the 25th of November, is being fought the real battle for the life of Ray Lamphere. Four days were required to decide upon a jury, a board of reviewers. Ten days more were consumed in the taking of evidence. During these ten days each side built its fleet. The prosecution constructed a powerful, first-class battleship. The defense adopted different tactics, relying on a multitude of small craft, such as torpedo boats and submarines, to do the damage, and so harass the maneuvers of the enemy as to render it incapable of infliction of serious damage.

"As of yet," concluded Darling, "the armor of the big warship has proved of sufficient thickness to resist the fire of innumerable theories from the opposing flotilla."[2]

Martin Sutherland, Prosecutor Smith's cocounsel, was the first to address the jury that day. Appealing to the jurors' "good common sense," he began by mocking the defense's contention that the female body found in the ashes was not Belle's. Joe Maxson's testimony proved that, besides the hired hand himself, Belle and her three children were the only ones in the house on the night of the fire. The next morning, "there were found four bodies in the debris. Ordinary common sense would lead us to believe that those were the bodies who inhabited that dwelling."

As for the teeth, they "were not false teeth, easily removed, but bridgework fastened to the natural teeth of Mrs. Gunness. Yet the defense has asked you to run with the imagination of Mr. Hutson, who testified that he recognized Mrs. Gunness even with two veils over her face," said Sutherland with an audible sneer. "It's very probable, isn't it, that Belle Gunness would come to La Porte, hire a livery wagon, and drive out to the scene of her murders! Gentlemen of the jury, your common sense teaches you better. And by using that same common sense, you will realize that we have established the *corpus delicti* beyond a reasonable doubt."

Turning next to the question of motive, Sutherland, his voice still laced with sarcasm, described the seemingly genial defendant as a man driven to exact murderous vengeance on his former lover, both for betraying him with Helgelien and for reneging on a promise of hush money after he witnessed the murder of the North Dakotan.

"Testimony we have introduced," said Sutherland, "shows that Lamphere, the easy-going Lamphere, the hard-drinking Lamphere, the fellow-about-town, had an easy berth out with Mrs. Gunness. Testimony further shows that Andrew Helgelien supplanted Lamphere in Mrs. Gunness's affections. This caused jealousy in the suspicious Lamphere, who did not want to trade his cozy berth with Mrs. Gunness for a hard bed offered by Liz Smith.

"On the night of January 14th Helgelien disappeared, never to be seen alive again," continued Sutherland. "Lamphere did not stay at Michigan City, as Mrs. Gunness had instructed him. The scene that he saw that night was such as to satisfy his desire of getting Helgelien out of the way. A compact was probably made over the body of Helgelien. What that was we have no positive evidence, but we have a right to infer that she agreed to pay him money. From receipts it was evident that there was no money due him for labor, yet his whole cry was that she owed him money and he would get even with her. The woman did not abide by this compact, did not pay Lamphere enough of the blood money, and the morning of April 28, Lamphere applied the torch to her house, sending her and her children to an awful death in a fiery furnace."

Lamphere's behavior immediately prior to the conflagration left no doubt about his guilt, argued Sutherland. "We find on the day before the fire, Mrs. Gunness was tracked by Lamphere," Sutherland stated. "Mrs. Gunness, weeping, entered Minich's store and bought some groceries. Lamphere, as an excuse for entrance, bought a five-cent plug of tobacco. Lamphere followed Mrs. Gunness out of the store, glaring at Mrs. Gunness.

"What is the evidence now to show that Lamphere committed the crime on the morning of April 28? We find Lamphere skulking and hiding before the fire started, then again after the fire started. We find Lamphere flatly contradicting himself in the stories he told to Deputy Sheriff Marr and Deputy Sheriff Antiss. First he told one thing and then he told another to the various officers. Finally, he practically made a confession of arson to Deputy Antiss.

"It is enough!" cried Sutherland, raising his voice for the first time.

Sutherland concluded with a dig at his opponents. "Now as to the defense," he said with a dismissive shrug, "if you are able to tell what it is, you can do better than the prosecution. They would attempt to prove by one witness that she was alive, and by the next witness that she was dead. By one witness they attempt to show that the teeth were clipped off and left in the fire, by another witness they attempt to show that they were not her teeth. The expert testified that he found poison in the mass of the stomachs, and Mr. Cutler testified that poisonous fluids were used in the bodies.

"From all these facts," concluded Sutherland, returning to his starting point, "we ask you to sum up the whole matter and use your good common sense."[3]

Next up was Wirt Worden's cocounsel, Ellsworth Weir. Son of a prominent local politician who had served both as a two-term state senator and mayor of La Porte, Weir was lucky to be there at all. Several years earlier, while representing a pretty young Cleveland woman, Mrs. Louise Brill, in a divorce suit, he had been shot at point-blank range by her estranged husband, Joseph—an "immensely rich" mine owner who accused the attorney of being "unduly intimate" with his wife and "stealing her affections." Newspapers throughout the Midwest reported that the wound was "probably fatal." Under the ministrations of a La Porte physician, however, Weir eventually made a full recovery.[4]

Now, attacking Sutherland for allowing a case of such vital importance to "degenerate into sarcasm," Weir angrily accused his opponent of "the greatest legal somersault of the present century!" For all his talk about common sense, Sutherland himself had taken "a flight into the realms of fancy," spinning a purely imaginary tale about Lamphere's involvement in Andrew Helgelien's murder. "He pictures the scene when Lamphere sees Mrs. Gunness killing Helgelien," Weir said derisively. "And then because they are partners in crime, they want to kill each other!"

It was possible, Weir conceded, that Mrs. Gunness had a confederate who assisted in her crimes, and who eventually had "a purpose in getting rid of" her. But the theory that Lamphere was her accomplice was "merely a guess, and you cannot guess this defendant into the penitentiary, or hang him by guessing!"

Turning to the issue of the teeth, Weir demanded to know why the prosecution had not produced the miner Louis Schultz. "Where is he now? Why do they not bring him here? The most important witness!" He also wondered why Dr. Norton had "made a diagram of the teeth" and provided it to Sheriff Smutzer "two weeks before the teeth were found." In that amount of time, Weir suggested darkly, a fake set "could have been made and substituted."

And what about the poison "that Mr. Sutherland brushes away with a wave of his hand? Granted that the undertaker used a pure arsenic powder," said Weir, "yet the eminent Dr. Haines testified that there was strychnine sufficient to have killed three people. For Lamphere to have committed the crime of murder, it would have been necessary for him to have gone into the house, administer the poison, and then carried Mrs. Gunness and her three children into the cellar and set fire to the building. But Lamphere could not have gained admission to that house. It was locked up tight!"

As Weir drew near the end of his remarks, his voice grew hoarse with emotion. "That a crime was committed we all agree," he said, "and as good citizens we feel that if the criminal can be apprehended, he should be convicted. But I do not believe that Ray Lamphere is guilty of the crime which is charged against him. So far as Ray Lamphere is concerned, there is no evidence that he did anything except occasionally to drink, and many men drink. Ray Lamphere may be ever so bad, but he did not commit this crime, and as he did not, he should be freed by you gentlemen."

By the time Weir reached his closing words, tears were coursing down his cheeks. "Tomorrow is Thanksgiving. You of the jury go home tomorrow, your task completed, to the hearts of your families. This man, if you condemn him, will have nothing before him! Think! Think long and hard before you seal the doom of a human life!"[5]

Worden, who spoke next, delivered what was by all accounts a moving appeal on behalf of his client. "Before a body of his peers, a man could have pled for his own life with no greater force," wrote one observer. "He fought for the prisoner as though the prisoner was his own brother." His powerful speech inspired a particularly head-scratching tribute from Harry Burr Darling, who praised the defense lawyer for leaving "no table unturned to make the jury 'fireproof' against the blazing bonfires in the face of Prosecutor Smith."[6]

Worden began by reminding the jurors of the concept of reasonable doubt. "This case against Ray Lamphere is entirely built up of circumstantial evidence," he stressed. "Therefore you must be satisfied that there is *no other* reasonable explanation of the evidence than the one presented in the indictment that Lamphere is guilty. Otherwise he is entitled to be acquitted."

Every point the prosecution had made, Worden argued, was open to doubt, beginning with its claim that Mrs. Gunness had died in the fire. "I firmly believe she is alive," Worden asserted. "She had abundant motive for the commission of this crime, in the coming of Asle Helgelien to find out about his brother. She made preparation for the fire. Even in her will she made provision for the disposal of her property in the event of the death of all her children. I am honest in saying that I believe the statement of D. M. Hutson and the two little girls.

"What of the four bodies?" he continued. "I believe it impossible for four bodies to fall from the second story, and still to be found together, laid out in regular rows. The remains of the piano were found on top of the bodies. If we are to believe the state, those bodies falling from the second floor beat the piano to the basement!"

By way of planting even more doubt in the minds of the jurors, Worden proffered a startling new suggestion: that Joe Maxson was somehow complicit in Mrs. Gunness's sinister scheme. "I am of the opinion that Joe Maxson knows more than he has been willing to tell. I believe he had his clothes on all night. There was no yelling, no cry of fire, no calling of the neighbors."

In regard to the teeth, Worden dismissed Dr. Norton's testimony as "prejudiced." "I say to you that these teeth never went through the fire!" he exclaimed. Everything connected to them, "from the manner in which they were found" to "the condition in which they are now," suggested that they were part of a diabolical plot to convince the world that Mrs. Gunness had perished in the flames.

Worden went on to dispute "the testimony of John Rye, who said Lamphere went back to the Gunness home on January 14" and "read aloud a statement by Lamphere that denied this."

His final words were delivered with "a ringing intensity of feeling": "They say that Lamphere made damaging admissions. Suppose you agree that Lamphere lied to Antiss. Would you hang him for lying? Then we must all prepare for death! But I believe if you act as your conscience dictates and according to the law and the evidence, there will be no question about your verdict!"[7]

State's Attorney Smith was the last to speak. In contrast to the impassioned tones of the defense attorneys, he began in an easy, conversational style, eschewing histrionics—at least for the moment.

"I'm not here to make a political speech," he told the jurors. "I want to talk to you a little bit about this case. I am going to show you beyond a reasonable doubt that Lamphere set fire to the house and burned up those people."

Like his cocounsel, Smith dismissed the defense arguments as hopelessly confused. "I cannot conceive on what theory the defense is trying this case," he said. "One moment they say Belle Gunness is alive and the next that she is dead." Addressing Worden's charge that the evidence against Lamphere was "entirely circumstantial," he repeated the line he had used in his opening statement. "Of course the evidence is circumstantial!" he exclaimed. "When men start out to burn houses or commit crimes, they do not give notice, nor go around with a brass band."

Smith responded to another of Worden's accusations by leveling one of his own. "Where is Louis Schultz?, they ask. Well, we ask: Where is Nigger Liz? Why don't they establish an alibi by her? What was the defendant doing during the one hour and forty-five minutes which, according to his own statement, was consumed in going a mile and a quarter? If the time that has been stated is not correct, why don't they bring in Nigger Liz? She knows. Why don't they bring her in?

"Where is there any evidence that Dr. Norton told anything but the absolute truth about the teeth?" Smith continued. "When the defense's own dental experts testified, they stated that the teeth had been made for and had been worn in the same mouth, and further that they had been through the fire."

Like Sutherland, he scoffed at Daniel Hutson's claim that Belle was easily recognizable despite the two veils hanging down to her chin. Next, he briefly recapped his reasons for believing that Lamphere was complicit in Andrew Helgelien's murder.

Then, in a moment made even more dramatic by the sudden shift in tone, he swiveled away from the jury box, jabbed a finger at Lamphere, and thundered: "What did you tell John Rye you would get even with the old woman for? Why did you tell Deputy Sheriff Antiss that you would plead guilty of arson were it not for the sake of your poor old mother? Why were you running around the Gunness place at night, and then pleading guilty to being out there, and paying fines for trespass?"

As Ray struggled, with limited success, to appear unshaken by this onslaught, Smith turned back to the jurors. Though the state had devoted much of its time to proving that Mrs. Gunness was murdered, Smith made it clear that he cared little about the woman. She was, after all, "rottener than hell." No, his "feelings were for the three innocent children, slain by a man who hides behind towers and sneaks about and sets a fire with such consequences!"

His final words, which rang with righteous indignation, could hardly fail to stir the blood of his listeners, most of whom were parents themselves. "I say to you that if you don't believe Lamphere is guilty beyond a reasonable doubt, then don't bring in a verdict of guilty. I do not ask you to vindicate that bad woman, but I have a right to plead in the name of God on behalf of those three innocent children!"[8]

In his instructions to the jury, Judge Richter defined "reasonable doubt," stressed that the defendant's failure to testify should "raise no presumption of any kind against him," and explained that circumstantial evidence was "to be regarded as quite as conclusive in its convincing power as direct and positive evidence." He then told the jurors that, under the law, they could bring in one of several verdicts:

Guilty of murder in the first degree—Death
Guilty of murder in the first degree—Life sentence
Guilty of murder in the second degree—Life sentence
Guilty of manslaughter—Two to twenty-one years
Guilty of arson—Two to twenty-one years
Not guilty

It took Richter fifteen minutes to read his instructions. At 5:30 p.m., Thanksgiving Eve, the jurors filed out of the courtroom to begin their deliberations.[9]

39.

VERDICT

After five hours of heated debate and four divided ballots, it was clear that the jurors were not about to reach a quick decision. At 10:45 p.m., they knocked off for the night, resuming their deliberations after breakfast on Thanksgiving Day.

Twice that day they requested additional information from Judge Richter. Twice they were told that the court could do nothing more than reread the instructions to them. Both times, the twelve men filed back into the courtroom, took their seats in the jury box, and listened intently while Judge Richter read through his instructions in their entirety.

By then, rumors had spread that jury was deadlocked. As the twelve men continued their deliberations into the afternoon, the rest of the participants dispersed for their holiday meals, and the lights of the emptied courtroom were extinguished.

As dusk came on, a group of newspapermen—milling about on the street, awaiting a decision—saw the courtroom windows suddenly light up from within. Words spread rapidly that a verdict was about to be returned, and people came swarming. The room was nearly filled when it became clear that the crowd had responded to a false alarm: Deputy Sheriff Antiss, entertaining some out-of-town friends curious to see the site of the notorious trial, had brought them up to the courtroom and turned on the lights.

Finally, at approximately 7:00 p.m.—fifteen minutes after returning from supper and twenty-six hours after beginning their deliberations—the jurors sent word to Bailiff Matz that they had come to a decision on their nineteenth ballot.

After notifying Judge Richter and the attorneys by telephone, Matz switched on the courtroom lights. By the time Richter and the lawyers arrived, the room was packed, every seat occupied, people standing in the aisle and lining the walls. A few minutes later, Lamphere was brought over from the jail by Deputy Sheriff Antiss, who seated himself directly behind the prisoner to ensure that Ray did not make any "undue movements" upon hearing the verdict.[1]

At 7:20, the jurors filed inside and took their seats in the jury box and the court was called to order.

"Gentlemen of the jury, have you reached an agreement?" asked the judge.

Rising to his feet, foreman Henry Mills confirmed that they had, but said that he "wished to make a statement before the verdict was read." Judge Richter replied that he was "not at liberty to hear any statement until the verdict was received and read."

A tense few moments of silence ensued as Foreman Mills passed the white slip of paper to Bailiff Matz, who handed it to Judge Richter. After entering the verdict upon the docket, Richter cleared his voice and read:

"We find the defendant guilty of arson."

The crowd, having been warned that no demonstration would be tolerated, heard the verdict in silence. Ray appeared to flush, then grow pale, and those watching him closely noticed a "slight tremor of his hands." Otherwise, he showed no reaction. His attorneys, however—who "seemed to take the blow harder than the prisoner himself"—started forward, as though about to offer an angry protest, before "check[ing] themselves."[2]

Having read the verdict, Judge Richter asked Foreman Mills if he still cared to make his statement, but Mills declined the offer, saying that "it would do no good now." After receiving the thanks of the judge and Prosecutor Smith for their "careful and conscientious consideration of the case," the twelve men were discharged and Lamphere was ordered to stand.

"Do you have any reasons to state why sentence should not be pronounced upon you?" asked Judge Richter.

Ray—his face haggard, his eyes downcast, his hands held before him "as if his wrists were still shackled"—slowly replied, "I have nothing to say at this time."

With that, Judge Richter sentenced him to the state prison in Michigan City for an indeterminate term of two to twenty-one years, fined him $5,000, and disenfranchised him for five years. The court then instructed the deputy sheriff to escort him back to the county jail.[3]

With a fair degree of hyperbole—and a certain civic pride in his city's newfound notoriety—Edward Molloy of the *La Porte Weekly Herald* declared that Ray's conviction "brought to a close one of the most famous murder trials in the history of the world":

> In every city, every town and every hamlet and even at the cross roads, in fact places, no matter how remote, to which the telegraph, the mails and the newspapers had access, the people were watching the trial. They had followed the case from its beginning. They had devoured every line printed by the newspapers and they had formed theories on the various features of the case. The newspapers and the news associations were wild to get all the news that was to be had. Within two minutes after Judge Richter read the verdict, it was flashed by wire to all points of the compass. The cables carried the news to Europe and to other foreign lands.[4]

Interviewed in his cell that night by Molloy, Ray seemed reconciled to his fate.

"It could have been worse," he said. "I don't have any particular complaint. The evidence was pretty strong against me, so I'm willing to take my medicine. Sure, I was hoping for an acquittal, but my conscience is clear, and that helps some."

Hoping to settle some of the controversial questions raised during the trial, Molloy asked Ray why he "didn't arouse the people when you saw the fire that morning if you didn't set it."

"Well," said Ray, "I suppose if I'd realized what was going to happen and knew what I know now, I guess I would've done so. I got scared and did things I shouldn't have done, and that made it look bad."

"Do you believe Mrs. Gunness is dead or alive?" Molloy asked.

"Oh, she's dead, all right," said Ray. "That was her body and the children they found in the fire."

"Tell me this, Ray," said Molloy. "What did you really see that night you returned from Michigan City, the night Helgelien disappeared?"

Ray was emphatic. "I didn't see anything," he said.

Molloy tried pressing him for more details on the matter, but at that point Ray clammed up, explaining that his attorney, Wirt Worden, "had told him not to make any admissions."

"But what does it matter, now that you've been convicted?" said Molloy. "They can't try you again."

Ray only shook his head and repeated that he was following his lawyer's instructions.

Once Molloy was gone, Ray asked Sheriff Smutzer for a sheet of paper, a pen, and some ink, and composed a letter to his mother.

"Dear Mother," he began. "I will try and write you a few lines to let you know how I am":

> I just got back from the courthouse where I went to get my sentence. I was somewhat disappointed, although the circumstances were against me, but Ma, I am not guilty and before God I am no criminal, even if I am in the eyes of the people. Don't worry about me, Ma, for it might have been worse. I have thought many times since I have been here in jail that it is a wonder I did not find a resting place in her private burying ground, so Ma, do not worry for I am among the living with a clear conscience, and know I never did any very great wrong to anybody. Now Ma, I know you are almost heartbroken, but try and console yourself in the fact that I am innocent. Of course it is hard for me but not half as hard as it would be if I were guilty.

"Now Ma, cheer up," he concluded. "Don't worry about me, and I will see you sometime. Goodbye from your son, Ray."[5]

With the trial behind him, Ray, relieved of the tension of uncertainty, slept soundly Thursday night. The letter had not yet been mailed the following morning when Ray was brought into Sheriff Smutzer's office. Moments later, his mother and his sister, Mrs. Pearl Steele, entered, the pair having traveled by train from South Bend to bid him goodbye.

Sheriff Smutzer made his office available for the sad occasion. Supported by her daughter, the seventy-year-old woman burst into tears as she embraced her boy.

"Ray, I know you are innocent," she said between sobs. "Your mother still believes in you."

Ray's eyes moistened, but otherwise he kept control of his emotions.

Moments later, knowing that "she might not live to see her wayward son again," the elderly woman was led from the office in a state of near collapse.[6]

Lamphere might have accepted his fate with equanimity, but the same could not be said of Wirt Worden, who gave free vent to his outrage. Speaking to reporters at the jail that morning, he denounced the verdict as "ridiculous.

"There were absolutely no grounds and no evidence to support," he said bitterly. "We're going to make a motion for a new trial on Monday. If that's denied, we'll take the appeal to the supreme court."

No one doubted Worden's sincerity, though an appeal seemed unlikely. To begin with, there was the expense—$500 for a transcript alone. Moreover, it would take at least two years for the case to reach the state supreme court, and by that time, as the *Herald* noted, "the minimum term of Lamphere's sentence would have expired and it would be better to work for his release on parole." Even if the decision were reversed on appeal and the state declined to retry the case, Ray could hardly count on walking away a free man, since Smith had made it clear that he was prepared to bring charges against Lamphere for the murder of Andrew Helgelien. The consensus among observers was that, once their emotions had cooled, Ray's lawyers would "realize that their client, by mere chance, had escaped a more severe punishment, and that . . . the best thing for [Lamphere] to do is to accept the verdict as gracefully as possible."[7]

The jury's decision, it emerged, had been a compromise between ten men who favored a verdict of murder in the second degree with a penalty of life imprisonment and two stubborn holdouts, one who argued for a verdict of arson, one who wanted to acquit.[8] Among editorial writers in newspapers throughout the Midwest, the consensus was that the decision made little legal or logical sense. In the words of one typical commentator, "The result of the trial was peculiar":

> According to the judgment of the jury, Lamphere was guilty of arson but was acquitted of the charge of murdering Mrs. Gunness and her children, who were incinerated in the conflagration. It imposes a severe strain upon the imagination to conceive how it would be possible for the defendant to be adjudged guilty of arson without being convicted of murder also . . . Under the circumstances, the return of a verdict of arson is a travesty of justice [and] cannot be viewed as being anything other than almost absurdly inconsistent.[9]

Apart from his die-hard defenders, virtually everyone seemed to feel that the jury had let Lamphere off easy. One wisecracking writer for the *Chicago Daily News* remarked that, had Mrs. Gunness been on trial instead of Lamphere, the jury would probably have found her guilty of nothing worse than operating an unlicensed graveyard.[10]

There was one editorialist who felt differently. He agreed that Lamphere should have been found guilty of murder. But, at least when it came to the "ogress," that was no reason for the jury to impose a harsh sentence. "If Lamphere took the life of Belle Gunness," the writer opined, "he should have been presented with a gold medal."[11]

Early Friday afternoon, Ray was taken by interurban streetcar to Michigan City. Along with Sheriff Smutzer, he was accompanied by several newspapermen. He chatted easily with them, repeatedly remarking that he was "going to prison with a clear conscience." When one of the reporters asked what he meant by that, Ray replied, "I didn't do any more than hundreds of other people would've done in my place"—a comment that, to the ears of his listeners, "sounded very near to a confession."

On the whole, he seemed relaxed, even surprisingly cheerful, at one point whistling "Wait 'Til the Sun Shines, Nellie" while gazing out the window. A car was waiting at the Michigan City streetcar stop to drive him the rest of the way. "I'm lucky to be here," he mused aloud as the prison came into view. "Mighty lucky. Why, I might've been chopped up and put in a hole in old woman Gunness' chicken yard."[12]

With Smutzer still at his side, he was escorted to the chief clerk's window, where his name was entered in the register and he was assigned his convict number: 4,140. He was then taken to the receiving room for a bath, photographed and measured in the Bertillon room, and issued his suit of prison gray.

Before being led off to his cell, he shook hands with Sheriff Smutzer, "thanked him for the excellent treatment he had received in the county jail during the six months he had been confined there and asked him to say a good word for him when his application should come before the parole board in a couple of years."

Even before he spent his first night behind the walls of that grim fortress, Ray, as the papers reported, was "looking forward to the end of his minimum sentence, when he would be eligible for parole."[13]

CONCLUSION

A MYSTERY NEVER TO BE
FULLY RESOLVED

40.

CONFESSIONS

In their ongoing battle for newsstand supremacy, William Randolph Hearst and his yellow-press rival, Joseph Pulitzer, packed their Sunday magazine supplements with the most sensationally attention-grabbing—and often wholly fabricated—stories. One favorite recurrent feature was the "confession" of a notorious murderer, presented as a major newspaper exclusive, though, more often than not, it was a shameless hoax concocted by some anonymous staff writer. Occasionally, the criminal in question was paid to certify to the authenticity of the piece, though often it was written and disseminated without the consent—or even the knowledge—of the prisoner who had supposedly provided it.

Typical of these brazen frauds was the two-page spread published with much fanfare in the May 9, 1909, *Sunday Magazine* of Pulitzer's *St. Louis Post-Dispatch* under the headline "Confession of Ray Lamphere." From the moment of his arrest, the story read, Lamphere—"the Sphinx of the Gunness case"—had maintained a steadfast silence. "Through the tense times following the discovery of the bodies at the Gunness farm he refrained from making any statement. He withstood hours of midnight sweating." Recently, however, he had been "seen by a staff correspondent from the *Sunday Post-Dispatch*," to whom—for reasons unexplained by the paper—Ray had decided to "unbosom" himself.

Despite the lurid illustration accompanying the piece—a black-and-white drawing of Ray sneaking down into a creepy cellar hung with drying cuts of meat that might be either ham or human flesh—the "confession" is little more than a dull rehash of familiar facts, spiced up with a few fabricated "revelations." In addition to claiming that Belle had offered "to marry me if I would get my life insured," the narrator describes the night when he had unexpectedly returned from Michigan City with John Rye, then proceeded by himself to the Gunness farm:

> I went around to the side of the house where the cellar steps were and went into the cellar. Mrs. Gunness and Helgelien were in the sitting room above. I could hear their voices, and now and then I could catch a word, but I could not tell what they were talking about. Sounds that I heard made me think that Helgelien was sick or drunk.
>
> I did not realize it then, but I have no doubt now that the woman had given him poison in beer and that it was beginning to take effect. She always kept bottled beer in the house and it would have been easy for her to put poison in a glass of beer. I stayed there between half an hour and an hour. All the time I could hear Helgelien making sounds as if he was sick . . . [The next morning] Helgelien was not there. Mrs. Gunness said he had gone home. I did not suspect then that she had killed him.

"For the first time," the newspaper trumpeted, it had obtained "direct testimony" proving that Mrs. Gunness "killed her victims by poison"—an impressive journalistic coup, had the heralded confession been authentic.[1]

Ray would never finish his two-year minimum sentence. The hemorrhage he suffered on the second day of the trial turned out to be, as his physician had recognized, the sign of incipient tuberculosis. By October 1909—less than a year after his conviction—it was clear that he was dying.

Hoping to win Ray's release, his brother-in-law, H. L. Finley of La Porte, traveled to Indianapolis for a meeting with Governor Thomas R. Marshall and was informed by Marshall's secretary, Mark Thistlewaite, that the state parole board would not meet until early December.

"Lamphere will come home in a box before then," was Finley's grim reply.

He then appealed to the governor for an immediate pardon. Taking the matter under advisement, Marshall contacted both Warden James D. Reid of the Indiana State Prison and William Antiss, now sheriff of La Porte. Reid believed that no good purpose would be served by freeing Lamphere, "since in prison he had the best of care and was more comfortable than he would be at home." Antiss felt that Lamphere was not deserving of a pardon, "for he had not told all he knew about the Gunness case."[2] He advised that Lamphere remain in prison until he "unseal[ed] his lips."

According to newspaper reports, authorities, among them State's Attorney Ralph Smith, were "convinced that [Lamphere] will make a confession clearing every detail of the Gunness death farm mystery when he realizes the end is at hand."[3]

Their confident prediction proved to be wishful thinking. On Thursday afternoon, December 30, Ray began to fail so rapidly that, though his sister, Mrs. Finley, was immediately notified by telephone, he was dead by the time she arrived a few hours later. He was thirty-eight years old.

"Died with Gunness Mystery Unsolved," the *Indianapolis News* reported on Friday:

> Whatever knowledge Lamphere had of the night when the Gunness house was burned to the ground went with him to the grave, for he made no statement before his death that would throw any light on the Gunness case. Those who expected that he would confess before he died were disappointed, as were also those who expected that in his dying moments he would prove his innocence.[4]

That Ray had been acquitted of the murder charges brought against him and died without admitting to any guilt did not prevent a number of newspapers from identifying him in their obituary notices as "Ray Lamphere, the slayer of Mrs. Belle Gunness and her children."[5]

Ray's wake was held at his sister's home on Sunday, January 2, 1910. Along with Mrs. Finley and her husband, attendees included Ray's brother and elderly mother. Afterward, his body was transported to Rossville Cemetery for interment. Officiating at the funeral was the Reverend C. R. Parker of the First Baptist Church, who chose as his theme a verse from Genesis 18, dealing with God's righteous destruction of Sodom and Gomorrah.[6]

During his long incarceration in the La Porte county jail while awaiting the start of his trial, Ray had been visited regularly by another man of the cloth: the Reverend Edwin A. Schell, until recently pastor of La Porte's First Methodist Church. A native of Deer Creek, Indiana, and graduate of Northwestern University, the forty-eight-year-old Schell, after a distinguished career as a minister, church administrator, and writer for popular magazines, had been appointed president of Iowa Wesleyan University just weeks before the Gunness fire.[7] On the day of Ray's arrest, he was one of the first people to come speak to the prisoner. Afterward, interviewed by reporters, Schell had vouched for Ray's essentially harmless character.

"He is not a vicious man," said Schell, "just a farmer's son who had picked up a little knowledge of the carpenter's trade and, of course, cannot be expected to rate high mentally. But there is little in his past life to believe that he would be guilty of the crime of firing a house containing four people. He is a toper, and his relations to women are open to criticism. But he is not a bad man."[8]

In the following weeks, Schell became Ray's closest confidant, engaging him in emotional conversations that sometimes lasted several hours. Badgered by reporters following one of these talks, Schell refused to repeat what Ray had told him, insisting that "Lamphere's communications to me are wholly privileged."[9]

On several subsequent occasions, however, Schell could not resist dishing out tantalizing bits of supposedly confidential information, stating unequivocally that "the Gunness children were chloroformed" before the fire and "the woman's body found in the ruins was not that of Mrs. Gunness," who was "still alive." Asked about Ray's involvement in the Gunness atrocities, Schell startled his listeners by replying that he "was sure that [Lamphere] was innocent of all but the Helgelien murder. But of the latter he was very jealous." When one reporter asked if Schell was saying that Ray had confessed to the Helgelien murder, Schell clammed up, solemnly declaring "it would not be right" to answer that question, since the facts divulged by Ray were "as inviolably sacred as the secrets of the confessional should be."[10]

Having hinted so strongly for so long that he was in possession of Ray's darkest secrets, Schell came under renewed pressure to disclose them once Ray was in the ground. As before, he was firm in his refusal. "It is the minister's duty to hear confession and to plead with the criminal to make restitution or urge him to make his statements to the courts," he told reporters on January 10. "If I should reveal this confidence, the ministry would be discredited and would lose some of their power to do good by hearing confessions. I expect to be criticized whether I decide to reveal the statement or not. The ministry and churchmen will criticize me if I reveal, and others of the public will criticize me if I do not."

All in all, Schell said with a sigh, he had come to wish that Ray had never confided in him at all. "I would give $500 if I had not heard the story told me by Lamphere."[11]

On Thursday, January 13, 1910—three days after Schell made this statement—the front page of the *St. Louis Post-Dispatch* carried a startling banner headline: "Confession Clears the Gunness Mystery. Details of Lamphere's Dying Statement Given to the *Post-Dispatch*."

According to the copyrighted story (which made no mention of the supposedly exclusive confession published by the paper eight months earlier), days before his death, "when he believed eternity was near," Ray Lamphere "had unburdened his soul by a confession which clears the Gunness mystery, the crime classic of a generation." The confession—"hitherto supposed to have been made only to the Rev. E. A. Schell"—was given "to a man of unassailable character and truthfulness, whose standing in the community is such that his word is accepted without question." This unimpeachable source—who, for "good reasons" of his own, insisted on anonymity—had been tracked down by "a staff correspondent for the *Post-Dispatch* in a quest extending over six states.

"The *Post-Dispatch* staff correspondent fully verified the fact that this man had such an interview with Ray Lamphere as he asserts he had, under conditions as he describes them," the article continued. The confession, dictated by Ray, "had been put into writing at the time it was given." Unfortunately, "only one copy" was made. That copy, "which was left with Lamphere," had evidently disappeared. Nevertheless, "though the *Post-Dispatch* has not been able to find the written record of the confession, it has come into possession of its essential details from such a source that there can be no question of its authenticity . . . There is no reason to doubt that the statements now made public for the first time are substantially as they fell from the lips of Ray Lamphere."[12]

In contrast to the ostensible confession that had appeared the previous May, which offered little in the way of new information, the present one was packed with dramatic revelations. Not long after Ray went to work for Belle—so the story went—a Norwegian man had arrived at the farm in response to one of her matrimonial ads. "This man went to sleep one night and never awoke. In the dark hour before dawn, Mrs. Gunness awakened Lamphere and ordered him to carry something in a gunnysack to the farmyard where a hole had been dug as an ostensible receptacle for rubbish. The gunnysack and the something in it were tumbled into the hole and a hummock of earth was shoveled on top of it."

Within a month, "another man came to the farm," bringing "all his money from Wisconsin or Minnesota." A "few nights later, there was another burying job for Lamphere." By the time Ray helped dispose of a third corpse-filled gunnysack, he had become a willing accomplice, remunerated for his services with enough money "to spend in drinking and gambling in the saloons of La Porte." Each time Belle expected a new arrival, she would send Ray into town to purchase chloroform, which she used to kill her victims in their sleep. On those occasions when "the chloroform did not of itself kill them," she would "sever their heads with a keen-edged ax.

"Then Andrew Helgelien came," the confession continued. Ordered to move out of the house, Ray waited until Helgelien and Mrs. Gunness were out driving one day, then snuck back in and

> bored a hole through the floor of the sitting room in such a position that it would not be discovered but would enable him to both hear and see what went on in the room. When Mrs. Gunness sent him to Michigan City on a fictitious errand and told him to stay all night, he suspected that Helgelien's time had come.
>
> He returned in the evening against her orders and crept into the cellar. Something Mrs. Gunness had given Helgelien

had made him sick. He was groaning in great distress. "For God's sake, call for a doctor," Lamphere heard him say, but Mrs. Gunness told him that he would soon be better. Presently he succumbed to the effect of the poison and dropped from his chair to the floor. Lamphere, staring through the hole in the floor, saw Mrs. Gunness strike the blow that ended Helgelien's life. He went away then and it was not until the next night that the woman called on him to help her bury a body sewed in a gunnysack.

When Lamphere demanded "a larger share of the profits," the two quarreled bitterly and "Mrs. Gunness ordered him off the farm." Repairing to his favorite watering hole, Lamphere began downing whiskeys and brooding over the money he felt entitled to. "He believed there was not less than $1500 hidden about the house . . . The more he drank, the more convinced he became that Mrs. Gunness had not given him a fair deal."

In the early hours of the morning of April 28, an inebriated Lamphere, equipped with "some of the chloroform that had been bought with Mrs. Gunness' money" and accompanied by a female companion, "crept up through the cedars toward the silent house on the hilltop . . . It was something that Lamphere, sober, would not have undertaken. But Lamphere, drunk, had enough bravado to essay it."

The Gunness dog, which would have set up a racket at the intrusion of a stranger, was "silenced with a word" from the familiar ex-farmhand. Sneaking into the bedrooms of Mrs. Gunness and her children, Lamphere—who had learned the technique from his former employer—chloroformed them all. Then he and his companion ransacked the house by candlelight. Much to their disappointment, they found less than seventy dollars. By then, dawn was beginning to break. Abandoning the search, they hurried away. As Lamphere headed toward the farm "where he was to work that day, he looked back and saw smoke and flames bursting from the house on the hill."

Ray insisted that he "did not intentionally start the fire." He "did not desire the death of the Gunness children. He was not such a monster that he could wish to burn sleeping children in their beds. He did not even intend to kill Mrs.

Gunness." Apparently, he had unwittingly left a burning candle behind, which sparked the conflagration.

Foremost among the facts supposedly established by the confession was "that Mrs. Gunness is dead":

> The adult body found in the smoking ruins of the Gunness farmhouse was the body of Mrs. Belle Gunness. She was under the influence of chloroform when the smoke crept up through the crevices and smothered her. She died with the head of her little boy pillowed on her breast. He, too, was chloroformed and died without waking. Neither of them knew aught of it when the two little girls, Myrtle and Lucy, not so thoroughly chloroformed as the woman and boy, awoke to their peril and ran into their mother's room and threw themselves on the woman, beseeching help. They perished there with the woman and the boy, mercifully suffocated by the smoke before the flames came licking at the tender flesh.

There was another, perhaps even more startling revelation. When Ray snuck into the Gunness farmhouse that night, he had found a fifth person asleep in one of the bedrooms—Jennie Olsen! Mrs. Gunness had in fact "sent Jennie away to school in California for a time, but she had returned, and Mrs. Gunness, for reasons of her own, had kept her concealed in the house. Lamphere found her when he went there that night and chloroformed her, and she died as she lay in her bed. With her slender body, the flames did their work so well that the searchers raking the hot debris the next day found only the other four bodies."

As for the girl exhumed from the Gunness graveyard and widely assumed to be Jennie, her identity "added another mystery to the case."[13]

Ray's purported confession made headlines in newspapers across the country, from the *Los Angeles Herald* to the *New York Times*. In La Porte, reaction was uniformly dismissive. "No one here believes the tale," reported the correspondent for the *Cincinnati Enquirer*. Both Wirt Worden and Ralph N. Smith scoffed at every supposed revelation, deriding the entire account as "a story of the cock-and-bull variety."[14]

Pressed to reveal the source of the confession, the editor of the *Post-Dispatch* stood by his refusal to disclose the person's name, defending his decision on the basis of long-standing journalistic practice. "In newspaper offices," he wrote, "it is well known that valuable information is often obtained under an inviolable pledge of confidence, and that such a pledge is never broken unless the newspaper is released by the person to whom it is made . . . the name of the man who received the confession from Lamphere will never be made known by the *Post-Dispatch* unless permission is given by this man, which seems highly improbable." He did, however, drop a very strong hint as to the identity of his anonymous source, declaring that "the Rev. Mr. Schell could verify the confession, if he would consent to break his silence."[15]

Besieged by reporters at his home in Burlington, Iowa, on Friday, January 14, Schell "reiterated that he had not divulged any such confession to any person."[16] The following day, however, he succumbed to the pressure. Summoning a reporter from the *Chicago Tribune* to his office at Iowa Wesleyan University, the pastor finally broke his long silence, dictating a statement that appeared on the front page of the next day's edition under the headline "Dr. Schell Bares Lamphere Secret."

"In view of the conflicting reports which continue to keep alive interest in the Gunness case," Schell began, "and the interrogations which must continually arise in the minds of sorrowing friends and recognizing that the principal facts already are made public, I have concluded to relieve myself of further responsibility by communicating to the public through the *Chicago Tribune* the details of my three conversations with the late Ray Lamphere in the jail at La Porte, the statements he made to me, and the circumstances under which they were made."

Schell recalled first hearing about the fire at the Gunness house "on the next to the last Monday morning" of April 1908 and described his sorrow at learning of the death of the three children, "who had been attending my Sunday school, a bright, winsome lad 5 years old and two girls, perhaps 7 and 9. I had seen the children driving around in a pony cart the previous fall and several times noticed the boy in the infant class. At the suggestion of J. P. Rupel, the Sunday school superintendent, we arranged a brief memorial service for the Sunday school the following Sunday morning."

A few days later, Ray Lamphere was arrested. That Friday, "at the suggestion of Prosecuting Attorney Smith and understanding it was Lamphere's wish,
I called at the jail to counsel with him and perhaps to receive his confession."

Lamphere, said Schell, "was agitated in the extreme. Beads of perspiration
were on his brow, his hands twitched, and his nervousness was plainly noticeable
. . . He said that he supposed they would hang him, but that he was innocent
of murder."

During that first conversation, Lamphere "denied that he set the house on
fire and related to me how he had slept at the house of a negress until 3 a.m. that
morning, then had started for the home of a relative in the country, and in passing by the Gunness home had seen that it was burning, but being angry at Mrs.
Gunness and no longer working for her, he hurried past. He then said he reached
his relative's place in the country, some four miles further, at about 4 o'clock."

After leaving Lamphere, Schell made some inquiries, then returned to the
jail "early after dinner the same day . . . and told him I had learned that he had
not reached his relative until after 6 o'clock that morning." Confronted with this
inconsistency, Ray now "said that on thinking it over, he remembered that he
went back to bed after waking up at 3 a.m. and that the negress got his breakfast about 4 o'clock a.m. and that he did not start as early as he thought, as he
remembered the Lake Erie train went by just as he crossed the track north of
the lake. He also said that instead of going directly by the house, as he had said
in the morning, he had taken the road farther east and on the other side of the
lake and only saw the house at a distance."

Gently chiding Lamphere for prevaricating, Schell "advised him that if he
wanted my sympathy, prayers, and help to remain silent or tell the exact truth.
I promised not to tell the prosecuting attorney." The two men then engaged in
"general conversation about Mrs. Gunness." Finally, "after some two hours,"
Lamphere opened up about the events of that fateful night.

He "had been intimate with Mrs. Gunness from June 1907," Ray explained.
"Three times at her request," he had purchased chloroform and once he "dug a
hole in the hog lot for her and helped her put in the body of someone who she
said had died suddenly about the house, and she thought the easiest way was to
cover him up and say nothing about it."

Ray insisted that he had "no suspicions of Mrs. Gunness having murdered
anyone until one night when he returned suddenly from Michigan City and,

having bored some holes through a wall, saw her administer some chloroform to a man and hit him in the back of the head with a hatchet. Fearing her after that, he had quit working for her and returned to the house only occasionally to get his wages still due."

When Schell responded that he was not fully convinced by the story—"that it was contradictory in too many particulars"—Ray admitted that he "had taken money from Mrs. Gunness several times, making her 'shell out' or he would tell on her. Once she gave him $50. At another time $15, and again $5. He would then go to saloons and when he was sober he would find the money all gone." On the Saturday night before the fire, he had come to her house and, reminding her that he had witnessed the Helgelien murder, demanded more hush money. "She refused to give him more than $1, and he told her that he would get even with her."

At Schell's prodding, Ray then went on to detail the events of the night of the conflagration:

> On Sunday night, after he and the negress had been drinking about 11 o'clock, the two went together to the Gunness house, letting themselves in by a key which he had and going quietly so as not to disturb another hired man who was in the house. With some of the chloroform which he had purchased for Mrs. Gunness before Helgelien disappeared and part of which he had kept in another bottle, the two gave Mrs. Gunness some chloroform, holding it under her nose until she became quiet. The little boy was in bed with her. They then gave some to the two girls who were in another room. He could not explain how all were together when found. He did not know, he was pretty drunk, but that was the way he remembered it.
>
> He and the negress then searched for the large sum of money which they were sure was hidden in the house, but found only a small amount. He did not set the house on fire, though he was not certain that the negress did not do it, for she was as drunk as he was. He stoutly protested that he had not arranged a candle so that it would burn down and later set fire to the place, and that he had nothing in his mind more

than to get enough money to have a "big time" with. He and
the negress left the house together, and at a certain point in the
road, she went home and he went running away, greatly afraid
because he saw the house burning.

After hearing Ray's statement, Schell went home and transcribed it from
memory on two sheets of paper, which he showed to Ray the following day.
Urged to share it with Prosecuting Attorney Smith "and save the county the cost
of the trial and his sisters the expense of defending him," Ray "agreed to sign it
and give it to the prosecuting attorney." Schell then met with Smith and "told
him that Lamphere was going to confess." That, according to the pastor, was the
end of his involvement with Lamphere.

"I still feel that the communication was privileged," Schell told the *Tribune*
reporter, "that I owed it to his sisters to refuse to make it public until now, and
that the church whose minister I was at La Porte had a right to expect silence
from me, and that failure on my part to keep the confidence a secret might deter
others needing the encouragement of a Christian preacher from opening his
heart to some man of God."[17]

The *Chicago Tribune*'s claim that it had scored a journalistic coup with Schell's
statement was greeted with scorn by the *St. Louis Post-Dispatch*, which asserted
that the *Tribune*'s ostensible "scoop" merely corroborated what the *Post-Dispatch*
had already published two days earlier. Far from redounding to the *Tribune*'s
credit, "the publication of the confession . . . emphasizes the *Post-Dispatch*'s
motto, 'First in Everything.'"[18]

Freed from its pledge of confidentiality, the *Post-Dispatch* now confirmed
what many had suspected all along: that its anonymous source was the Reverend
Schell. In a front-page story on Saturday, January 15, F. A. Behymer, the reporter
who had gotten the confession from Schell, gave a full account of the episode—a
"fascinating story of newspaper resource and enterprise" that had led to "this
notable achievement in newsgathering."

Behymer—who went to work for the paper as an eighteen-year-old and
would remain on the staff for the next sixty-four years until his retirement in

1952[19]—traveled to Schell's Iowa home on Sunday, January 9, where he learned from the pastor's wife that her husband "had gone to Adair, 200 miles up the state, to dedicate a church. Mrs. Schell said that her husband had spoken the last word about Lamphere's confession and it would be useless to see him."

Undeterred, Behymer proceeded to Adair, where he found the pastor "at a home at which he was being entertained." "Following a planned line of attack," Behymer then engaged Schell in a discussion of the crime. Sensing that the pastor "thought the world ought to know the truth" but felt constrained by his pledge of confidentiality, Behymer proceeded by indirection. Instead of asking straightforward questions, he put forth theoretical propositions about what might have occurred. Schell responded in kind, filling in details "not as one giving information but as one suggesting theoretical explanations.

"Both of us were playing parts," Behymer explained. "I was seeking facts by asking for theories, and Dr. Schell was imparting information under the guise of hypothesis. But it was a harmless masquerade, because neither was deceiving the other but only playing at it."

Given their little charade, it was unclear to Behymer "how much of the information had been given involuntarily and how much intentionally." But "it did not matter. I had the Lamphere confession, and Dr. Schell knew I had it, and said so, but he asked me not to reveal the source of my information. I promised and kept the promise until Dr. Schell, by revealing the source of the information himself, released me from the obligation."[20]

Questioned by reporters following the publication of Schell's statement, Wirt Worden responded with a snort. "I went to see Lamphere in jail immediately upon hearing that he had been talking with Dr. Schell," Worden explained. "I asked him if he had confessed. Lamphere was holding the Bible given to him by Dr. Schell, and standing there with his hand on the book, he laughed and said he would never tell the clergyman anything he wouldn't tell me. He then repeated what he had told the preacher. It was the same story he clung to all through the case, absolutely denying that he had killed Mrs. Gunness or set her house on fire. Lamphere insisted that was all he told the pastor."[21]

A local physician, interviewed by the *La Porte Argus-Bulletin*, was equally dismissive. Schell's story, he said, "was the most ridiculous thing I ever saw in print. No matter how deep might have been their sleep, it's impossible that Lamphere and the negress could have chloroformed Mrs. Gunness and her three children without awakening them. And if Mrs. Gunness had been awakened, there would have been screaming, and Maxson would have heard it."[22]

Prosecuting Attorney Smith was of a different opinion. "I know it's authentic," he said about Schell's statement. "There are remarks in the story which Schell made to me after his talks with Lamphere, quoted exactly."

Even so, there was one element of the confession that Smith questioned. "Schell told me to arrest a certain negress," Smith told reporters. "He didn't tell me why, but now I know. In my opinion, however, Lamphere lied to Schell when he told that this colored person went to the Gunness house with Lamphere and assisted him in the murder of the woman and her children. I think this person helped plan the thing, but she was too wise a girl to go to the house with Lamphere and assist in the execution."[23]

41.

THE SKULL

The "negress" referred to in Schell's statement was, of course, Elizabeth Smith—"Nigger Liz," as her neighbors had no compunctions about calling her. Immediately following the publication of Ray's reported confession on Saturday, January 15, 1910, she was arrested at home on the order of Judge Richter and subjected to a four-hour "sweating" at the county jail. She admitted that Ray had spent part of the night of April 27 at her home but fiercely denied that she had accompanied him to the Gunness house or had anything to do with the fire. She was then released on a five-hundred-dollar bond.

She was expected to give grand jury testimony the following Thursday, January 22, but failed to appear. She was "sick at home," the newspapers reported, "and her physicians say she may not be able to undergo an inquisition for weeks. Worry over her position in the affair and the action of the authorities has made her seriously ill."[1]

She was still "prostrated" on February 4 and unable to appear before the grand jury that had been called to examine her. One month later, on Saturday, March 5, State's Attorney Smith announced that, owing to the lack of "tangible evidence on which to hold her for trial, the decision had been reached to drop the case against Elizabeth Smith for alleged complicity in the crimes committed at the Gunness farm."[2]

That same day, Wirt Worden had his own announcement to make, telling reporters that "there would be sensational developments shortly in connection with the Gunness case," ones that confirmed his long-held belief "that she is alive."

The big news promised by Worden broke the following day: Belle Gunness had been located in Grand Rapids, Michigan, identified by a local police officer, Louis Richmond. "This woman has by her peculiar actions caused at least three others to suspect that she is Mrs. Gunness," declared Richmond, who immediately wrote to Sheriff Antiss in La Porte, urging him "to send a deputy to the Michigan city to arrest the woman."[3]

This announcement was greeted with widespread and well-justified skepticism. Just two months earlier, in January, papers throughout the Midwest had trumpeted the news that Belle had been arrested in Willmar, Minnesota, where she was working under an alias as housekeeper for a farmer named Gus Kirby. In mid-February, word came from Washington State that the "archmurderess" had been "found on a ranch, sixteen miles from Bellingham by United States Marshal Andrew Williams."[4]

As in both those previous instances, the Michigan story proved to be false, the woman in question having been identified as Belle for no better reason than that she "was a Norwegian and had inserted advertisements in Norwegian newspapers seeking a husband."[5] Despite these repeated mirages, sightings of "La Porte's Lucretia Borgia" would continue unabated. Before the year was out, she would be reported as living in Moscow, Idaho; Greenville, Illinois; Palouse, Washington; and Galcon, Oklahoma, where she was ostensibly cohabiting "with a man who is the possessor of a fur coat, two revolvers, two rifles, and two shotguns."[6]

Each of these supposed discoveries was scrupulously investigated by La Porte authorities at the behest of State's Attorney Smith. Though Smith remained convinced that Belle was dead, he insisted on running down every lead, intent on proving "that every clue brought up by those who cling to the belief that Mrs. Gunness is alive is without foundation."[7]

Wirt Worden—one of those who clung most tenaciously to that belief—got a seemingly significant boost in December 1912, when a prisoner named Harry

Myers, doing time in the Michigan City penitentiary, came forward with a startling story.

A convicted burglar and horse thief, Myers had been put to work in the prison and, while nursing the dying Ray Lamphere, had obtained—so he claimed—a "deathbed statement" from Ray. According to Myers, Ray insisted that Belle Gunness was alive. The headless adult body found in the ruins was that of a Chicago woman brought to the Gunness farm as a housekeeper and poisoned a few days later. She was then decapitated "to make identification almost impossible." Her head—wrapped in a piece of carpet and placed inside a wooden box containing "three other heads, two of them that looked as if they had been dead some time"—was given to Lamphere, who "buried it in a field of rye." Belle had killed her three children, also with poison, to "keep them from talking" about all the male visitors who had vanished so mysteriously.

On the night of the conflagration, Ray had driven Belle "in a two-seated rig drawn by a pony to a point nine miles from La Porte, where another man whom he did not know met her and drove her to Chicago." She was carrying "two large valises and a small basket. In the basket was a box made of tin containing a large pile of paper money, the smallest denomination being $100 bills." After he "delivered Mrs. Gunness to the other man," Ray "returned to the Gunness farm and set fire to the house in which were the bodies of the Chicago woman and three children." For his work, he received $500.[8]

Myers's widely publicized revelation brought a new flood of reported sightings. Within two weeks, "at least twenty Mrs. Gunnesses [had] been seen in different parts of the country and reported to police."[9] Most of these tips were so patently implausible that La Porte authorities paid no attention to them. One, however—a telegram from police in Lethbridge, Alberta, Canada, claiming that the notorious fugitive was living in a small mining village ten miles away—was taken seriously enough that the La Porte police chief, William Meinke, was dispatched to Lethbridge to confirm her identity. The woman in question, according to information conveyed by a Norwegian miner named Foreland, "weighed about the same as Mrs. Gunness and is of the same age. She has three trunks, kept securely locked in her basement, that correspond to those which were told about by witnesses at the time the murders were discovered." Foreland also claimed that he was "in possession of a letter written to the woman which commenced with the words 'Dear Belle.'"

Meinke's trip up north, however, proved to be in vain. He returned to La Porte on January 27, 1913, and announced that "the woman is not Mrs. Gunness."[10]

Shortly before five p.m. on Friday, March 17, 1916, Elizabeth Smith—"the only person in the world who might have lifted the veil of mystery from the Gunness case"[11]—died at the home of a friend. No one, including herself, knew her exact age, though, as she told the doctor who attended her in her final illness, she suspected it was "pretty near eighty." A few days earlier, while lying on her cot beside the stove in the only habitable room of her tumbledown shack on Pulaski Street, an errant spark set the mattress on fire. Neighbors, hearing her screams, rushed to her aid and, after swiftly extinguishing the fire, carried her to her friend's home. Though the burns she suffered weren't life-threatening, the shock of the experience, combined with her frail physical condition, proved too much for the "aged negress."[12]

Knowing that her end was near, Smith asked to see Wirt Worden. Over the years, she had promised him repeatedly that, when she knew she was dying, she "would tell him everything she knew of Belle Gunness and the murder farm." As luck would have it, however, Worden was in Louisiana on a business matter. By the time he got back to La Porte, Elizabeth Smith was in the ground.[13]

In announcing her death, newspapers recounted the salient facts of her life: her childhood spent with her widowed mother, an ex-slave known as "Granny" Olmstead, who lived to be 104 and claimed to have known George Washington; her marriage to a Union army cook who died early, leaving her with a federal pension of $24 a month; her own shrewdness as a businesswoman that allowed her to acquire six houses and a savings account of several thousand dollars. And, of course, her youthful reputation as a "colored beauty" who had "dazzled many a white man."[14]

In the latter years of her life, Smith, like many old people, had become what we now call a compulsive hoarder. A newspaperman, visiting her shack sometime after her death, was shocked at its condition. "There are tons and tons of rubbish in the old shack," he reported. "The front door was piled high with rubbish of all kinds, all absolutely valueless. The floor was covered several feet deep with papers, broken lamps, chairs, benches, tin cans, bits of window screen, rags, and filth and dirt of every kind and description. Rubbish was piled high around the little stove in one room, where she was finally compelled to live because all the others were so full of rubbish. Her coal ashes were dumped on the floor by the stove."[15]

The shack being beyond salvation, plans were made to tear it down and sell the lumber, studs, and sheathing. A man named Andrew Harness was retained to clean the place out and demolish it. Eventually, he would sell nearly a thousand pounds of rags and scrap metal to local junk dealers and cart twenty wagonloads of refuse to the town dump.

On Friday, May 5, while rummaging about in the knee-deep debris of Smith's shack, Harness turned up a human skull—a "musty, cob-webby" relic, missing its lower jaw and with "only a few rotted roots to mark the upper set of teeth."[16] Newspapers throughout the country immediately announced a possible solution to the Gunness mystery. Should the skull prove to be Belle's, its discovery would confirm one widely held theory: "that Ray Lamphere and Elizabeth Smith, his black paramour, murdered Mrs. Gunness and her children, dragged the bodies to the cellar and then severed the head of Mrs. Gunness from the body so that it might not be identified and suspicion fall upon her for the deed." Alternatively, wrote the *Chicago Tribune*, "if experts can prove that the skull found in the shack of 'Nigger Liz' fits that of the torso found, then it may be established that Mrs. Gunness escaped the fire."[17]

The excitement provoked by Harness's find, however, was exceedingly short-lived. Within twenty-four hours, doctors examining the skull declared that it was at least forty years old, while neighbors of Smith's affirmed that it had been in her possession "long before she knew there was such a woman as Belle Gunness." Smith, it seemed, was what the newspapers quickly labeled a "voodoo doctor" who "used the skull to conjure with."

"My mother, she's dead now," said one of Smith's acquaintances, "but she often told me about how she'd see Nigger Liz sitting up at night with the light shining through the holes in the skull and Nigger Liz she'd sit and read to it out of the Bible." Others testified that it was Smith's "custom to write the names of those persons upon whom she wished to work a malicious charm upon the skull and go through her mysterious ceremonies over the pencil marks." There were, in fact, a number of names inscribed in pencil on the cranium of the skull, one of which—"Phil Bungers"—appeared to refer to a long-retired La Porte police officer, Phil Bongerz, "whom [Smith] hated most fiercely."[18]

Unconstrained by anything as banal as verifiable fact, the *Chicago Tribune* proclaimed that Smith—"a known 'voodooist,' a worker of charms and incantations—was a friend of Mrs. Gunness and often visited her":

> Papers dug from the dirt in her shack lead to the belief that she may have been engaged in the same practices as Mrs. Gunness, or may even have been the latter's mentor in crime. There are letters containing proposals of marriage from men she evidently got into communication with through marriage newspapers. There are recipes for weird charms and love philters, and papers on hypnotism and clairvoyance. Then there is the question of how she obtained enough money to acquire almost a whole block of La Porte property, as well as a comfortable bank account. Was the money obtained in the same way as Mrs. Gunness', or did she share in the latter's wealth for some part she played in helping fill the graves on the "death farm"?[19]

The source of the skull would never be determined, though one individual came forward with a colorful, if highly dubious, explanation. His name was C. F. Russell. A Barnumesque character who ran a "traveling show" that toured the army outposts of the western frontier, Russell claimed that, twenty-five years earlier, Elizabeth Smith had been suffering from "a tumor in the abdomen" and had consulted "an old dark mammy," who provided her with a surefire cure: a magical incantation to be recited while rubbing the skull of a murderer:

> Rub-a-dub-dub-dub
> Murderer's skull to rub
> And fair or foul
> Or foul or fair
> You can have it
> As you care.

As it happened, Russell himself was in possession of just such a skull. A former member of the Seventh Calvary under General George Armstrong Custer—or so he claimed—Russell had been "wounded in a fight with Sitting Bull's men and discharged for disability." As a result, he "was not with his regiment" at the Little Big Horn massacre. During one of his subsequent tours out west, he "visited the battlefield where my comrades had been wiped out" and discovered "the skull of a chief," which he kept "as a souvenir."

Somehow, Smith learned that he was in possession of the skull and, figuring "that nobody was more of a murderer than the Indians who killed Custer and all those soldiers," she sought out Russell and begged to borrow the skull. "I'd never heard of her," Russell told his interviewer, "but she promised to return it, and so I gave her the skull."

When he went to retrieve it about a year later, however, she told him that it had been stolen. "I had no reason to believe she wasn't telling the truth," explained Russell, "so I let the relic go."[20]

Though some newspapers persisted in reporting that the skull might yet "provide a key to the famous Gunness case," most agreed that Elizabeth Smith had "taken the secrets of the murder farm to the grave." Wirt Worden expressed particular frustration. "I knew of Ray's friendship with the old woman and tried my best to get her to talk," he told one reporter. "If only I hadn't been away when Liz died, the whole mystery would have been solved by now."[21]

42.

MRS. CARLSON

Throughout the years, anyone connected with the Gunness story was likely to find his name in the newspapers. In January 1915, Joe Maxson—the last of Belle's handymen and survivor of the farmhouse fire—was arrested by La Porte police, charged with beating his wife and threatening to kill her and their children. Eight years later, on October 31, 1923, he died on the job at the Indiana Moulding Company, fatally struck on the head by a piece of falling lumber.[1]

The following year, a nephew of Belle's, twenty-six-year-old Adolph Gunness, was much in the news. An ex-soldier who had been gassed and shell-shocked in the Great War, Adolph was a patient at the Speedway Hospital for disabled veterans in Chicago, where he met and began a romance with a nurse named Anna Furness. They were married on July 20, 1923. Several months later, he absconded with $1,400 of her money and fled to Madison, Wisconsin, where, it turned out, he had another wife, the former Ella Mathewson, to whom he had been wed in 1920. Arrested and brought back to Chicago, he was convicted of bigamy and sentenced to one to five years in the Joliet penitentiary.[2]

In late 1930, a Russian immigrant named John A. Nepsha, who had arrived in La Porte two years after the Gunness affair, purchased the former "murder farm" and began constructing a house where Belle's home once stood. Nepsha, newspapers reported, "laughed at the superstitions which have kept the property vacant the last two decades. He thinks so little of such ghost stories that he plans to make a garden of the graveyard which yielded body after body of the woman's victims." Confirming, in the view of some La Porteans, that the place was accursed, Nepsha became embroiled in a bitter divorce proceeding a few years later and eventually "filed suit, asking Judge Russell W. Smith to partition between himself and his former wife seven tracts of land totaling sixty-four acres and including the Gunness farm."[3]

Sporadic sightings of Mrs. Gunness were reported over the next twenty years. The "Vamp Slayer" (as she was now dubbed in the press) was spotted in Colorado, Canada, Mississippi, New York. When, in 1928, Los Angeles detectives discovered that a string of missing boys had been molested and slain at a chicken ranch in the nearby community of Wineville, speculation ran high that Belle Gunness, recently reported as living in California, was somehow connected to the horrors.[4]

The continuing failure of these supposedly promising leads did nothing to shake Wirt Worden's conviction that Belle was still alive. He was totally convinced by the deathbed confession that Ray Lamphere had supposedly made to Harry Myers and that was published in its entirety for the first time in July 1930.[5] Worden never abandoned the hope that the multimurderess would someday be apprehended. And in the spring of 1931, that hope finally seemed to be fulfilled.

On the night of February 9, 1931, Peter H. Lindstrom, a Chicago meat packer, received a telephone call informing him that his father, August, had died suddenly late that afternoon at his home in the Los Angeles suburb of Lomita. On the face of it, there seemed nothing suspicious about the elder Lindstrom's death. A retired lumber dealer and former resident of Williams, Arizona, Lindstrom was eighty-two years old, a ripe age at any time and especially in a day when the life expectancy for a US male born in the mid-1800s was less than fifty. Still, the news came as a shock to Peter. Just one day earlier, he had received a letter from his father, who declared that he was "feeling fine" and "expected to live to be 100 years old."[6]

August's body was transported to the Stone & Myers funeral home, where the deputy chief coroner signed the death certificate, ascribing the cause to heart failure. The remains were then shipped to Williams, Arizona, where they were interred on February 11.

A few days after the funeral, Peter traveled to Los Angeles to look more closely into the circumstances of his father's death and take care of the old man's estate. His first stop was the home of Mrs. Esther Carlson, the sixty-two-year-old widow who had worked as August's housekeeper for the past fifteen years.

Mrs. Carlson's late husband, Charles, had been close friends with August, their bond having been forged years earlier when Lindstrom was the superintendent of a logging camp near Williams and Carlson the proprietor of a local saloon. One day, after firing a gang of Mexican workers and replacing them with a bunch of his fellow Swedes, Lindstrom, according to newspaper accounts, was attacked by the Mexicans on the main street of Williams. Breaking free, he ran into Carlson's saloon with the Mexicans at his heels. "Carlson, standing behind the bar, drew a revolver and killed three of the Mexicans." From that point on, the two men had been "almost inseparable companions." They were neighbors in Hemet, California, when Carlson died after a prolonged illness in 1925. Soon after, Lindstrom moved to Lomita, taking the widow Carlson with him as his housekeeper.

Now, conferring with Mrs. Carlson, Peter Lindstrom learned that, on the afternoon of February 9, she had telephoned a local physician, Jesse A. Lancaster, and "informed him that Lindstrom was violently ill. Dr. Lancaster instructed her to come to his residence, where he gave her a powder for the patient. About a half hour later, she phoned again and stated Lindstrom was dying. Dr. Lancaster went to the home and found Lindstrom dead."[7]

The story struck Peter as odd. His suspicious were raised to an even higher pitch when he discovered something else: a week before his father's death, Mrs. Carlson had arranged with the Lomita branch of the California Bank to make Lindstrom's $2,000 account a joint account for herself and her employer. No sooner had August been buried than a close friend of hers, forty-two-year-old Mrs. Anna Erickson, appeared at the bank with a letter of authority from Mrs. Carlson and withdrew the entire sum.[8]

Peter immediately shared his suspicions with his brother, Charles, a state highway official in Williams. On Wednesday, February 18, August's body was exhumed and taken by train back to Los Angeles, arriving early Thursday. That same morning, Esther Carlson and Anna Erickson were brought in for questioning by Captain William Bright of the sheriff's homicide detail. Afterward, the two women repaired to Mrs. Carlson's place for coffee.[9]

Early Friday, following the autopsy on August Lindstrom, the county chemist, R. A. Abernathy, reported to Deputy District Attorney George Stahlman that he had found two and a half grains of arsenic in Lindstrom's stomach—"enough to kill forty men"—along with "a quantity of split-pea soup."[10] Warrants for the arrest of Esther Carlson and Anna Erickson on a charge of suspicion of murder were immediately issued. By then, however, Erickson had been stricken with violent convulsions and rushed to General Hospital. When her stomach was pumped and the contents analyzed by Abernathy, the county chemist, he discovered that she had ingested "a strong dose of arsenic." Doctors expressed little hope of her survival.

It was shortly after midnight when Esther Carlson was taken into custody. Under questioning by Captain Bright and Deputy D. A. Stahlman, she remained tight-lipped about Lindstrom. As for Erickson, all she would say was: "She got me into this."[11]

Defying the dire predictions of her physicians, Anna Erickson not only survived but felt strong enough by Sunday, February 22, to point the finger of guilt at Mrs. Carlson. Speaking to Stahlman from her hospital bed, Erickson claimed that, about three weeks before August Lindstrom's death, Carlson had told her that "she couldn't stand him any longer and wished he was out of the way." Lindstrom had also "been talking of giving up his home and going back to Williams, Arizona, to live with his son, Charles"—a move that would have left his longtime housekeeper without a job.[12]

Two days later, on Tuesday the twenty-fourth, Stahlman took another written statement from Anna Erickson, who leveled even more incriminating charges against her former friend. As the deputy D.A. told reporters following this second bedside interview, Erickson claimed "that Mrs. Carlson had often remarked that she was sick of taking care of old men. She said that Mrs. Carlson had made this statement not only in referring to Lindstrom but to her husband, Charles Carlson, and another man, both of whom are reported to have died in Hemet in 1925 within a short time of each other."[13]

The other man, as newspapers soon revealed, was an eighty-year-old Swedish immigrant named Gustav Ahlzen. Soon after arriving in this country, Ahlzen fell ill and was taken into the home of the Carlsons, then living in Hemet, California. A doctor was summoned, who diagnosed the problem as heart disease and prescribed a then-common drug for the condition: strychnine tablets, to be taken one at a time as needed.

A short time later, however, Ahlzen was found dead. "It was generally accepted that he had taken the entire box of tablets at once," the *Los Angeles Times* reported, "either by accident or with suicidal intent." Some months later, Charles Carlson died, reportedly of stomach cancer. Thanks to Anna Erickson's latest accusations, however, Deputy D.A. Stahlman announced plans to travel to Hemet to look into the deaths of both men.[14]

That same Tuesday, beginning at 11:00 a.m., an inquest was held into August Lindstrom's death at the county morgue. Along with the dead man's two sons, witnesses included county chemist Abernathy; undertaker Charles Myers; B. A. Peckham, the bank manager who had turned over the $2,000 to Anna Erickson at Esther Carlson's written order; and Deputy Sheriff Harry Brewster, who testified that he had "found an empty strychnine bottle in a sewing bag belonging to Mrs. Carlson."

Carlson herself refused to testify, on the advice of her attorney. Erickson, who had just been discharged from the hospital, was there, too. After initially declining, she agreed to testify. Aided by another deputy sheriff, Hazel Brown, she tottered to the witness stand, where she "admitted that she had given Lindstrom a piece of apple pie on the morning of his death but declared that she had given another neighbor a piece of the same pie."

The coroner's jury was unpersuaded by her professions of innocence. Though ruling that Lindstrom died from poison "administered with homicidal intent by a person or persons unknown to us," they recommended that "Mrs. Esther Carlson and Mrs. Anna Erickson be held pending further action in this case." That evening, immediately following the all-day inquest, Stahlman issued murder charges against the pair.[15]

The next morning, shortly after their arraignment, Stahlman left for Hemet, where he discovered that Esther Carlson had purchased "a quantity of poison" from a local pharmacist in 1922. Inspecting the medical records of Gustav Ahlzen, he learned that—though the old man's death was officially ascribed to natural causes—"the same symptoms as in arsenic poisoning were present before he died." Stahlman was also told of unverified "reports indicating that strychnine poisoning may have caused Charles Carlson's death." Before returning home that night, the deputy D.A. announced to reporters that the "bodies of both men may be exhumed."[16]

On the first Monday of March, another pharmacist—L. L. Willis of Long Beach, who had been following the case in the newspapers—came forward to report that, a month earlier, Mrs. Carlson and her friend had attempted to purchase arsenic from him. "Suspicious of their motive," he "declined to make the sale." His disclosure prompted police to make another search of Carlson's home, where they found a piece of stationery inscribed with a recipe for ant poison:

> 3 cupfuls of sugar in jar
> 2 cupfuls boiling water on sugar
> Add 2 teaspoonfuls of sodium of arsenite
> Put in little cans

Deputy D.A. Stahlman immediately declared his intention "to show the formula to numerous druggists in Los Angeles, Long Beach, Redondo and other nearby towns in an effort to ascertain whether or not the women used it as a pretext for purchasing sodium of arsenite."[17]

That Friday, the preliminary hearing was held in Municipal Court. By then, Anna Erickson was fully recovered. It was Esther Carlson who appeared desperately weak and unsteady—the result, as newspaper readers were informed, of an advanced case of pulmonary tuberculosis.

County chemist Abernathy was the first to take the stand, testifying that Lindstrom's body was "saturated with arsenic." Lindstrom's son, Charles, described the suspicions that had led him to have his father's body exhumed and returned to California for examination by the coroner. "Mrs. Carlson told me that my father came home ill one day, refused to eat lunch, was violently sick during the afternoon," Charles told the jury. "She said that he refused to allow her to call a doctor. She finally did so about 7:00 p.m., when his condition grew much worse. But he was dead when the physician arrived."

The physician in question, Dr. Jesse A. Lancaster, told of giving Mrs. Carlson medicine for Lindstrom on the day of his death. He confirmed that, when he arrived at Lindstrom's home shortly after 7:00 that evening, the old man was dead.

"Several days afterwards," he continued, "I was called to attend Mrs. Erickson, who was ill. I found her sick and vomiting and administered treatment, removing her to the hospital. A chemical test of the contents of her stomach showed arsenic. She told me she became ill after drinking part of a cup of coffee which Mrs. Carlson gave her."

At the close of the hearing, Judge H. Parker Wood ordered that both women be held for trial on charges of murder. Denying their lawyers' request, he refused to release them on bail. Three weeks later, the defendants pleaded not guilty when brought before Superior Judge William C. Doran, who ordered them to go to trial on April 30 in Department Three of Superior Court.[18]

Before that date arrived, however, something happened that propelled Esther Carlson—up until then a figure of strictly local notoriety—onto the front pages of newspapers around the country and touched off a controversy that would resonate for the next seventy years.

Besides the recipe for ant poison, police had found something else of interest during their second search of Esther Carlson's home: a battered trunk containing an old photograph of two little girls and a boy. Exactly how the photo came to be shown to Mrs. Mary Kruger of Huntington Park is unclear. What is certain is that Mrs. Kruger, a former resident of La Porte who claimed to have known the Gunness family well, positively identified the children as Belle's son, Phillip, and her daughters, Myrtle and Lucy.[19]

Informed of this startling fact, Deputy D.A. Stahlman and his boss, Buron Fitts, immediately let it be known that they were launching an investigation into the possibility that Esther Carlson was the notorious Mrs. Gunness. Throughout the nation, headlines trumpeted the dramatic development: "L.A. Woman May Be Famous Murderess," "Slayer in Los Angeles May Be Belle Gunness," "Mrs. Carlson Called 'Murder Farm' Woman."[20] Newspapers ran side-by-side photographs of the two women: the famous formal portrait of the glowering, moon-faced "Female Bluebeard" and various shots of the scarecrowish Mrs. Carlson, who—allowing for the passage of years and the ravages of disease—might well have been an old, emaciated Belle. In the twenty-three years since the Gunness horrors came to light, sightings of the multimurderess had averaged one a month, according to the *Los Angeles Times*. "Of all those Gunness suspects," the paper reported, "Mrs. Carlson appears to be 'the hottest.'"[21]

Confined to her bed in the prison ward of the County Hospital, Mrs. Carlson—whose condition had taken a marked turn for the worse—denied, with all the vigor she could muster, that she was Belle Gunness. Interviewed by Stahlman, she asserted that her maiden name was Johnson. Born in Sweden in 1867, she immigrated to America in 1892 at the age of twenty-five and for the next seventeen years worked as a housemaid for the Asa V. Cook family of Hartford, Connecticut. In 1907, she married a Hartford man, Charles Hanson. Just nine months later, her new husband drowned in the Agawam River near Springfield, Massachusetts. In 1909, she came to Los Angeles and soon afterward moved to Williams, Arizona, where, in 1911, she met and married Charles Carlson. Following his death in 1925, she moved back to Los Angeles. She insisted that she had never lived in Indiana, or indeed, ever set foot in the state.[22]

Authorities were unconvinced. "Mrs. Gunness dropped from sight in 1908," Stahlman said, "and with Sheriff McDonald of La Porte and the authorities in Connecticut and Massachusetts we shall investigate those seventeen years she says she spent in the employ of the Cook family."

In La Porte—where, as newspapers reported, the populace had been whipped into a state of high excitement by the possibility that the ogress had finally been found[23]—Sheriff Tom McDonald expressed his doubts about the dying woman's denials. "If Mrs. Carlson was not Mrs. Gunness, the case is the strangest one could imagine because so many details dovetail," he declared. "The ages, the nationalities, and many of the racial features, the fact that each woman had three children, two girls and a boy, with ages corresponding and, from pictures, with similar features, these things are responsible for my strong feeling that Mrs. Carlson may be Mrs. Gunness."[24]

Besides sending Stahlman photographs and a detailed physical description of Belle, McDonald promptly contacted two men, former residents of La Porte, currently living in the Los Angeles area: John "Dennis" Daly, a seventy-year-old boilermaker, a neighbor of Belle's between 1902 and 1908 "who had met and talked with her hundreds of times," and John A. Yorkey, a onetime La Porte saloonkeeper who had often seen her around town. On Thursday, May 7, 1931, bearing introductory telegrams from Sheriff McDonald, Daly and Yorkey appeared in Stahlman's office and were immediately taken to view Esther Carlson in the hope that they could settle the question of her true identity.

By then, however, Esther Carlson was dead. She succumbed to her illness on Wednesday, May 6, a week after Anna Erickson went on trial for August Lindstrom's murder.[25] Learning from doctors that Mrs. Carlson had only a few hours to live, Stahlman had rushed to her bedside, accompanied by Anna Erickson's defense attorney, Joseph Marchetti. Hoping that, at the last, Carlson would clear up the mystery of August Lindstrom's death, Stahlman bent close to the semiconscious woman's ear and asked if she had poisoned Lindstrom. A barely audible sound—variously described as a mumble, sigh, and croak—escaped her lips. Stahlman thought it sounded like "Yes."

"You admit you gave him arsenic?" he asked. She answered with the same muffled sound.

Satisfied that Carlson had made a deathbed confession, Stahlman stepped aside and Marchetti took his place.

"Mrs. Carlson," the lawyer asked, "you mean you did *not* kill Mr. Lindstrom, don't you?"

When she emitted the very same sound, Stahlman, letting out a sigh of his own, was forced to concede that the dying woman had no idea what she was being asked.

A few hours later, as newspapers reported, "death sealed her lips forever." Her body was removed to the county morgue to await transport to Hemet for burial.

Driven to the morgue by Stahlman, Dennis Daly and John Yorkey each spent about forty minutes viewing the corpse. Afterward, speaking to reporters, Daly declared that he was positive that the dead woman was Belle Gunness. "I haven't the slightest doubt about it," he said. "She had a peculiar twist to her mouth that was very noticeable. Her eyes are the same color. Her hair, although faded by age, is the same general color and texture. The cheekbones are high, too. The height of the woman is the same. The last time I saw Mrs. Gunness she was rather heavy, but the tuberculosis could have worn the body down through the years."[26]

John Yorkey was equally emphatic in his identification. On Monday, May 11—the same day that Esther Carlson was laid to rest in Valley Cemetery beside her second husband, Charles—Yorkey sent a letter to Wirt Worden. "I am sorry

I did not go and see her while alive," he wrote, "but you can bet all you got that was Belle Gunness of the old murder farm."[27]

43.

THE MYSTERY OF INIQUITY

Wirt Worden died of a heart attack in January 1943 at the age of sixty-nine. For the last eight years of his life, he had been a judge in the La Porte Circuit Court and had played a small part in the notorious case of D. C. Stephenson, former grand dragon of the Indiana branch of the Ku Klux Klan, whose conviction for the murder of a young woman, Madge Oberholtzer, dealt a death blow to the Klan's growing political influence in the state. In recalling Worden's accomplishments, however, newspaper obituaries gave greatest prominence to his role in the Gunness case and his successful defense of Ray Lamphere on the murder charge.[1]

Worden never abandoned his belief that Belle had escaped, though whether he accepted John Yorkey's confident assertion is unknown. In any event, another eighty years would pass before proof emerged that Yorkey was wrong. In 2014, Knut Erik Jensen, a native of Selbu, Norway—Belle's birthplace—embarked on a research mission to settle the question of Esther Carlson's true identity. After consulting census books, cemetery records, city directories, and various other documents, he definitively established that the story the dying Carlson told about her background was true in every detail. She was not Belle Gunness.[2]

———— ⟩⟨⦾⟩⟨ ————

In my previous book, *Man-Eater*—about the nineteenth-century Colorado cannibal and convicted mass murderer Alfred Packer, whose guilt or innocence remains a matter of heated dispute—I referred to the innate human need for what psychologist Arie Kruglanski was the first to label "cognitive closure," which he defined as "the individual's need for a firm answer to a question and aversion to ambiguity."[3] The sheer popularity of detective stories, a genre first brought to life in Edgar Allen Poe's "The Murders in the Rue Morgue," is testimony to the power of this basic psychological hunger, our deep-seated longing to arrive at—or be provided with—tidy solutions to vexing puzzles.

In contrast, of course, to the seemingly impossible riddles neatly unraveled by the ratiocinative genius of a C. Auguste Dupin or a Sherlock Holmes or a Hercule Poirot, real life often presents us with criminal mysteries that stubbornly, even maddeningly, resist solution. Foremost among these is the identity of Jack the Ripper, and the regular appearance of books promising the long-sought revelation suggests just how difficult it is for us to tolerate the unknowable. Other cases shrouded in uncertainty that continue to elicit purported solutions include those of Lizzie Borden, the Lindbergh baby kidnapping, and most recently, the JonBenét Ramsey murder.

Though less well known nowadays than these others, the Gunness case continues to attract the fascinated attention of crime buffs. In 2008, for example, a pair of forensic anthropologists, after exhuming the remains from Chicago's Forest Home Cemetery, employed DNA analysis in an attempt to determine if the headless body was that of Mrs. Gunness. The results were "inconclusive."[4] When I embarked on this project, I fantasized that my own research might produce a solution of the century-old mystery. At one point, I believed I had stumbled on an exciting lead: a newspaper clipping revealing that Gunness had sometimes placed her matrimonial advertisements under the pseudonym "Belle Hinckley."[5] Further digging led to the discovery that a woman by that name was residing in Wisconsin in 1915. I thought I might be on to something, but my excited hopes were quickly dashed when it turned out that there was absolutely no connection between the two Belles.

My next hope was that, by the time I finished writing my book, I would arrive at some relatively firm conclusion about precisely what happened on the night of the Gunness fire. To my chagrin, I must now confess to failure even on that far more modest score. After several years of being deeply immersed in every detail of the Gunness case, I am unable to venture even an informed opinion on the matter.

To be sure, Lamphere's reported confession to the Reverend Schell strikes me as highly implausible. Beyond that, however, various possibilities seem equally credible to me: that Belle staged her own death and escaped, that she died in a fire deliberately set by Ray, or that she immolated herself and her children in a final act of suicidal desperation. An editorial published in the *Cleveland Plain Dealer* following the horrific discoveries on the murder farm has proved to be prescient: "The La Porte case may always remain one of the most puzzling things in the annals of crime."[6] I trust that, at the very least, my reconstruction of the crime will allow readers to arrive at their own opinions about the mystery of Belle Gunness's ultimate fate.

Of course, there is a deeper mystery at work here. What kind of woman— what kind of person—could commit the kind of atrocities perpetrated by Belle Gunness? To be sure, other female psychopaths have killed at least as many victims. Just seven years before the Gunness horrors came to light, "Jolly" Jane Toppan, a respected and popular New England nurse, confessed to thirty-one murders, making her America's most prolific serial murderer before John Wayne Gacy. Earlier women poisoners like Lydia Sherman and Sarah Jane Robinson— "American Borgias," as they were called—subjected husbands, siblings, and their own children to slow, agonizing deaths by arsenic.

What distinguished Belle from her homicidal predecessors, however— indeed what makes her a unique figure in the annals of female criminality, at least in our nation—is the butchery she performed on her victims, the desecration of their corpses, hacked to pieces and dumped in the muck of her hog lot. Reducing other people to subhuman status is the very essence of evil, and students of her crimes have struggled to account for its origins in Belle: the vicious assault she ostensibly suffered in adolescence that ignited her hatred of men; the pathological greed that transformed her into a "Bluebeard with a profit motive."[7] These and other theories clearly cannot begin to explain evil on the scale of the Gunness horrors, confronting us with a mystery far more profound than the question of whether she survived the fire: what the Bible calls "the mystery of iniquity."

I leave the last words on the subject to the editor of the *La Porte Weekly Herald*, who wrote them on the day after the Lamphere verdict: "The mystery that hangs about the murderous operations of Mrs. Gunness is likely to never be fully dispelled . . . in conception and brutality of execution, the crimes of Mrs. Gunness are unparalleled. She is entitled to be known to future generations as the arch fiend of the twentieth century."[8]

NOTES

PROLOGUE

1. Charles Perrault, *The Complete Fairy Tales in Verse and Prose* (Mineola, NY: Dover, 2002), p. 78.

2. Francis Parkman, *La Salle and the Discovery of the Great West* (Boston: Little, Brown, and Company, 1908), pp. 211–14.

3. Jasper Packard, History of La Porte County, Indiana, and Its Townships, Towns and Cities (La Porte, IN: S. E. Taylor & Company, 1870), p. 36.

4. Ibid., p. 37.

5. Charles C. Chapman, *History of La Porte County, Indiana; Together with Sketches of Its Cities, Villages, and Townships, Educational, Religious, Civil, Military, and Political History; Portraits of Prominent Persons and Biographies of Representative Citizens* (Chicago: Chas. C. Chapman & Co., 1880), p. 616.

6. Rev. E. D. Daniels, *A Twentieth Century History and Biographical Record of La Porte County, Indiana* (Chicago: The Lewis Publishing Company, 1904), p. 126.

7. Packard, pp. 443–58.

8. Daniels, p. 132.

9. Daniels, pp. 237, 239, 241, 242, 258, and 263.

10. Capsule biographies of these and other prominent La Porteans can be found in a bound volume at the La Porte County Historical Society.

11. Packard, pp. 47 and 72.

12. Chapman, pp. 514–15.

13. Packard, p. 73.

14. Chapman, p. 517.

15. *Fort Wayne Daily News*, December 1, 1902, pp. 1 and 2, and December 4, 1902, p. 1.

16. *Fort Wayne Daily News*, December 18, 1902, p. 2.

17. *La Porte Weekly Herald*, May 14, 1908, p. 2.

CHAPTER ONE

1. Donald L. Miller, *City of the Century: The Epic of Chicago and the Making of America* (New York: Simon & Schuster, 1996), p. 141.

2. Theodore Dreiser, *Newspaper Days* (New York: Horace Liveright, 1922), p. 210.

3. Bessie Louise Pierce, *A History of Chicago, Volume III: The Rise of a Modern City, 1871–1893* (New York: Alfred A. Knopf, 1957), p. 22.

4. Harold M. Mayer and Richard C. Wade, *Chicago: Growth of a Metropolis* (Chicago: University of Chicago Press, 1969), p. 22.

5. See Theodore C. Blegen, *Norwegian Migration to America: The American Transition* (Northfield, MN: The Norwegian-American Historical Association, 1940), p. 481, and Odd S. Lovoll, *A Century of Urban Life: The Norwegians in Chicago before 1930* (Champaign, IL: University of Illinois Press, 1988), pp. 15 and 77.

6. Lovoll, p. 65.

7. A. T. Andreas, *History of Chicago. From the Earliest Period to the Present Time. In Three Volumes. Volume II—From 1857 until the Fire of 1871* (Chicago: The A. T. Andreas Company, 1886), p. 444. As it happened, the coroner's jury—though concluding that "some wicked boys" were "accessory to the death" of little Knud—found no definitive evidence that the victim had been "purposely drowned" for his refusal to steal. The death was ruled accidental, and the plan for a monument abandoned.

8. See A. E. Strand, *A History of the Norwegians of Illinois: A Concise Record of the Struggles and Achievements of the Early Settlers together with a Narrative of what is now being done by the Norwegian-Americans of Illinois in the Development of Their Adopted Country* (Chicago: John Anderson Publishing Company, 1905), p. 217; Blegen, p. 434; and Lovoll, pp. 20–21, 54, and 93.

9. Lovoll, p. 82; Strand, p. 245.

10. Jean Skogerboe Hansen, "*Skandinaven* and the John Anderson Publishing Company," *Norwegian-American Studies*, Vol. 28 (1979), pp. 35–68.

11. Strand, p. 228 and 231–33; Lovoll, pp. 5, 130–31, 184, and 186.

12. Strand, p. 180. At the time, Oslo was still known as Christiana.

13. Irving Cutler, *Chicago: Metropolis of the Mid-Continent* (Carbondale, IL: Southern Illinois University Press, 2006), p. 74; Ann Durkin Keating, *Chicago Neighborhoods and Suburbs: A Historical Guide* (Chicago: University of Chicago Press, 2008), p. 174.

14. Pierce, p. 31. To be more precise, the percentage of arrests for Norwegians was 1.09 in 1880 and 1.26 in 1890. By way of comparison, the percentages for Germans were 11.84 in 1880 and 11.07 in 1890; for the Irish, 17.62 in 1880 and 10.33 in 1890.

15. According to genealogical records, Paul and Berit's children were Marit Paulsdatter Størset, Peder Moen, Ole Paulsen, Olina Paulsdatter Størset (later Nellie Larson), Marit Leangvollen, Brynhild Paulsdatter Størset (the future Belle Gunness), and "one other," name unknown. See http://www.geni.com/people /Belle-Gunness/6000000010140315276.

16. Kjell Haarstad, letter to Janet Langlois, March 29, 1976, on file at the La Porte County Historical Society. See also Janet Langlois, *Belle Gunness: The Lady Bluebeard* (Bloomington, IN: Indiana University Press, 1985), pp. 2–4.

17. M. S. Emery, *Norway Through the Stereoscope: A Journey Through the Land of the Vikings* (New York: Underwood and Underwood, 1907), pp. 197–98.

18. See Haarstad letter; Langlois, p. 2.

19. See Haarstad letter.

20. Langlois, p. 3; Emery, p. 97.

21. See Haarstad letter. Quoted in Langlois, p. 2.

22. See, for example, Sylvia Perrini, *She Devils of the USA: Women Serial Killers* (Goldmineguides.com, 2013), p. 58, and Ilene Ingbritson Wilson, *Murder in My Family* (Bloomington, IN: Trafford Publishing, 2004), p. 9.

23. Langlois, p. 3.

CHAPTER TWO

1. Highly detailed information on the transatlantic crossing is available on the website *Norway-Heritage: Hands Across the Sea*, www.norwayheritage.com.

2. Ibid.; Odd S. Lovoll, "'For People Who Are Not in a Hurry': The Danish Thingvalla Line and the Transportation of Scandinavian Emigrants," *Journal of American Ethnic History*, Vol. 13, No. 1 (Fall 1993), pp. 48–67.

3. All legal documents from this period show her name as Bella, including her marriage license to Mads Sorenson and the 1898 lawsuit she and Mads filed against the Yukon Mining & Trading Co. (see below, Note 23). Also see the article "Mrs. Gunness Changed Name," *Chicago Daily Tribune*, May 17, 1908, p. 5.

4. Odd S. Lovoll, *A Century of Urban Life: The Norwegians in Chicago before 1930* (Champaign, IL: University of Illinois Press, 1988), p. 155.

5. Theodore Dreiser, *Sister Carrie* (New York: Bantam Books, 1958), pp. 17–18.

6. *Chicago Examiner*, May 7, 1908, p. 2.

7. *Chicago Tribune*, May 7, 1908, p. 1.

8. Most sources say Mads worked as a department store watchman (or detective). Others, however, describe him as a floor manager. See, for example, *Indianapolis News*, May 12, 1908, p. 8.

9. Marriage License of Anthon [*sic*] Sorenson and Bella Peterson, Illinois Regional Archives Depository, Northeastern Illinois University, Chicago. For unexplained reasons, the certificate shows Bella's age as twenty-nine and Mads's age as thirty-four. For the Rev. Torgersen's obituary, see "Cupid's Noted Aid Dead," *Chicago Daily Tribune*, November 12, 1905, p. 8.

10. Langlois, p. 4.

11. *La Porte Argus-Bulletin*, May 7, 1908, p. 1.

12. Ibid.

13. *Chicago Daily Journal*, May 8, 1908, p. 1.

14. Langlois, p. 77.

15. *Chicago Examiner*, May 6, 1908, p. 2.

16. *Chicago Tribune*, May 7, 1908, p. 2.

17. Ibid.

18. Ann Jones, *Women Who Kill* (New York: Fawcett Crest, 1980), p. 137; *La Porte Argus-Bulletin*, May 7, 1908, p. 1. Previous sources say that the Sorensons bought the Alma Street property in 1896. Records show, however, that it was purchased in September 1895. Moreover, Bella is listed as sole owner of the property. See tract book, vol. 106A, p. 196, Cook County Recorder of Deeds, Chicago, Illinois.

19. Caroline was born in March 1896; Myrtle on February 6, 1897; Axel in January 1898; and Lucy on Christmas Day, 1898.

20. *La Porte Argus-Bulletin*, May 6, 1908, p. 2.

21. By contrast, the US infant mortality rate in 2015 was fewer than six deaths for every one thousand live births. The causes of death for Caroline and Axel can be found in the official Records of Interments at the Forest Home Cemetery, Chicago, Illinois.

22. "*Sorenson et al. vs. Yukon Mining & Trading Company*, Bill in Chancery, Filed June 3, 1898, Circuit Court of Cook County," on file at the Circuit Court Archives, Cook County, Chicago, Illinois.

23. "*Bella Sorenson et al. vs. Yukon Mining & Trading Company et al.*, Notice, Motion, and Affidavits of Hogenson, Anderson, & Rosenberg, Filed June 16, 1898, in Circuit Court, Cook County," on file at the Circuit Court Archives, Cook County, Chicago, Illinois.

24. "*Bella Sorenson et al. vs. Yukon Mining & Trading Company et al.*, Copy of Decree," on file at the Circuit Court Archives, Cook County, Chicago, Illinois.

25. *Chicago Tribune*, April 11, 1900, p. 1.

26. *Chicago Daily Journal*, May 8, 1908, p. 2; *Chicago Tribune*, May 8, 1908, p. 2; Record of Interments, August 1900, Forest Home Cemetery, Chicago, Illinois.

27. *Chicago Inter Ocean*, May 7, 1908, p. 3.

28. *La Porte Argus-Bulletin*, May 7, 1908, p. 1.

CHAPTER THREE

1. Langlois, pp. 34–36.

2. *Chicago Daily News*, May 9, 1908, p. 1.

3. *Indianapolis News*, May 9, 1908, p. 4; Sylvia Shepherd, *The Mistress of Murder Hill: The Serial Killings of Belle Gunness* (Bloomington, IN: 1stBooks Library, 2001), p. 17.

4. Langlois, pp. 37–40.

5. Ibid., p. 37.

6. Lillian de la Torre, *The Truth About Belle Gunness* (New York: Fawcett/Gold Medal Books, 1955), p. 13.

7. See *Duluth News-Tribune*, May 13, 1908, p. 2, and *Chicago Daily Journal*, May 9, 1908, p. 1.

8. "Indiana's Murder Farm," *Harper's Weekly*, Vol. LII, No. 268 (May 30, 1908), p. 23.

9. Records of Interments, August 1902, Forest Home Cemetery, Chicago, Illinois.

10. Albert Nicholson's recollections were transcribed on July 28, 1951. The typescript is filed in the archives of the La Porte County Historical Society, as is the full transcript of the coroner's inquest held on December 17, 1902, which contains the testimony of both Swan Nicholson and Jennie Gunness. See also de la Torre, pp. 41–45.

11. *Fort Wayne Daily News*, December 1, 1902, pp. 1 and 2, and December 4, 1902, p. 1. Also see *La Porte Argus-Bulletin*, December 16, 1902, p. 1, and December 17, 1902, p. 1.

12. Bowell's postmortem report is contained in the transcript of the coroner's inquest, December 17, 1902, filed in the archives of the La Porte County Historical Society.

13. *La Porte Argus-Bulletin*, December 19, 1902, p. 1.

14. Langlois, p. 108.

15. de la Torre, p. 45.

16. Ibid.

17. Coroner's inquest, archives of the La Porte County Historical Society.

18. de la Torre, p. 45.

CHAPTER FOUR

1. Langlois, pp. 56–57.

2. *Duluth News-Tribune*, May 13, 1908, p. 2.

3. Langlois, pp. 45–48.

4. Ibid., pp. 49–50.

5. Langlois, p. 58.

6. Ibid., pp. 60, 61–62, and 66–67. See also Stuart Holbrook, *Murder Out Yonder: An Informal Study of Certain Classic Crimes in Back-Country America* (New York: Macmillan, 1941), p. 127.

7. Shepherd, p. 69.

8. *Decatur Herald,* May 23, 1908, p. 1.

9. Paula K. Hinton, "'Come Prepared to Stay Forever': The Tale of a Murderess in Turn-of-the-Century America," diss. (Miami University, Oxford, Ohio, 2001), p. 41.

10. Ibid.

11. *"Coroner's Inquisition, Unidentified Person, Gunness Farm, Henry Gurholt?, Deposition of Witness Martin Gurholt, Exhibit 'B,'"* on file in the archives of the La Porte Historical Society Museum.

12. "Coroner's Inquisition, Deposition of Witnesses, Exhibit 'C,' Chris Christofferson, May 26, 1908," on file in the archives of the La Porte Historical Society Museum.

CHAPTER FIVE

1. A facsimile of one of these ads is on display in the Belle Gunness exhibit at the La Porte County Historical Society.

2. *La Porte Weekly Herald*, May 14, 1908, p. 8; Shepherd, p. 64; Hinton, p. 34.

3. Hinton, p. 46.

4. *Richmond Times Dispatch*, June 10, 1908, p. 1.

5. Hinton, p. 46; de la Torre, p. 55.

6. *La Porte Argus-Bulletin*, May 8, 1908, p. 1.

7. *Grand Forks Evening Times*, May 15, 1908, p. 3. Moe's last name is sometimes reported as "Moo."

8. de la Torre, p. 16; *New York Tribune*, May 10, 1908, p. 1; Shepherd, p. 53.

9. *Otago Daily Times*, November 30, 1908, p. 5; Hinton, p. 31; *La Porte Argus-Bulletin*, May 11, 1908, p. 1.

10. Shepherd, p. 52.

11. *La Porte Weekly Herald*, May 14, 1908, p. 8; Langlois, pp. 77–78; Shepherd, pp. 51–52; Anon., *The Mrs. Gunness Mystery!* (Chicago: Thompson & Thomas, 1908), pp. 66–67.

CHAPTER SIX

1. de la Torre, p. 17.

2. *La Porte Argus-Bulletin*, May 11, 1908, p. 1; de la Torre, p. 18.

3. *New York Sun*, May 10, 1908, p. 2; *La Porte Argus-Bulletin*, May 14, 1908.

4. de la Torre, p. 18; Anon., *The Mrs. Gunness Mystery!*, pp. 84–85; Troy Taylor, *"Come Prepared to Stay Forever": The Madness of Belle Gunness*. Hell Hath No Fury, Book 5 (Decatur, IL: Whitechapel Press, 2013).

5. de la Torre, p. 19.

6. *La Porte Argus-Bulletin*, May 18, 1908, p. 1.

7. *Marion Daily Mirror*, May 19, 1908, p. 2; *Washington Herald*, May 10, 1908, p. 3.

CHAPTER SEVEN

1. All contemporary newspaper articles on the case, as well as virtually all succeeding accounts, spell the name "Helgelein." However, on the Find-a-Grave website, there is a photograph of Andrew's gravestone in which his last name is spelled "Helgelien." There is a note on the site stating: "The name Helgelien as spelled on the gravestone is confirmed by family members to be correct. An alternate spelling (e.g., Helgelein) seen elsewhere is not correct."

2. Asle Helgelien, Andrew's brother, said that he had found eighty letters from Belle among his brother's belongings. During Ray Lamphere's trial, however, newspapers reported that the prosecution was in possession of seventy-five letters from Belle to Andrew. See *La Porte Argus-Bulletin*, May 18, 1908, p. 1, and November 19, 1908, p. 3.

3. Ted Hartzell, "Belle Gunness' Poison Pen," *American History*, Vol. 43, No. 2 (June 2008), p. 50.

4. *Chicago Evening American*, November 18, 1908, p. 3.

5. *Indianapolis Star*, May 7, 1908, p. 3; *Chicago Daily Journal*, May 8, 1908, p. 1. Some accounts say that Helgelien robbed and torched the post office not in Red Wing but in Norway, Minnesota.

6. My thanks to Katherine Ramsland for providing me with typed transcripts of Belle's surviving letters to Helgelien.

7. Hartzell, p. 53.

CHAPTER EIGHT

1. de la Torre, p. 19.

2. Shepherd, p. 30.

3. de la Torre, p. 104.

4. Shepherd, p. 28; *Altoona Morning Tribune*, November 18, 1908, p. 1; *La Porte Argus-Bulletin*, May 14, 1908, p. 1.

5. *La Porte Weekly Herald*, May 14, 1908, p. 1.

CHAPTER NINE

1. *La Porte Argus-Bulletin*, November 17, 1908, p.1.

2. *Chicago Tribune*, May 8, 1908, p. 1. Some accounts spell her last name "Cone."

3. *La Porte Argus-Bulletin*, November 17, 1908, p.1.

4. Compare, for example, *La Porte Argus-Bulletin*, May 9, 1908, p. 1, and *La Porte Weekly Herald*, November 26, 1908, p. 1.

5. *La Porte Argus-Bulletin*, April 29, 1908, p. 1, May 9, 1908, p. 1, and November 19, 1908, p. 1.

6. Transcripts of this and other letters between Asle Helgelien and Belle Gunness were provided to me by Dr. Katherine Ramsland.

7. *La Porte Argus-Bulletin*, May 9, 1908, p. 1; de la Torre, p. 107. Belle's original "Statement Alleging Insanity" is on file at the La Porte County Historical Society.

8. Josh Chaney, "Story About Belle Gunness," unpublished manuscript on file at the La Porte County Historical Society Museum; Hinton, p. 89; *La Porte Argus-Bulletin*, May 9, 1908, p. 1.

9. de la Torre, p. 21; *La Porte Argus-Bulletin*, May 9, 1908, p. 1.

10. de la Torre, p. 107.

11. *La Porte Argus-Bulletin*, May 13, 1908, p. 8.

CHAPTER TEN

1. *La Porte Weekly Herald*, May 14, 1908, p. 16. The *La Porte Argus-Bulletin* of May 8, 1908, reports the teacher's name as Jennie Garwood.

2. *Chicago Inter Ocean*, April 30, 1908, p. 12; de la Torre, p. 21. A transcript of Belle's will is in the archives of the La Porte Historical Society Museum.

3. Chaney, p. 27.

4. *La Porte Weekly Herald*, May 14, 1908, p. 15.

5. *La Porte Argus-Bulletin*, November 18, 1908, p. 1; de la Torre, p. 109.

6. *La Porte Argus-Bulletin*, November 18, 1908, p. 1; de la Torre, p. 111.

CHAPTER ELEVEN

1. *La Porte Argus-Bulletin*, May 4, 1908, p. 1, and November 18, 1908, p. 1; de la Torre, pp. 7 and 112; "Coroner's Inquisition, Deposition of Witness Joseph O. Maxson, April 29, 1908," on file in the archives of the La Porte Historical Society Museum.

2. "Coroner's Inquisition, Deposition of Witness William Clifford, April 29, 1908," on file in the archives of the La Porte Historical Society Museum.

3. "Coroner's Inquisition, Deposition of Witness William Humphrey, April 29, 1908," on file in the archives of the La Porte Historical Society Museum.

4. "Coroner's Inquisition, Deposition of Witness Daniel Marion Hutson, April 29, 1908," on file in the archives of the La Porte Historical Society Museum.

5. de la Torre, p. 10.

6. "Coroner's Inquisition, Deposition of Witness Joseph O. Maxson, April 29, 1908"; de la Torre, pp. 3 and 10.

7. *La Porte Argus-Bulletin*, April 28, 1908, p. 1.

8. de la Torre, p. 10; *La Porte Argus-Bulletin*, April 28, 1908, p. 1.

9. *La Porte Argus-Bulletin*, April 28, 1908, p. 1.

CHAPTER TWELVE

1. Thomas Dreier, "The School That Teaches Boys How to Live," *The Business Philosopher*, Vol. VI, No. 2 (February 1910), p. 75.

2. Carter H. Manny, "Gone Are the Days," unpublished memoir on file at La Porte Historical Society Museum; *La Porte Weekly Herald*, April 30, 1908, p. 1.

3. *La Porte Weekly Herald*, April 30 1908, p. 1.

4. "Coroner's Inquisition, Deposition of Witness William Humphrey, April 29, 1908."

5. *La Porte Argus-Bulletin*, April 28, 1908, p. 1.

6. *La Porte Weekly Herald*, April 30, 1908, p. 1.

7. *La Porte Argus-Bulletin*, April 29, 1908, p. 1; *Indianapolis Star*, April 30, 1908, p. 4.

CHAPTER THIRTEEN

1. *La Porte Argus-Bulletin*, November 20, 1908, p. 1; de la Torre, pp. 125–26.

2. *Chicago Daily Tribune*, April 30, 1908, p. 5; *La Porte Argus-Bulletin*, November 20, 1908, p. 1; de la Torre, p. 126.

3. Leonard J. Moore, *Citizen Klansmen: The Ku Klux Klan in Indiana, 1921–1928* (Chapel Hill: University of North Carolina Press, 1991), p. 56.

4. *Indianapolis Star*, March 19, 1916, p. 4.

5. de la Torre, p. 23; Langlois, pp. 41–42.

6. *La Porte Argus-Bulletin*, April 30, 1908, p. 1.

7. *La Porte Argus-Bulletin*, April 30, 1908, p. 1; *Fort Wayne News*, April 29, 1908, p. 1; *Cleveland Plain Dealer*, April 29, 1908, p. 1.

8. *La Porte Argus-Bulletin*, April 30, 1908, p. 1.

9. "Coroner's Inquisition, Deposition of Witness Daniel Marion Hutson, April 29, 1908."

10. *La Porte Argus-Bulletin*, April 30, 1908, p. 1; *La Porte Weekly Herald*, May 7, 1908, p. 1.

11. *Chicago Daily Tribune*, May 1, 1908, p. 5; *La Porte Argus-Bulletin*, May 1, 1908, p. 1.

CHAPTER FOURTEEN

1. *La Porte Weekly Herald*, May 7, 1908, p. 14.

2. Ibid.

3. "Coroner's Inquisition, Deposition of Witness Dr. J. Lucius Gray, May 12, 1908," on file in the archives of the La Porte Historical Society Museum.

4. *La Porte Argus-Bulletin*, May 1, 1908, p. 1.

5. *Chicago Inter Ocean*, May 2, 1908, p. 3.

6. *La Porte Argus-Bulletin*, May 1, 1908, p. 1.

7. *La Porte Argus-Bulletin*, May 1, 1908, p. 1; *Chicago Inter Ocean*, May 2, 1908, p. 3.

8. Shepherd, pp. 9 and 10; Hinton, p. 28.

CHAPTER FIFTEEN

1. "Coroner's Inquisition, Deposition of Witness Asle K. Helgelein, May 5, 1908," on file in the archives of the La Porte Historical Society Museum; Hinton, p. 29; Shepherd, pp. 11–12.

2. "Coroner's Inquisition, Exhibit 'A,' May 5, 1908."

3. de la Torre, p. 32.

4. Ibid.

5. "Coroner's Inquisition, Deposition of Witness Asle K. Helgelein, May 5, 1908."

6. "Coroner's Inquisition, Exhibit 'B,' May 18, 1908."

7. *Brooklyn Daily Eagle*, May 6, 1908, p. 1; de la Torre, p. 31.

CHAPTER SIXTEEN

1. See Charles K. Mavity, *The Bellville* [sic] *Tragedy: Story of the Trial and Conviction of Rev. W. E. Hinshaw for the Murder of His Wife* (Indianapolis: Sentil Print Co., 1895).

2. Historian Paula Hinton notes that "newspapers as far away as Cuba and Germany carried the story. In fact, the *Daily Herald* had a Cuban newspaper with the story on display in its window." See Hinton, p. 58.

3. de la Torre, pp. 35–36.

4. *Chicago Inter Ocean,* May 5, 1908, pp. 1 and 3.

5. *Chicago Tribune*, May 6, 1908, p. 3; *Chicago American*, May 6, 1908, p. 30; de la Torre, pp. 32–33.

6. *New York Times*, May 8, 1908, p. 2; *La Porte Weekly Herald*, May 14, 1908, p. 1.

CHAPTER SEVENTEEN

1. *Chicago Inter Ocean*, May 7, 1908, p. 3.

2. "Coroner's Inquisition, Unidentified Adult, Gunness Farm, May 6, 1908, 'Exhibit A,'" on file in the archives of the La Porte Historical Society Museum; *Chicago Daily News,* May 6, 1908, p. 1.

3. *Chicago Inter Ocean*, May 7, 1908, p. 3.

4. *Chicago Tribune*, May 7, 1908, p. 2.

5. *Chicago Daily American*, May 7, 1908, p. 1; *Cleveland Plain Dealer*, May 8, 1908, p. 1; *San Francisco Call*, May 12, 1908, p. 1; *Pittsburgh Press*, May 7, 1908, p. 1; *Chicago Evening American*, May 8, 1908, p. 3.

6. *Chicago Examiner*, May 7, 1908, p. 1.

7. *Chicago Daily Journal*, May 7, 1908, p. 1.

8. *Chicago Inter Ocean*, May 7, 1908, p. 1; Chicago *Daily American*, May 7, 1908, p. 2.

9. *La Porte Argus-Bulletin*, May 9, 1908, p. 1.

10. *Chicago Daily News*, May 7, 1908, p. 1.

11. New York Times, May 6, 1908, p. 1.

12. *Chicago Examiner*, May 7, 1908, p. 1.

13. *Chicago Daily Journal*, May 6, 1908, p. 3; *Chicago Examiner*, May 7, 1908, p. 2.

14. *Chicago Daily News*, May 7, 1908, p. 1.

15. Arthur Alden Guild, *Baby Farms in Chicago: An Investigation Made for the Juvenile Protection Agency* (Chicago: The Juvenile Protection Agency, 1917).

16. Alison Rattle and Allison Vale, *The Woman Who Murdered Babies for Money: The Story of Amelia Dyer* (London: André Deutsch, 2011).

17. *Chicago Inter Ocean*, May 8, 1908, p. 1.

18. *Chicago Examiner*, May 7, 1908, p. 2.

CHAPTER EIGHTEEN

1. *Chicago American*, May 7, 1908, p. 1.

2. *Chicago Tribune*, May 8, 1908, p. 2; *Los Angeles Herald*, May 8, 1908, p. 1.

3. *Chicago Tribune*, May 8, 1908, p. 2.

4. Shepherd, p. 39.

5. Ibid, p. 40; *La Porte Argus-Bulletin*, May 6, 1908, p. 1; *Chicago Tribune*, May 7, 1908, p. 1.

6. *Chicago Tribune*, May 7, 1908, p. 1. A friend of the Budsberg family, a hardware dealer named Edwin Chapin, accompanied Mathias and Oscar on the trip.

7. de la Torre, p. 32.

8. *La Porte Argus-Bulletin*, May 7, 1908, p. 1.

9. *New York Times*, May 8, 1908, p. 1.

10. Ibid.; *La Porte Weekly Herald*, May 14, 1908, p. 1.

11. *Chicago Evening American*, May 8, 1908, p. 1.

12. *Chicago Daily Journal*, May 7, 1908, p. 1; *Chicago Tribune*, May 8, 1908, p. 5.

13. *Chicago Tribune*, May 8, 1908, p. 5.

14. *Los Angeles Herald*, May 8, 1908, p. 1.

15. *Pittsburgh Press*, May 7, 1908, p. 1.

16. *Los Angeles Herald*, May 8, 1908, p. 1.

CHAPTER NINETEEN

1. *Chicago Tribune*, May 8, 1908, p. 1.

2. See *The Federal Reporter: Cases Argued and Determined in the Circuit Court of Appeals and Circuit and District Courts of the United States,* Vol. 177 (St. Paul, MN: West Publishing Co., 1910), pp. 679–84.

3. Pamela Ilyse Epstein, *Selling Love: The Commercialization of Intimacy in America 1860s–1900s* (diss., New Brunswick Rutgers, The State University of New Jersey, 2010), pp. 127–28.

4. Clifton R. Wooldridge, *Twenty Years a Detective in the Wickedest City in the World* (Chicago, IL: Chicago Publishing Co., 1908), p. 119.

5. *Chicago Tribune*, May 9, 1908, p. 1.

6. Wooldridge, p. 132.

CHAPTER TWENTY

1. *Chicago Inter Ocean*, May 8, 1908, pp. 1 and 2; *Chicago Daily Journal*, May 9, 1908, pp. 1 and 3.

2. *Chicago Inter Ocean*, May 9, 1908, p. 1.

3. *Chicago Daily News*, May 8, 1908, p. 1.

4. Ibid.; *La Porte Argus-Bulletin*, May 8, 1908, p. 1.

5. *Los Angeles Herald*, May 10, 1908, p. 1; *Chicago Tribune*, May 10, 1908, p. 1.

6. *Washington Herald*, May 9, 1908, p. 3.

7. *Washington Herald*, May 13, 1908, p. 3.

8. *Washington Herald*, June 6, 1908, p. 3.

9. *Washington Herald*, May 22, 1908, p. 3.

10. *La Porte Argus-Bulletin*, May 11, 1908, p. 2.

11. *Paducah Evening Sun*, May 15, 1908, p. 5; *Washington Times*, May 9, 1908, p. 2; *Salt Lake Herald*, May 12, 1908, p. 3; *Washington Herald*, May 22, 1908, p. 3; Hinton, pp. 47–52.

12. Hinton, p. 35; "Coroner's Inquisition, Unidentified Person, Gunness Farm, Henry Gurholt?, Deposition of Witness Martin Gurholt, Exhibit 'B.'"

13. *New York Sun*, May 12, 1908, p. 5; Hinton, p. 43.

14. Hinton, p. 36.

15. *Richmond Times-Dispatch*, June 10, 1908, p. 1.

16. *Chicago Inter Ocean*, May 8, 1908, p. 2.

17. *La Porte Argus-Bulletin*, May 9, 1908, p. 3.

18. *La Porte Argus-Bulletin*, May 20, 1908, p. 1.

19. *La Porte Argus-Bulletin*, May 16, 1908, p. 4.

20. *La Porte Argus-Bulletin*, May 11, 1908, p. 1; *Salt Lake Herald*, May 12, 1908, p. 1.

21. *Chicago Tribune*, May 10, 1908, p. 3.

22. Ibid.

23. *Chicago Inter Ocean*, May 8, 1908, pp. 1 and 2.

CHAPTER TWENTY-ONE

1. *La Porte Argus-Bulletin*, May 9, 1908; *Chicago Tribune*, May 7, 1908, p. 3

2. See, for example, *Grand Forks Daily Herald*, May 19, 1908, p. 1.

3. *La Porte Argus-Bulletin*, May 9, 1908, p. 5, and May 11, 1908, p. 3.

4. *Chicago Examiner*, May 24, 1908, Sunday magazine, p. 6.

5. "A Symposium on Mrs. Belle Gunness," *The Phrenological Journal and Science of Health Magazine,* Vol. 121, Number 8 (August 1908), pp. 251–53.

6. *La Porte Argus-Bulletin*, May 8, 1908, p. 7.

7. Harold Schechter, *The Devil's Gentleman: Privilege, Poison, and the Trial That Ushered in the Twentieth Century* (New York: Random House/Ballantine Books, 2007), p. 139.

8. *Chicago Tribune*, June 3, 1908, p. 1.

9. *La Porte Argus-Bulletin*, May 18, 1908, p. 1.

CHAPTER TWENTY-TWO

1. Dr. Walter S. Gaines, letter to Charles S. Mack, July 13, 1908, filed in the archives of the La Porte Historical Society Museum. See also *La Porte Argus-Bulletin*, May 9, 1908, p. 1.

2. See Langlois, p. 1.

3. A. I. Schutzer, "The Lady-Killer," *American Heritage*, Vol. 15, Issue 6 (October 1964), pp. 36–39 and 91–94.

4. Ibid., p. 37.

5. *Chicago Daily Journal*, May 8, 1908, p. 3.

6. *La Porte Argus-Bulletin*, May 9, 1908, p. 3; *La Porte Weekly Herald*, May 21, 1908, p. 5.

7. For an excellent account of the Bender case, see Robert H. Adleman, *The Bloody Benders* (New York: Stein and Day, 1970).

8. See, for example, the *Chicago Daily Tribune*, May 10, 1908, p. 2.

9. *Chicago Daily Tribune*, May 9, 1908, p. 8.

CHAPTER TWENTY-THREE

1. *La Porte Argus-Bulletin*, May 9, 1908, p. 1; *New York Times*, May 10, 1908, p. 2; *Chicago Inter Ocean*, May 10, 1908, p. 1; *Chicago Examiner*, May 9, 1908, pp. 1 and 2.

2. *New York Times*, May 10, 1908, p. 2; *Chicago Examiner*, May 9, 1908, p. 2.

3. *La Porte Argus-Bulletin*, May 9, 1908, p. 2.

4. *Chicago Evening American*, May 9, 1908, p. 1.

5. *La Porte Argus-Bulletin*, May 9, 1908, p. 1.

6. Ibid., p. 7.

7. *Grand Forks Daily Herald*, May 10, 1908, p. 3.

8. *Columbus Enquirer Sun*, May 12, 1908, p. 2.

9. *Aberdeen Daily American*, May 18, 1908, p. 1.

10. *The Bellingham Herald*, May 26, 1908, p. 1.

11. *Duluth New Tribune*, May 16, 1908, p. 3; *Belleville New Democrat*, June 1, 1908, p. 1; *Lexington Herald*, May 19, 1908, p. 1; *Saskatchewan Sunday Tribune*, June 14, 1908, p. 2; *Columbus Enquirer Sun*, June 10, 1908, p. 1.

12. *Chicago Evening American*, May 9, 1908, p. 1.

13. Hinton, p. 95.

14. Ibid., p. 94.

15. *Chicago Inter Ocean*, May 10, 1908, p. 1; *Chicago Tribune*, May 10, 1908, p. 1.

16. *La Porte Argus-Bulletin*, May 9, 1908, p. 1, and May 10, 1908, p. 1; *Scranton Republican*, May 10, 1908, p. 1.

17. *Chicago Tribune*, May 10, 1908, p. 2.

CHAPTER TWENTY-FOUR

1. *Chicago Inter Ocean*, May 11, 1908, p. 1.

2. *La Porte Weekly Herald*, May 14, 1908, p. 14.

3. *La Porte Argus-Bulletin*, May 11, 1908, p. 1; *New York Times*, May 11, 1908, p. 2.

4. *Chicago Inter Ocean*, May 11, 1908, p. 1.

5. *La Porte Argus-Bulletin*, May 11, 1908, p. 1.

6. *La Porte Weekly Herald*, May 14, 1908, p. 3.

7. *Chicago Inter Ocean*, May 11, 1908, p. 1.

8. *New York Times*, May 11, 1908, p. 2.

9. *La Porte Argus-Bulletin*, May 11, 1908, p. 1; *La Porte Weekly Herald*, May 14, 1908, p. 14; *New York Times*, May 11, 1908, p. 2.

10. *La Porte Argus-Bulletin*, May 13, 1908, p. 2; *Chicago Inter Ocean*, May 11, 1908, p. 1; Hinton, pp. 64 and 65.

11. *La Porte Weekly Herald*, May 14, 1908, p. 3.

12. *La Porte Weekly Herald*, May 21, 1908, p. 2.

13. See, for example, the advertisement for the Lyric Theater in the *Concordia (Kansas) Daily Blade*, November 23, 1908, p. 4.

CHAPTER TWENTY-FIVE

1. *La Porte Weekly Herald*, May 21, 1908, p. 4.

2. *Chicago Inter Ocean*, May 11, 1908, p. 2.

3. *Chicago Daily Journal*, May 11, 1908, p. 1.

4. *La Porte Argus-Bulletin*, May 14, 1908, p. 8.

5. *Salt Lake Herald*, May 15, 1908, p. 3.

6. de la Torre, p. 51.

7. *Chicago Daily Journal*, May 13, 1908, p. 2.

8. *La Porte Weekly Herald*, May 14, 1909, p. 8.

9. Ibid.

10. *New York Times*, May 25, 1908, p. 3.

11. de la Torre, p. 52.

12. Anon., *The Mrs. Gunness Mystery! A Thrilling Tale of Love, Duplicity & Crime. Being a recital of the strange story of the career of Mrs. Belle Gunness. It tells in detail everything regarding her career of crime; how she, by representing herself as a charming and rich widow, lured matrimonial victims to her farm, only to murder them in cold blood. Also containing accounts of other noted murder mysteries, including the Bender Case, the Holmes Castle Mystery, and others* (Chicago: Thompson & Thomas, 1908), pp. 10–13.

13. Ibid., pp. 44–45.

14. Ibid., pp. 68–69.

15. Ibid., p. 81.

16. Ibid., p. 176.

CHAPTER TWENTY-SIX

1. Holbrook, p. 140; de la Torre, p. 48.

2.   *Chicago Daily Examiner*, May 10, 1908, p. 1; *La Porte Herald Weekly*, May 21, 1908, p. 1. Accounts differ in the number of watches found in the ruins, with some newspapers putting the total at eleven.

3.   *La Porte Argus-Bulletin*, May 11, 1908, p. 1.

4.   Ibid., May 23, 1908, p. 1; *Chicago Inter Ocean*, May 28, 1908, p. 3.

5.   *Chicago Daily Tribune*, May 16, 1908, p. 3; *La Porte Weekly Herald*, May 21, 1908, p. 4.

6.   *La Porte Argus-Bulletin*, May 13, 1908, p. 4.

7.   *Chicago Daily Examiner*, May 20, 1908, p. 3; *Chicago Inter Ocean*, May 20, 1908, p. 2.

8.   *Chicago Daily Tribune*, May 20, 1908, p. 6.

9.   *La Porte Argus-Bulletin*, May 19, 1908, p. 1.

10. Ibid., May 15, 1908, p. 1.

11. Ibid., May 21, 1908, p. 2.

12. *Chicago Inter Ocean*, May 23, 1908, p. 2; *New York Times*, May 23, 1908, p. 2. Appended to these six indictments was a seventh, charging Lamphere with assisting Belle Gunness in disposing of Helgelien's body.

CHAPTER TWENTY-SEVEN

1.   *La Porte Argus-Bulletin*, May 21, 1908, p. 8.

2.   Langlois, pp. 23 and 26–27.

3.   de la Torre, pp. 61–62.

4.   Shepherd, p. 126.

5.   *New York Times*, May 30, 1908, p. 2; *Chicago Inter Ocean*, May 30, 1908, p. 3; Hinton, pp. 61–62; Shepherd, pp. 125–26.

6.   Shepherd, pp. 125–26.

7.   *La Porte Weekly Herald*, June 25, 1908, p. 4.

8.   *La Porte Argus-Bulletin*, May 21, 1908, p. 1.

9.   *Detroit Free Press*, July 10, 1908, p. 2; *La Porte Argus-Bulletin*, July 10, 1908, p. 1, and July 11, 1908, p. 1; *Spanish Fork Press*, July 16, 1908, p. 1; *Chicago Inter Ocean*, July 18, 1908; *La Porte Argus-Bulletin*, July 29, 1908, p. 1; *Wichita Daily Eagle*, October 9, 1908, p. 1.

CHAPTER TWENTY-EIGHT

1. *Chicago Inter Ocean*, November 8, 1908, p. 8. For unknown reasons, no transcript of Ray Lamphere's trial exists. My account of the proceedings draws on the extensive coverage by the La Porte and Chicago newspapers.

2. *La Porte Argus-Bulletin*, November 12, 1908, p. 1; de la Torre, pp. 65–66.

3. *La Porte Weekly Herald*, November 12, 1908, p. 7.

4. de la Torre, p. 63; *La Porte Weekly Herald*, November 12, 1908, p. 3; *La Porte Argus-Bulletin*, November 10, 1908, p. 1.

5. *Fort Wayne Journal-Gazette*, March 9, 1905, p. 1; *Cincinnati Enquirer*, April 11, 1905, p. 1.

6. *Fort Wayne News*, January 22, 1906, p. 8; *Argos Reflector*, January 26, 1998, p. 1.

7. *La Porte Weekly Herald*, November 12, 1908, p. 3.

8. Ibid., November 13, 1908, p. 1.

9. Ibid., November 10, 1908, p. 1.

10. *Chicago Evening American*, November 10, 1908, p. 1; *Chicago Examiner*, November 10, 1908, p. 1.

11. *Chicago Daily Journal*, November 11, 1908, p. 3.

12. Shepherd, pp. 127–28; de la Torre, p. 50; *Boston Daily Globe*, June 1, 1908, p. 8.

13. *St. Louis Post-Dispatch*, June 1, 1908, p. 2.

14. *Cincinnati Enquirer*, June 2, 1908, p. 2; *New York Times*, June 3, 1908, p. 3.

15. *La Porte Argus-Bulletin*, November 10, 1908, p. 1.

16. Ibid., November 12, 1908, p. 1, and November 13, 1908, p. 1.

CHAPTER TWENTY-NINE

1. *La Porte Argus-Bulletin*, November 13, 1908, p. 1.

2. de la Torre, p. 70.

3. *La Porte Argus-Bulletin*, November 12, 1908, p. 1.

4. *La Porte Argus-Bulletin*, November 13, 1908, p. 1; *La Porte Weekly Herald*, November 19, 1908, p. 1.

CHAPTER THIRTY

1. *La Porte Argus-Bulletin*, November 13, 1908, p. 3, and *La Porte Daily Herald*, November 13, 1908, p. 8.

2. *Chicago Inter Ocean*, November 8, 1908, p. 8.

3. de la Torre, p. 75.

4. *Indianapolis Star*, May 11, 1930, p. 1.

5. *La Porte Argus-Bulletin*, November 10, 1908, p. 1.

6. *La Porte Argus-Bulletin*, November 13, 1908, p. 3.

7. de la Torre, p. 79.

8. *La Porte Weekly Herald*, November 19, 1908, pp. 1 and 3; de la Torre, p. 79.

9. *La Porte Weekly Herald*, November 19, 1908, p. 2.

10. Ibid.

11. de la Torre, p. 85.

12. Ibid., pp. 85–86.

13. *La Porte Argus-Bulletin*, November 13, 1908, p. 4.

CHAPTER THIRTY-ONE

1. *La Porte Argus-Bulletin*, November 14, 1908, p. 2.

2. Daniels, p. 722.

3. *Indianapolis Star*, December 12, 1912, p. 2; January 20, 1913, p. 8; February 23, 1913, p. 16.

4. de la Torre, p. 86.

5. Ibid.; *La Porte Weekly Herald*, November 19, 1908, p. 2.

6. *Indianapolis Star*, August 17, 1940, p. 14.

7. See, for example, *Dental Digest*, Vol. XI, No. 5 (May 1905), p. 520.

8. *La Porte Weekly Herald*, November 19, 1908, p. 3; *La Porte Argus-Bulletin*, November 16, 1908, p. 3.

9. *La Porte Argus-Bulletin*, November 16, 1908, p. 3.

CHAPTER THIRTY-TWO

1. *La Porte Weekly Herald*, November 19, 1908, p. 3.

2. *La Porte Argus-Bulletin*, November 16, 1908, pp. 1 and 4.

3. de la Torre, p. 100; *La Porte Argus-Bulletin*, November 16, 1908, p. 8; *La Porte Weekly Herald*, November 19, 1908, p. 5.

4. de la Torre, p. 93; *La Porte Weekly Herald*, November 19, 1908, p. 3.

5.   *La Porte Argus-Bulletin*, November 16, 1908, p. 4; *La Porte Weekly Herald*, November 19, 1908, p. 3.

6.   de la Torre, p. 94.

7.   *La Porte Argus-Bulletin*, November 16, 1908, p. 4.

8.   Ibid.

9.   *La Porte Argus-Bulletin*, November 16, 1908, p. 8.

10. *Carroll (Iowa) Herald*, May 13, 1908, p. 3.

11. *La Porte Argus-Bulletin*, November 17, 1908, p. 1.

12. *Chicago Daily Journal*, November 17, 1908, p. 2.

CHAPTER THIRTY-THREE

1.   Washington Irving, "Rip Van Winkle," in *Selected Writings of Washington Irving* (New York: The Modern Library, 1984), p. 48.

2.   *La Porte Weekly Herald*, November 19, 1908, p. 5.

3.   *Evansville Press*, May 12, 1908, p. 1; *Pittsburgh Press,* May 7, 1908, p. 1; de la Torre, p. 101.

4.   *La Porte Weekly Herald*, November 19, 1908, p. 5.

5.   Ibid.

6.   *La Porte Argus-Bulletin*, November 18, 1908, p. 1; *La Porte Weekly Herald*, November 19, 1908, p. 5; de la Torre, pp. 103–4.

7.   *La Porte Argus-Bulletin*, November 18, 1908, p. 1.

8.   Ibid.; de la Torre, p. 114.

9.   *La Porte Argus-Bulletin*, November 18, 1908, p. 1.

10. de la Torre, p. 116.

11. Ibid., p. 126.

12. *Chicago Examiner*, November 20, 1908, p. 4.

CHAPTER THIRTY-FOUR

1.   *La Porte Argus-Bulletin*, November 20, 1908, p. 1.

2.   Ibid.; *Chicago Daily Journal*, November 20, 1908, p. 2.

3.   For a capsule biography of Ball, see Fern Eddy Schultz, "La Porte County's first 'native son,'" at http://www.heraldargus.com/community/columnists/fern_eddy _schultz/la-porte-county-s-first-native-son/article_fbe8c5f2-51b6-57eb-b1ca -009cdb20059f.html.

4. Shepherd, p. 178.

5. *La Porte Argus-Bulletin*, November 21, 1908, p. 1; *Alexandria Times-Tribune*, November 21, 1908, p. 1.

6. de la Torre, pp. 134–36.

7. *La Porte Argus-Bulletin*, November 21, 1908, p. 1.

8. *The Daily Republican*, November 21, 1908, p. 7.

9. Shepherd, p. 185.

10. *Chicago Daily Examiner*, November 21, 1908, p. 5.

CHAPTER THIRTY-FIVE

1. *Chicago Examiner*, November 18, 1908, p. 6; *Indianapolis News*, November 21, 1908, p. 3.

2. *La Porte Argus-Bulletin*, November 20, 1908, p. 1.

3. *La Porte Weekly Herald*, November 26, 1908, p. 14.

4. Ibid., p. 15.

5. Ibid., p. 11.

6. *Chicago Daily Tribune*, November 23, 1908, p. 2.

7. *Chicago Daily Journal*, November 22, 1908, p. 2.

CHAPTER THIRTY-SIX

1. *Chicago Examiner*, November 22, 1908, p. 1; *Chicago Inter Ocean*, November 22, 1908, p. 11; *La Porte Argus-Bulletin*, November 23, 1908, p. 1.

2. *Indianapolis Star*, November 22, 1908, p. 5; de la Torre, p. 139.

3. *Cincinnati Enquirer*, November 24, 1908, p. 9.

4. *St. Louis Post-Dispatch*, November 23, 1908, 5; de la Torre, p. 144.

5. *La Porte Argus-Bulletin*, November 23, 1908, p. 1; Shepherd, p. 187; de la Torre, p. 144.

CHAPTER THIRTY-SEVEN

1. *Chicago Daily Tribune*, January 28, 1923, p. 11.

2. *Unity: Freedom, Fellowship and Character in Religion*, Vol. XIV, No. 2 (September 16, 1884), p. ii.

3. See, for example, *Oshkosh Daily Northwestern*, June 13, 1895, p. 1.

4. See, for example, *The American Law Register*, Vol. 51, Philadelphia: Department of Law, University of Pennsylvania, 1903, pp. 465–66.

5. Robert Loerzel, *Alchemy of Bones: Chicago's Luetgert Case of 1897* (Urbana and Chicago: University of Illinois Press, 2003), p. 126; John Buckingham, *Bitter Nemesis: The Intimate History of Strychnine* (Boca Raton, FL: CRC Press, 2008), p. 193; Edward H. Smith, *Famous Poison Mysteries* (New York: The Dial Press, 1927), p. 183.

6. *Louisville Courier-Journal,* November 22, 1908, p. 1.

7. *La Porte Argus-Bulletin,* November 24, 1908, p. 1.

8. *Wichita Daily Eagle,* November 25, 1908, p. 1; *Cincinnati Enquirer,* November 25, 1908, p. 2; Shepherd, pp. 191–92; *Chicago Examiner,* November 25, 1908, p. 1.

9. *Wilkes-Barre Record,* November 25, 1908, p. 1.

10. *Detroit Free Press,* November 25, 1908, p. 2.

CHAPTER THIRTY-EIGHT

1. *La Porte Argus-Bulletin,* November 25, 1908, p. 1.

2. Ibid.

3. Ibid.; *Chicago Daily Examiner,* November 25, 1908, p. 2; *Chicago Tribune,* November 25, 1908, p. 1; de la Torre, pp. 149–51.

4. *Marshall County Independent,* January 25, 1901, p. 1; *Fort Wayne Journal-Gazette,* January 27, 1902, p. 1; *Waterloo Press,* January 31, 1901, p. 2; *Leader Courier*, July 18, 1901, p. 1. Brill, charged with attempted murder, was allowed to plead guilty to assault and battery and got off with a $500 fine, plus costs.

5. de la Torre, pp. 152–53; *La Porte Argus-Bulletin*, November 25, 1908, p. 1.

6. *La Porte Argus-Bulletin.* November 26, 1908, p. 1.

7. de la Torre, pp. 153–54; Shepherd, pp. 196–97.

8. *La Porte Weekly Herald,* December 3, 1908, p. 4; de la Torre, pp. 155–56; Shepherd, pp. 196–98.

9. *Chicago Daily Tribune,* November 26, 1908, p. 2; *Chicago Inter Ocean,* November 26, 1908, p. 4; Shepherd, pp. 199–200; de la Torre, pp. 156–57.

CHAPTER THIRTY-NINE

1. *Chicago Inter Ocean,* November 27, 1908, p. 1.

2. *La Porte Weekly Herald,* December 3, 1903, p. 1.

3. *Chicago Inter Ocean,* November 27, 1908, p. 2.

4. *La Porte Weekly Herald*, December 3, 1903, p. 1.

5. *La Porte Argus-Bulletin*, December 3, 1908, p. 1.

6. *Raleigh Times*, November 27, 1908, p. 1.

7. *La Porte Weekly Herald*, December 3, 1903, p. 8.

8. *Chicago Daily Journal*, November 27, 1908, p. 2.

9. The comments on the outcome were collected and published by the *La Porte Weekly Herald*, December 3, 1908, p. 8.

10. Ibid.

11. Ibid.

12. *La Porte Argus-Bulletin*, November 28, 1908, p. 1.

13. Ibid.; *Fort Wayne Journal-Gazette*, November 28, 1908, p. 1; *Culver Citizen*, December 10, 1908, p. 2.

CHAPTER FORTY

1. *St. Louis Post-Dispatch Sunday Magazine*, May 2, 1909, pp. 55–56.

2. *Belvedere Daily Republican*, October 7, 1909, p. 1; *Indianapolis News*, December 31, 1909, p. 2.

3. *Dakota County Herald*, October 8, 1908, p. 1.

4. *Indianapolis News*, December 31, 1909, p. 2.

5. See, for example, *Warren Times Mirror*, December 31, 1909, p. 1.

6. Shepherd, p. 211.

7. See Edwin A. Schell, *Historical Sketch and Alumni Record of Iowa Wesleyan College* (Mount Pleasant, IA: Mount Pleasant News-Journal, 1917), p. 38.

8. Shepherd, p. 32.

9. *Indianapolis News*, May 13, 1908, p. 8.

10. Ibid.; *Evansville Press*, May 13, 1908, p. 1; Shepherd, p. 104.

11. Shepherd, pp. 212–13.

12. *St. Louis Post-Dispatch*, January 13, 1910, pp. 1 and 2.

13. Ibid.

14. *Cincinnati Enquirer*, January 14, 1910, p. 4.

15. *St. Louis Post-Dispatch*, January 13, 1910, p. 2; *Houston Post*, January 14, 1910, p. 4.

16. *Cincinnati Enquirer*, January 14, 1910, p. 4.

17. *Chicago Daily Tribune*, January 15, 1910, pp. 1 and 2.

18. *St. Louis Post-Dispatch*, January 16, 1910, p. 2.

19. Ibid., June 22, 1956, p. 17.

20. Ibid., January 16, 1910, p. 2.

21. Shepherd, p. 219; *Indianapolis Star*, January 16, 1910, p. 5.

22. Shepherd, p. 220.

23. Ibid., p. 219.

CHAPTER FORTY-ONE

1. *Brazil (Indiana) Daily Times*, January 22, 1910, p. 6.

2. *Indianapolis Star*, March 7, 1910, p. 5.

3. Ibid.

4. *Daily Republican*, January 31, 1910, p. 3; *Indianapolis News*, February 16, 1910, p. 3.

5. *Fort Wayne News*, February 16, 1910, p. 9.

6. *Indianapolis Star*, June 23, 1910, p. 3; *Culver Citizen*, September 22, 1910, p. 6; *Pullman Herald*, July 8, 1910, p. 5; *Indianapolis Star*, August 16, 1910, p. 5.

7. *Indianapolis News*, February 16, 1910, p. 3.

8. An abbreviated version of Myers's statement first appeared in 1912. See, for example, *Indianapolis Star*, December 18, 1912, p. 6. It was not until eighteen years later that the complete statement was published. See *Indianapolis News*, July 17, 1930, p. 17.

9. *Fort Wayne News*, December 21, 1912, p. 11.

10. *Bismarck Tribune*, December 24, 1912, p. 5; *Calumet News*, January 27, 1913, p. 3.

11. *La Porte Argus-Bulletin*, March 18, 1916, p. 1.

12. *Chicago Daily Tribune*, May 6, 1916, p. 8.

13. *Atlanta Constitution*, May 7, 1916, p. 14.

14. *La Porte Argus-Bulletin*, March 18, 1916, p. 1; *Indianapolis Star*, March 19, 1916, p. 4.

15. *La Porte Argus-Bulletin*, May 5, 1916, p. 1.

16. *Chicago Daily Tribune*, May 6, 1916, p. 1.

17. *La Porte Argus-Bulletin*, May 5, 1916, p. 1; *Chicago Daily Tribune*, May 6, 1916, p. 8.

18. *La Porte Argus-Bulletin*, May 5, 1916, p. 1.

19. *Chicago Daily Tribune*, May 6, 1916, p. 8.

20. *La Porte Argus-Bulletin*, May 8, 1916, p. 1.

21. *Chicago Daily Tribune*, May 6, 1916, p. 8.

CHAPTER FORTY-TWO

1. *Indianapolis Star*, January 8, 1915, p. 11; *Seymour Tribune*, October 31, 1923, p. 6.

2. *Capital Times*, January 2, 1924, p. 2; *Cincinnati Enquirer*, July 3, 1924, p. 4.

3. *Garrett Clipper*, October 2, 1930, p. 5; *Indianapolis Star*, February 14, 1936, p. 11.

4. See *Indiana Evening Gazette*, September 26, 1928, p. 1. The perpetrator of the so-called Wineville Chicken Coop Murders turned out to be a twenty-two-year-old pedophile and Canadian immigrant named Gordon Stewart Northcott. For a good account of the case (which served as the basis of the 2008 Clint Eastwood–directed movie *Changeling*), see *Anthony Flacco, The Road Out of Hell: Sanford Clark and the True Story of the Wineville Murders* (New York: Diversion Books, 2009).

5. *Indianapolis News*, July 17, 1930, p. 17; *La Porte Herald Argus*, April 28, 1933, p. 1.

6. *Los Angeles Times*, February 21, 1931, p. 14. The elder Lindstrom's full name was Carl August Lindstrom. Newspaper accounts, however, consistently refer to him as August Lindstrom.

7. Ibid.

8. Ibid.

9. *Los Angeles Times*, February 19, 1931, p. 23.

10. *Los Angeles Times*, February 21, 1931, p. 14.

11. *Oakland Tribune*, February 21, 1931, p. 2.

12. *Los Angeles Times*, February 22, 1931, p. 21; *San Bernardino County Sun*, February 22, 1931, p. 5.

13. *Oakland Tribune*, February 24, 1931, p. 25. Though he was known as "Charles," Esther Carlson's husband, coincidentally or not, had the same first and middle name as her victim: Carl August.

14. *Los Angeles Times*, February 25, 1931, p. 16.

15. *Los Angeles Times*, February 24, 1931, p. 21; *Prescott Evening Courier*, February 25, 1931, p. 2.

16. *Los Angeles Times*, February 26, 1931, p. 26.

17. *Los Angeles Times*, March 6, 1931, p. 21.

18. *Modesto News-Herald*, March 7, 1931, p. 1; *Los Angeles Times*, March 7, 1931, p. 20, and March 27, 1931, p. 20.

19. *Oakland Tribune*, May 3, 1931, p. 3; *San Matteo Times*, May 2, 1931, p. 2.

20. *San Matteo Times*, May 2, 1931, p. 2; *Albuquerque Journal*, May 3, 1931, p. 1; *Los Angeles Times*, May 8, 1931, p. 16.

21. *Los Angeles Times*, May 9, 1931, p. 14.

22. Ibid.

23. Ibid.

24. Ibid.

25. After deliberating for just under five hours, the jury found Erickson not guilty on May 13, 1931. See *Modesto News-Herald,* May 14, 1931, p. 1.

26. *San Francisco Chronicle*, May 8, 1931, p. 14.

27. *Los Angeles Times*, May 13, 1931, p. 15. Yorkey's letter to Worden is in the archives of the La Porte Historical Society Museum.

CHAPTER FORTY-THREE

1. *Indianapolis Star*, January 4, 1943, p. 20.

2. Jensen's findings were delivered in a lecture at the La Porte County Historical Society Museum in October 2014. His talk is available on YouTube: https://www.youtube.com/watch?v=nKa78XVyqJs&feature=youtube.

3. See Maria Konnikova, "Why We Need Answers," *New Yorker,* April 30, 2013, http://www.newyorker.com/tech/elements/why-we-need-answers.

4. *Indianapolis Star*, May 14, 2008, p. B6.

5. *Chicago Inter Ocean,* May 14, 1908, p. 1.

6. See *La Porte Weekly Herald,* May 28, 1908, p. 1.

7. Jones, p. 165.

8. *La Porte Weekly Herald*, December 3, 1908, p. 7.

BIBLIOGRAPHY

Adleman, Robert H. *The Bloody Benders*. New York: Stein and Day, 1970.

Andreas, A. T. *History of Chicago. From the Earliest Period to the Present Time. In Three Volumes. Volume II—From 1857 until the Fire of 1871*. Chicago: The A. T. Andreas Company, 1886.

Anon. *The Mrs. Gunness Mystery! A Thrilling Tale of Love, Duplicity & Crime. Being a recital of the strange story of the career of Mrs. Belle Gunness. It tells in detail everything regarding her career of crime; how she, by representing herself as a charming and rich widow, lured matrimonial victims to her farm, only to murder them in cold blood. Also containing accounts of other noted murder mysteries, including the Bender Case, the Holmes Castle Mystery, and others*. Chicago: Thompson & Thomas, 1908.

Bailey, Frankie Y., and Steven Chermak, eds. *Famous American Crimes and Trials. Volume 2: 1860–1912*. Westport, CT: Praeger, 2004.

Bass, Arnold. *Up Close and Personal: A History of La Porte County*. Bloomington, IN: AuthorHouse, 2006.

Baumann, Edward, and John O'Brien. *Murder Next Door: How Police Tracked Down 18 Brutal Killers*. New York: Diamond Books, 1993.

Blegen, Theodore C. *Norwegian Migration to America: The American Transition*. Northfield, MN: The Norwegian-American Historical Association, 1940.

Brewster, Hank. *On the Road to the Murder Farm: The Hunt for Belle Gunness.* NP, 2012.

Buckingham, John. *Bitter Nemesis: The Intimate History of Strychnine.* Boca Raton, FL: CRC Press, 2008.

Burt, Olive Wooley. *American Murder Ballads and Their Stories.* New York: Oxford University Press, 1958.

Chapman, Charles C. *History of LaPorte County, Indiana; Together with Sketches of Its Cities, Villages, and Townships, Educational, Religious, Civil, Military, and Political History; Portraits of Prominent Persons and Biographies of Representative Citizens.* Chicago: Chas. C. Chapman & Co., 1880.

Compton, Samuel Willard. *Robert De La Salle.* New York: Chelsea House, 2009.

Cutler, Irving. *Chicago: Metropolis of the Mid-Continent.* Carbondale, IL: Southern Illinois University Press, 2006.

Daniels, Rev. E. D. *A Twentieth Century History and Biographical Record of LaPorte County, Indiana.* Chicago: The Lewis Publishing Company, 1904.

de la Torre, Lillian. *The Truth About Belle Gunness.* New York: Fawcett/Gold Medal Books, 1955.

Dine, S. S. *The Philo Vance Murder Cases: 2—The Greene Murder Case & The Bishop Murder Case.* Leonaur Books, 2007.

Dreier, Thomas. "The School That Teaches Boys How to Live." *The Business Philosopher*, Vol. VI, No. 2 (February 1910), pp. 75–79.

Dreiser, Theodore. *Newspaper Days.* New York: Horace Liveright, 1922.

———. *Sister Carrie.* New York: Bantam Books, 1958.

Emery, M. S. *Norway Through the Stereoscope: A Journey Through the Land of the Vikings*. New York: Underwood and Underwood, 1907.

Epstein, Pamela Ilyse. *Selling Love: The Commercialization of Intimacy in America 1860s–1900s*. Diss., New Brunswick Rutgers, The State University of New Jersey, 2010.

Guild, Arthur Alden. *Baby Farms in Chicago: An Investigation Made for the Juvenile Protection Agency*. Chicago: The Juvenile Protection Agency, 1917.

Hansen, Jean Skogerboe. "*Skandinaven* and the John Anderson Publishing Company." *Norwegian-American Studies*, Vol. 28 (1979), pp. 35–68.

Hartzell, Ted. "Belle Gunness' Poison Pen." *American History*, Vol. 43, No. 2 (June 2008), pp. 46–51.

Hermansson, Casie E. *Bluebeard: A Reader's Guide to the English Tradition*. Jackson, MS: University Press of Mississippi, 2009.

Hinton, Paula K. "'Come Prepared to Stay Forever': The Tale of a Murderess in Turn-of-the-Century America." Diss., Miami University, Oxford, Ohio, 2001.

Holbrook, Stuart. *Murder Out Yonder: An Informal Study of Certain Classic Crimes in Back-Country America*. New York: Macmillan, 1941.

Irving, Washington. *Selected Writings of Washington Irving*. New York: The Modern Library, 1984.

Jones, Ann. *Women Who Kill*. New York: Fawcett Crest, 1980.

Keating, Ann Durkin. *Chicago Neighborhoods and Suburbs: A Historical Guide*. Chicago: University of Chicago Press, 2008.

Kelleher, Michael D., and C. L. Kelleher. *Murder Most Rare: The Female Serial Killer.* Westport, CT: Praeger, 1998.

Langlois, Janet. *Belle Gunness: The Lady Bluebeard.* Bloomington, IN: Indiana University Press, 1985.

Loerzel, Robert. *Alchemy of Bones: Chicago's Luetgert Case of 1897.* Urbana and Chicago: University of Illinois Press, 2003.

Lovoll, Odd S. *A Century of Urban Life: The Norwegians in Chicago before 1930.* Champaign, IL: University of Illinois Press, 1988.

————. *Norwegian Newspapers in America: Connecting Norway and the New Land.* St. Paul, MN: Minnesota Historical Society Press, 2010.

Mavity, Charles K. *The Bellville Tragedy: Story of the Trial and Conviction of Rev. W. E. Hinshaw for the Murder of His Wife.* Indianapolis: Sentil Print Co., 1895.

Mayer, Harold M., and Richard C. Wade. *Chicago: Growth of a Metropolis.* Chicago: University of Chicago Press, 1969.

Miller, Donald L. *City of the Century: The Epic of Chicago and the Making of America.* New York: Simon & Schuster, 1996.

Moore, Leonard J. *Citizen Klansmen: The Ku Klux Klan in Indiana, 1921–1928.* Chapel Hill: University of North Carolina Press, 1991.

Packard, Jasper. *History of LaPorte County, Indiana, and Its Townships, Towns, and Cities.* LaPorte, IN: S.E. Taylor & Company, 1870.

Parkman, Francis. *La Salle and the Discovery of the Great West.* Boston: Little, Brown, and Company, 1908.

Perrault, Charles. *The Complete Fairy Tales in Verse and Prose*. Mineola, NY: Dover, 2002.

Perrini, Sylvia. *She Devils of the USA: Women Serial Killers*. Goldmineguides. com, 2013.

Pictorial and Biographical Record of LaPorte, Porter, Lake and Starke Counties, Indiana: Containing Biographical and Genealogical Records of Leading Men, Women and Prominent Families of the Counties Named, and of Other Portions of the State; Together with a Number of Valuable Portraits. Chicago: Goodspeed Brothers, 1894.

Pierce, Bessie Louise. *A History of Chicago, Volume III: The Rise of a Modern City, 1871–1893*. New York: Alfred A. Knopf, 1957.

Ramsland, Katherine. *Many Secrets, Many Graves*. Notorious USA, 2014.

Rattle, Alison, and Allison Vale. *The Woman Who Murdered Babies for Money: The Story of Amelia Dyer*. London: André Deutsch, 2011.

Rowe, Theresa. *Red on the Hoosier Moon*. Bloomington, IN: 1stBooks Library, 1998.

A. I. Schutzer, "The Lady-Killer." *American Heritage*, Vol. 15, Issue 6 (October 1964), pp. 36–39 and 91–94.

Shepherd, Sylvia. *The Mistress of Murder Hill: The Serial Killings of Belle Gunness*. Bloomington, IN: 1stBooks Library, 2001.

Smith, Edward H. *Famous Poison Mysteries*. New York: The Dial Press, 1927.

Strand, A. E. *A History of the Norwegians of Illinois: A Concise Record of the Struggles and Achievements of the Early Settlers together with a Narrative of what is now being done by the Norwegian-Americans of Illinois in the*

Development of their Adopted Country. Chicago: John Anderson Publishing Company, 1905.

Taylor, Troy. *"Come Prepared to Stay Forever": The Madness of Belle Gunness.* Hell Hath No Fury, Book 5. Decatur, IL: Whitechapel Press, 2013.

Thomas, George C., and Richard A. Leo. *Confessions of Guilt: From Torture to Miranda and Beyond.* New York: Oxford University Press, 2012.

Wilson, Ilene Ingbritson. *Murder in My Family.* Bloomington, IN: Trafford Publishing, 2004.

Wooldridge, Clifton R. *Twenty Years a Detective in the Wickedest City in the World.* Chicago, IL: Chicago Publishing Co., 1908.

ACKNOWLEDGMENTS

My thanks, as always, to my agent, David Patterson. In sharing her material with me, Janet Langlois couldn't have been more gracious. Katherine Ramsland was equally generous in providing me with transcripts of the correspondence between Belle and Andrew Helgelien. Krista Reynen and Meg Moss supplied invaluable research assistance. I owe a special debt of thanks to Susie Richter of the La Porte County Historical Society, as well as to historian Bruce Johnson.

Mostly, as ever, I wish to convey my gratitude, appreciation, and everlasting love to my wonderful wife, Kimiko Hahn.

INDEX

D

E

F

L

M

MacDonald, F. W., 151

Mack, Charles S.
    Gunness declared dead by, 147
    in the inquest, 77
    testimony of, 169–171, 173
    on victims' bodies, 84–86

magic lantern show, 135

Mandel Brothers, 11, 15

Mann, Jacob J., xiii

Manny, Carter Hugh, 70–71

Marchetti, Joseph, 256

Marr, Leroy, 74
    in the inquest, 77
    investigation of Truelson, 161
    Lamphere questioned by, 74–75
    Lamphere's collapse and, 158
    testimony of, 188

Marshall, Thomas R., 228–229

Martin, Clyde, 179

Martin, H. H., 21

Mathewson, Ella, 248

matrimonial agencies, 104–106

Maxson, Joseph, 53, 248
    on Belle's last day, 59–60
    Belle's last day and, 61
    in the body search, 83–85, 107–108
    complicity of, 213
    in the fire, 65–67, 166–167
    in the inquest, 77
    looters chased by, 97–98
    in the search for bodies, 84–86, 90–91
    testimony of, 184–186, 192
    on the tooth search, 202–203

McAlester, Henry R., 126

McDonald, Tom, 255

McGill, S. H., 179

Meinke, William, 243–244

Mennen, Frederick C., xiii

Meyer, J. H. William, 93, 173–175

Michael, Charles H., 145

Miller, Fred, xiv

Miller, J. C., 16, 94

Miller, William P., 203

Mills, Henry, 218

Minich, John, 60–61

ABOUT THE AUTHOR

Harold Schechter is an American true-crime writer who specializes in serial killers. Twice nominated for the Edgar Award for Best Fact Crime, he is the author of the nonfiction books *Fatal, Fiend, Bestial, Deviant, Deranged, Depraved, The Serial Killer Files, The Mad Sculptor,* and *Man-Eater*. Schechter attended the State University of New York in Buffalo, where he earned his PhD under the direction of Leslie Fiedler. He is a professor of American literature and popular culture at Queens College of the City University of New York. Schechter is married to poet Kimiko Hahn and has two daughters, the writer Lauren Oliver and professor of philosophy Elizabeth Schechter.